Britain and Its Mandate over Palestine

By the Same Author

Basic Laws on the Structure of the Soviet State
The Soviet Foreign Trade Monopoly
Law After Revolution
Palestine and Israel: A Challenge to Justice
The Ruses for War: American Interventionism Since World War II
Flight into the Maelstrom: Soviet Immigration to Israel and Middle East Peace
Genocide in Cambodia: Documents from the Trial of Pol Pot and Ieng Sary
The Case for Palestine: An International Law Perspective
The Genocide Convention: An International Law Analysis
Consular Law and Practice
The Law of Consular Access: A Documentary Guide
The Statehood of Palestine: International Law in the Middle East Conflict
The Six-Day War and Israeli Self-Defense: Questioning the Legal Basis for Preventive War
The International Diplomacy of Israel's Founders: Deception at the United Nations in the Quest for Palestine
Foreigners on America's Death Rows: The Legal Combat over Access to a Consul
The Legality of a Jewish State: A Century of Debate over Rights in Palestine

Britain and Its Mandate over Palestine

Legal Chicanery on a World Stage

John Quigley

ANTHEM PRESS

Anthem Press
An imprint of Wimbledon Publishing Company
www.anthempress.com

This edition first published in UK and USA 2022
by ANTHEM PRESS
75–76 Blackfriars Road, London SE1 8HA, UK
or PO Box 9779, London SW19 7ZG, UK
and
244 Madison Ave #116, New York, NY 10016, USA

British Library Cataloguing-in-Publication Data
A catalogue record for this book is available from the British Library.

Library of Congress Cataloging-in-Publication Data
A catalog record for this book has been requested.

ISBN-13: 978-1-83998-463-1 (Hbk)
ISBN-10: 1-83998-463-5 (Hbk)

Credit line: Library of Congress

This title is also available as an e-book.

CONTENTS

PREFACE

On a summer morning in 1999, I received an unexpected telephone call from London at my office. Israel and the Palestine Liberation Organization had agreed to begin talks for a final peace to settle the conflict over Palestine. A treaty was anticipated. The British Government was concerned that while Israel had a staff of lawyers competent in international law, the Palestinians did not. A treaty could more readily be agreed upon if the Palestinians had solid legal backup. A panel of lawyers assembled by the British Government had just met to make plans for legal consultation. At the meeting, my name was mentioned as a possible addition to the panel.

Two months later, I found myself sitting down for an exploratory meeting with officials of the Palestine Liberation Organization. One of the British lawyers opened the session by quipping that Prime Minister Tony Blair was backing the project to make amends for the Balfour Declaration. On the other side of the table, the quip was received politely for the icebreaker that it was intended to be. The question of whether Britain's issuance and implementation of the Balfour Declaration might indeed have been less than legal hung in the air for only a moment, before the conversation turned to the matters at hand.

As participants on both sides of the table knew, however, it was a question at the very heart of the conflict over Palestine that began when Britain took the territory from Turkey. A change in the complexion of Palestine's population under Britain's tenure generated the conflict that the anticipated treaty was to end. During the interwar years, when it governed Palestine, Britain went to considerable lengths to establish itself legally and to frame its implementation of the Balfour Declaration as legitimate. That effort, which involved arrangements with other powers of the day and with the League of Nations, was largely successful as a matter of public relations. That success set the stage for the United Nations to make a recommendation about Palestine's future.

Much ink has been spilled over Britain's role in Palestine from a policy perspective, but less attention has been devoted to whether Britain's governance and the changes it brought about were based in legality, such that they could appropriately serve as a basis for a territorial disposition in the country. This book examines long forgotten communications and documentation to ask whether Britain's hold on Palestine was indeed based in law. While the clock of history cannot be made to run in reverse, the legality of what was done in the 1920s remains at the heart of the conflict between Israelis and Palestinians in the twenty-first century. An inquiry may offer direction for resolving what has been the most intractable territorial conflict of modern times.

The inquiry is based largely on governmental and intergovernmental documentation of the period, much of which was classified at the time. It is the author's hope that readers will follow up and explore on their own the treasure trove of material that is now largely accessible, either at research libraries or through a digitization program of the United Kingdom National Archives. League of Nations documents are available digitally from the League of Nations Archive, maintained by UN Archives Geneva.

In my own efforts to access this material, I have been aided by the library staff of the Ohio State University's Moritz College of Law and in particular by librarians Natasha Landon, Matt Cooper, Corazon Britton, and Kaylie Vermillion. Dima Hajj Ahmad, JD 2023 at the College, tracked down additional source material of the era.

I have profited from Victor Kattan's major scholarship on legal issues in Britain's governance of Palestine. I owe a special debt to Blake Alcott, who generously shared from his collection of documents on Palestine, and who provided invaluable insight by reviewing an early draft of mine.

Full citations are given in each chapter to sources referenced in the text. If a source is cited more than once, the subsequent citations are in shortened format. One oddity to bring to readers' attention is that in the text I quote from two Belgian lawyers both named Henri Rolin, and both of whom wrote about legal issues in Palestine. To distinguish the two in citations to their writings, I give a middle initial for one, and each time I cite them I give their dates. In citations to British cabinet documents, "C.P." means "Cabinet Paper"; "CAB" means "Cabinet."

SETTING THE STAGE: WAS BRITAIN'S RULE IN PALESTINE LEGAL?

A particular narrative about Britain's rule in Palestine shaped the discussion in 1947 at the United Nations over Palestine. No one has compiled this narrative in a single document, and one will not find it called by this name in the existing literature. Some of the elements of the narrative were invented and promoted by the British Government. Others were embellishments added by adherents of a movement that sought Jewish statehood in Palestine. This narrative, in any event, has been at the center of international consideration of Palestine from the beginnings of conflict there to the present day. For ease of identifying it, we will refer to it using a capital "n."

The Narrative runs that during the World War I, as the British Army was poised to take Palestine from Turkey, Britain decided that it would promote Jewish statehood there. That determination was expressed in 1917 in a letter sent over the name of A. J. Balfour, the Foreign Secretary. The letter came to be called the Balfour Declaration. It was a binding commitment on Britain's part to the Jewish people of the world. At war's end, the Zionist Organization, which promoted Jewish statehood, was invited to present its case to the Paris Peace Conference, in a sign of international acceptance of Jewish rights. The League of Nations, which was created at the Paris Peace Conference, decided that territory being taken from Turkey should be administered subject to the League's oversight under a regime called "mandates." The League placed Palestine under this regime after Britain's Allies decreed that Britain should rule there. Britain's legal standing in Palestine was confirmed by the League and was reconfirmed in a peace treaty concluded with Turkey.

The arrangement between Britain and the League of Nations, the Narrative continues, was memorialized in a document called the Palestine mandate that required Britain to implement the Balfour Declaration. By the terms of this mandate document, Britain was granted Palestine, and the right of the Jewish people to Palestine was formally attested by the international community. The League issued a mandate to Britain, thereby endorsing the

Balfour Declaration and guaranteeing Jewish territorial rights. The mandate document was a treaty binding on the League and on the international community generally. Following World War II, the United Nations, in a special provision of the UN Charter, confirmed and carried forward the territorial rights of Jewry in Palestine. In that fashion, a legal basis was confirmed for a UN General Assembly recommendation for Jewish statehood and for a declaration of statehood for a state to be called Israel.

The Narrative continues to be recounted in the twenty-first century as underpinning a legal rationale for Jewish statehood in Palestine. It is accepted as valid by governments as they ponder solutions to the continuing conflict between Israelis and Palestinians. Palestinian claims to self-determination and sovereignty are assessed against what is assumed to be a commitment made to the Jewish people by the international community in the 1920s.

The Narrative, however, is not based in reality. There is no point in it that cannot be challenged in light of what actually transpired. The Balfour Declaration reflected no intent on Britain's part to bind itself to any particular course of action. The document was issued not to proclaim Jewish rights, but to counter measures by Germany to solidify the loyalty of its own Jewish population for Germany's war effort. The Paris Peace Conference invited the Zionist Organization to make a public statement but did not endorse its aims. The League of Nations did not appoint Britain to rule Palestine and did not give it territorial or any other rights there. Britain's efforts to convince its Allies to endorse the Balfour Declaration were rebuffed. Britain wrote up a document as a blueprint for its rule in Palestine and sought approval of that document from the League of Nations. The League said, however, that Britain first needed sovereign rights for Palestine before Britain could rule under the League's mandate system. Sovereignty was held by Turkey. Britain tried unsuccessfully for three years to gain sovereign rights from Turkey. The League's Council approved the terms of Britain's mandate document, but the League's Council lacked a power to approve the terms on which Britain would govern Palestine.

When Turkey did finally agree to a peace treaty, Turkey refused to grant sovereignty to Britain. As a result, Britain never acquired a right to rule Palestine. The League of Nations expressed no opinion in favor of Jewish entitlement in Palestine. It did not purport to require Britain to implement any rights that might have adhered to Jewry. Britain never considered itself legally bound by any arrangement it had with the League. Britain's mandate document in any event was inconsistent with the League's requirements for a mandate, first because it allowed for no central indigenous governing authority in Palestine, and second because the Palestine population was not consulted in the choice of an outside power to govern. As a result, the mandate document lacked any standing in law. The absence of any international endorsement of Jewish rights in the League era meant that there were no such rights to carry forward into the era of the United Nations. The underlying rights of the majority population of Palestine therefore remained unaffected by anything Britain had done.

The Narrative crystallized from an effort by the British Government to give its governance of Palestine a framework that would make it seem lawful and from a simultaneous effort by the Zionist Organization to portray Jewish territorial entitlement as being guaranteed by law. Some elements of the Narrative find their origin in positions taken by Britain, while others are a product of the Zionist Organization. The Narrative is a broad-brush depiction of a history that emerged from the combined efforts of the British Government and the Zionist Organization that then impacted the United Nations.

Analysts who argue that the British Government, and the Zionist Organization along with it, violated rights of Palestine's majority Arab population put forward a highly plausible claim to self-determination for that population. But even they leave key elements of the Narrative unchallenged.

A few words on how Britain became involved in Palestine may be helpful before we deconstruct the Narrative. The story begins with World War I. Turkey, Germany's ally against Britain, held territory in the Arab world that it had incorporated four centuries earlier into the Turkish Empire, sometimes referred to as the Ottoman Empire. The latter designation was based on the name of an early leader, Osman. Palestine, an area on the eastern shores of the Mediterranean Ocean that dated from ancient times, was part of the empire's Arab provinces.

By early twentieth century, discontent was growing against Turkish rule in its Arab provinces. Britain hoped to take advantage of this sentiment by encouraging rebellion, which in turn would help it against Turkey. The Arabs wanted assurance of independence for themselves, an independence to which Britain was prepared to agree.[1] At the same time, Britain and its ally, France, agreed between themselves that if they prevailed, they would assume a governance of these provinces.[2] The Arabs, under Hussein bin Ali, Sherif of Mecca, were willing to give Britain economic preferences in a future pan-Arab state.[3] The Arabs did revolt in aid of Britain and contributed to Britain's ultimately successful effort to drive Turkish forces out of the Arab provinces.

Complicating its commitment to the Arabs, however, the British Government issued a statement that it favored what it called a "national home" in Palestine "for the Jewish people."[4] At the time of its policy statement, Britain was engaging Turkish forces from the south of Palestine, though it would take another year to drive them out of Palestine entirely.

Tilting the scale back in favor of Arab independence, however, the United States, as ally to Britain and France, called for self-determination as a desired outcome of the War. "The Turkish portions of the present Ottoman Empire," said US President Woodrow Wilson, "should be assured a secure sovereignty."[5]

On 30 October 1918, two weeks before Britain concluded an armistice with Germany, it did the same with Turkey.[6] The United States took the lead in fashioning a new international organization, the League of Nations, to keep the peace in future. At US initiative, France and Britain agreed to a provision in the League's founding document, called its Covenant, for a system of governance by outside powers in Turkey's Arab provinces, whereby they would be regarded "provisionally" as "independent nations." The outside power would give "administrative advice and assistance" for a period of time, leading to independence. This system of governance—one that was new in international relations—was given the name "mandate" in the Covenant.[7]

The Covenant set principles for mandate governance in only general terms. The Covenant suggested that Turkey's Arab provinces should be governed under the mandate system but did not actually require it. The Covenant established no procedure to force a state in occupation of a portion of Turkey's Arab provinces to submit to the mandate system. The Covenant provided no procedure for determining whether a particular territory would fall under the system. It did not give the League a role in deciding which outside states would take which territories. It did not divide Turkey's Arab territories into distinct territorial entities. The Covenant's silence on these points left it to the states with troops on the ground—and that meant principally Britain—to decide whether to utilize the mandate system and how to implement it.

To the good fortune of Britain, the United States decided to keep out of the League of Nations. That abstention removed from League governance what might have been a strong voice in favor of self-determination for the Arab populations. Britain and France, the two states hoping to keep Turkey's Arab provinces, had a strong history as colonial rulers that inclined them to expect commercial advantage for themselves and a strong hand in governance.

The League structure imposed only minimal constraints. The Covenant provided for an Assembly of all the member states, but the Covenant provision on mandate territories gave this Assembly no role. The only League organ mentioned in the provision on mandate territories was its Council, in which membership was held by eight states, four of them permanently—Britain, France, Italy, and Japan. The Covenant gave the Council a minimal role in setting terms for mandate governance of a particular territory, plus a role to receive periodic reports from the administering states. The Council could adopt decisions only on the basis of unanimity, so no Council action adverse to Britain could be taken without its consent.

While the mandate system as enshrined in the Covenant inclined in the direction of protecting dependent populations, it did not sway far from colonialism as that institution had been developed by the European powers. Colonialism was rationalized by the colonizing powers as an institution that protected human rights.[8] The French espoused what they called a "mission civilisatrice," meaning that they would assist development for the local population. The British called it the "white man's burden." Some early analysts of the mandate system saw it as less than a fundamental break with the past, since colonialism was already rationalized as benefiting indigenous populations.[9] One student of colonialism referred to the mandates as "colonial mandates." He called them "a novelty," but only within "the terminology of colonial law."[10]

The flexibility left by the Covenant and the lack of enforcement power on the part of the League of Nations let Britain draw the Zionist Organization into governance in Palestine. Taking its name from Mt. Zion, a hill in Jerusalem, the Zionist Organzation sought a "home" for "the Jewish people" that would be "secured under public law."[11] The impetus for this aim was a concern that the discrimination faced by Jews in Europe would not be eradicated and that protection could be achieved only by gaining territory elsewhere, as explained by one of the movement's founders, Theodor Herzl, in a pamphlet titled *Der Judenstaat* (The State of the Jews).[12]

Herzl asked Turkey for territory in Palestine. He tried to enlist Germany to use its influence with Sultan Abd al-Hamid because Germany had financial interests in Turkey. He dangled the prospect of economic benefit for Turkey. "The implementation of the Zionist plan must mean welfare for Turkey as well," Herzl wrote in a plea to the German Government for sponsorship of a company he hoped to form. "Energies and material resources will be brought to the country; a magnificent fructification of desolate areas may easily be foreseen; and from all this there will arise more happiness and more culture for many human beings. We are planning to establish a Jewish Land-Company for Syria and Palestine, which is to undertake the great project, and request the protection of the German Kaiser for this company."[13] Herzl met with the Kaiser in 1898 while the Kaiser was visiting Jerusalem, and the Kaiser did raise the issue with the Sultan.

Herzl arranged a visit with the Sultan himself in 1901, offering to find funds to pay off the substantial debt that Turkey owned to banks in Europe. "The thorn, as I see it," Herzl told the Sultan, according to Herzl's entry in his diary, "is your public debt. If that could be removed, Turkey would be able to unfold afresh its vitality, in which I have great faith." When the Sultan expressed interest, Herzl explained that he "would have this operation carried out by my friends on all the stock exchanges of Europe."[14] Herzl had no such contacts, and nothing came of his entreaties to the Sultan.

During World War I, with the prospect that Palestine might change hands, the Zionist Organization turned its attention to Britain. A Russian emigré chemist named Chaim Weizmann, who was by then a leading figure in the Zionist Organization, was helping Britain build explosive devices for use in the war. Weizmann took advantage of his war work to lobby officialdom to take an interest in Palestine as a potential Jewish state. His efforts were opposed by British Jews who feared that their status in Britain might be eroded if a state for Jews was established elsewhere. Within Jewry, the greater support for the plan was in Eastern Europe because discrimination there against Jews was more overt. In the Russian Empire, which at the time included Poland, Jews faced severe limitations in choice of profession and place of residence. In the early years of the twentieth century, mob attacks occurred against Jews, notably in the cities of Kishinev and Kiev.

In the latter stage of the War, the British Government issued a statement to the Zionists, saying that it favored a "national home" for Jewry in Palestine and would work to achieve it. The document came to be called the Balfour Declaration. It was not clear whether the project of a national home was consistent with the plans with the Arabs. "National home" was a term the Zionists used to describe their aim of Jewish statehood in Palestine, but Britain did not indicate that it understood the term in that way.

Britain's reasons for advancing the cause of the Zionists are debated by historians. In other territory then recently taken, prominently Rhodesia and Kenya, Britain encouraged settlement by its own people. In Palestine, a hopefully loyal population might solidify what Britain knew would be its unwelcome presence there. For the Zionists, attaching their star to Britain gave them the backing of the government in control of Palestine's territory. As result of Britain's aspiration to control Palestine and the Zionists' aspiration for territory, the British Government and the Zionists formed a symbiotic relationship in which each saw advantage.[15] Within the British Government, as one analyst described, there was "an implicit assumption," never clearly articulated, "that there was an unbreakable link between the British presence in Palestine and the British commitment to Zionism."[16]

The Narrative, in any event, merits the attention of anyone trying to understand the conflict over Palestine. It was accepted as true at the United Nations as reason to partition Palestine. It is taken as fact even today as the international community seeks a path toward a peace that partition did not bring. If the Narrative is faulty, those efforts rest on false premises.

To unravel the facts, this book examines the main historical inflection points and the principal contentions that make up the Narrative. The Narrative will be broken down into twenty component propositions. Each proposition forms one chapter of the book. The title of each chapter is a statement of the proposition. The chapter explains the proposition and then refutes it, adducing historical evidence to show why the proposition is false. This style—title chapters that make statements that the author considers erroneous—is admittedly unorthodox. It will let a reader gain an understanding of each proposition that makes up the Narrative before seeing the evidence that shows why it is false.

Chapter 1

THE BALFOUR DECLARATION IS THE FOCAL POINT FOR THE LEGAL SITUATION OF PALESTINE

In documentation it presented to the League of Nations, as we will see in more detail shortly, the British Government highlighted its 1917 statement, the Balfour Declaration. The Balfour Declaration plays a central role in the Narrative. It was highlighted as well in 1948, in a statement issued in Tel Aviv to proclaim a Jewish state in Palestine. That statement recited that in 1897, "the First Zionist Congress convened and proclaimed the right of the Jewish people to national rebirth in its own country." The statement then continued, "This right was recognized in the Balfour Declaration of the 2nd November, 1917."[1]

A prominent Israeli jurist described the Balfour Declaration as the starting point for analysis of legal rights in Palestine. "From an international legal perspective," wrote Yoram Dinstein, "the first step for any meaningful discussion of the Palestine Question is the Balfour Declaration of 2 November 1917."[2] The "Palestine Question" was the title of the agenda item for Palestine in documents of the United Nations, when it began dealing with the situation in 1947. Dinstein, long-time professor of international law at Tel Aviv University, was familiar with the work of the United Nations on Palestine, having served there in Israel's delegation.

The Balfour Declaration occupies a central place in the Narrative, as a font of Jewish entitlement claims in Palestine. It would, to be sure, be important in the subsequent history of Palestine. Only one sentence in length, it reads:

> His Majesty's Government views with favour the establishment in Palestine of a national home for the Jewish people, and will use their best endeavours to facilitate the achievement of this object, it being clearly understood that nothing shall be done which may prejudice the civil and religious rights of existing non-Jewish communities in Palestine, or the rights and political status enjoyed by Jews in any other country.[3]

This statement was made by Britain's War Cabinet, a small coterie of top officials that managed the conduct of the war against Germany and its ally Turkey. The statement came to be known by the name of the Secretary of State for Foreign Affairs, A. J. Balfour. Whether it should be the focal point for Palestine's status, analyzing from an international legal perspective, is not obvious.

It was a statement that related to control of territory. For an analysis of the status of a particular territory, or of what can lawfully be done in a particular territory, one needs to ask where sovereignty lies. Britain had no sovereignty when the Balfour Declaration was issued, even though it would, as we shall shortly see, try to gain it. The statement was an expression of intent as to what Britain might do, whether or not it gained sovereignty, to bring about what it called a "national home for the Jewish people."

In ascertaining rights in a particular territory, one also needs to ask about the people who inhabit it. By early twentieth century, it was coming to be accepted that the population of a territory had certain rights. An important legal ruling was issued on this point just as World War I ended. The Aaland Islands in the Baltic Sea between Sweden and Finland were inhabited by Swedes but were under sovereignty of Finland. The islanders wanted the islands to be Swedish. A special international panel was appointed since Sweden and Finland could not come to agreement.

The panel ruled that by the standards of international law, the islands were part of Finland. Had it been the situation that there was no territorial sovereignty residing in any state, they continued, "the principle of self-determination may be called into play." They noted "the principle recognising the rights of peoples to determine their political fate."[4]

The panel did not regard that principle as trumping sovereignty, however. When the War Cabinet composed the statement, Palestine was firmly under Turkey's sovereignty. Turkey, to be sure, was close to losing a war, but the territory of Palestine belonged to it by the standards of the international community to determine sovereignty. Turkey's Arab provinces participated in its legislative assembly through elected representatives. Until and unless Turkey might cede sovereignty under a peace treaty, the sovereignty situation was clear.

The Palestine Question must be approached from the standpoint of sovereignty, if one is to analyze from an international legal perspective. After a war, territory can change hands. It need not necessarily change hands. The parties to a war may come to terms in a fashion that leaves territory under the existing sovereignty. In the case of Palestine, a peace treaty with Turkey would not be concluded until 1923, as we shall see in later chapters. It is the sovereignty situation in any event that is the focal point to analyze Palestine's status, not a statement by a state like Britain, even if Britain, as it did, had designs on the territory.

It must remain to later chapters to see how sovereignty played out for Palestine. The trajectory on Palestine's sovereignty would be far from a straight line. Britain would decree at a certain point that it planned to govern Palestine on the basis of the League Covenant's mandate concept. Whether that aim affected Palestine's legal status is a matter we will have to explore.

Britain, as we shall see, did understand the question of sovereignty, and that it could not govern without it. Britain would try to gain sovereignty for itself in a peace treaty, but events would intervene. Britain would try to carry through with the Balfour Declaration and to draw the League of Nations into acceptance of it. Whether any of that activity impacted Palestine's legal status must be part of an analysis.

One also needs to ask about the people, as the panel did in the Aaland Islands case. Colonial empires were still firmly in place, operated principally by France and Britain, the two states seeking Turkey's Arab provinces. The Covenant of the League of Nations, however, characterized the populations of Turkey's Arab provinces as "independent nations," at least "provisionally." In Palestine, Jews were about 10 percent of the population, while Arabs counted close to 90 percent. It would be that population with entitlement. The Balfour Declaration referred to "the Jewish people" without defining further. If the term was meant, as it doubtless was, to include Jews in Europe, they would not have been part of the population under the Covenant. So, the Balfour Declaration might run headlong into self-determination, at least if the "national home" contemplated for the Jewish people was to be territorial in character.

Sovereignty and the emerging doctrine of self-determination are the keys to analyzing the Palestine Question. The Balfour Declaration plays a role, but from a legal perspective the Balfour Declaration is not the starting point. Analysis of the status of a territory cannot begin with a statement of future intent by a state lacking sovereignty. Nonetheless, and to this extent there is a germ of truth in the Narrative as explicated by Dinstein, the Balfour Declaration enters the picture because it would be promoted by Britain as central to its plans for Palestine. Britain would seek acceptance of the national home concept from other states. In that way, the character and meaning of the Balfour Declaration relate not only to Britain but to the broader international community, and what it made of the Balfour Declaration. We must therefore move to several questions about the Balfour Declaration that one finds in the Narrative. One is whether the Balfour Declaration had any standing in law. Another is the question just mentioned, whether the "national home" meant a territorial state. Still another is whether the Balfour Declaration was issued to promote rights of world Jewry, or whether its aim was elsewhere. The Narrative has clear answers on all three questions. The Narrative's propositions occupy us in the next three chapters.

Chapter 2

THE BALFOUR DECLARATION WAS A BINDING COMMITMENT TO THE JEWISH PEOPLE

The reference to the Balfour Declaration in the 1948 statement proclaiming Israeli statehood was premised on the Balfour Declaration as a document carrying normative force. As we saw, the 1948 statement began from the 1897 assertion of Jewish rights and then said that that assertion of rights was recognized in the Balfour Declaration. As for the British Government, its view of the Balfour Declaration was less clear. It would seek, as we shall see, to gain acceptance of the national home concept by others but without claiming legal force for the Balfour Declaration itself. Moreover, as we shall see in Chapter 17, the British Government appeared to regard the Balfour Declaration as a policy statement, a policy that could be reversed if circumstances warranted.

Nonetheless, the supposedly binding nature of the Balfour Declaration became an element of the Narrative. Britain was said to have committed itself to a national home for the Jewish people in Palestine. Yoram Dinstein provided a legal underpinning. The Balfour Declaration, Dinstein wrote, "had a binding force as far as that country was concerned." Dinstein said that this was so because later British governments said so. "The British intention to be bound by the text (formally acknowledged and reiterated by successive British governments) can easily be ascertained." The commitment was based, Dinstein wrote, on the international law principle that a state can be bound by a promise it makes, so long as it intended to bind itself. "Under international law (as elucidated in two subsequent decisions of the International Court of Justice, in the *Eastern Greenland* case and in the *Nuclear Tests* cases)," he continued, "a unilateral declaration issued by the competent authorities of a state can have a binding effect upon that state, if such was the intention behind it."[1] The Balfour Declaration hence was said to be binding not as a two-party legal act, but as a unilateral commitment.

Dinstein's argument to that point was sound. A state can indeed be bound by a commitment made unilaterally. The Balfour Declaration did include the statement that Britain intended to apply its "best endeavours" to "facilitate" a national home" for the "Jewish people" in Palestine, hence Dinstein could find a way to see it as a unilaterally made commitment. States often say they will do one thing or another, however, and in most instances, they are not imposing a legal obligation on themselves. To be binding, the statement must be addressed to another state, not to a private group. The statement must be phrased in wording that shows that the state issuing it intended to take on a legal obligation. The obligation being undertaken must be clear. The statement must be issued with a certain level of formality and it must be made public. None of these factors was present with the Balfour Declaration.

The *Eastern Greenland* case that Dinstein mentioned, dating from 1933 (a case heard actually in the Permanent Court of International Justice, not in the International Court of Justice) involved a statement made to another state.[2] Denmark was claiming territory in the eastern sector of Greenland and was concerned that Norway might challenge that claim. As Norway's foreign minister and Denmark's ambassador to Oslo were discussing the matter, Norway's foreign minister said that Norway would not "make difficulties" over Denmark's claim. Norway later said that this statement was not a binding commitment. The Permanent Court of International Justice ruled, however, that it was. The Permanent Court stressed the fact that the addressee was a state. "A reply of this nature given by the Minister for Foreign Affairs on behalf of his Government in response to a request by the diplomatic representative of a foreign Power," the judges said, was "binding upon the country to which the Minister belongs."[3] The Court's implication was that the Foreign Minister's reply would not have been binding on Norway had its Foreign Minister been addressing a non-governmental group as opposed to a representative of Denmark as a state.

That difference was stressed by a deputation of Palestine Arab representatives meeting with Winston Churchill as Secretary of State for the Colonies in 1921. They demanded repudiation of the Balfour Declaration, saying that it lacked the force of law, since it was addressed not to a state, but to a private group. "One of the great laws governing international treaties," the representatives objected, "is that the two parties should possess the quality of government. A treaty between a governing Power and an individual cannot have international force."[4] The Balfour Declaration, they said, was directed to "a company of men who are neither a Power nor a nation."[5]

The Norwegian Government's statement, moreover, showed that Norway intended to be undertaking an obligation. Norway was committing itself to refraining from contesting a Danish sovereignty claim. The Balfour Declaration, on the other hand, did not reflect clearly what Britain might have been committing itself to do. The letter recited that Britain planned to use its "best endeavours" in the direction of a national home, but "best endeavours" could have meant very little. This formulation did not bespeak a commitment to take a particular action.[6] We shall see in Chapter 17 that within a short time, the British Cabinet seriously considered dropping the Balfour Declaration, with no concern that doing so would violate any legal obligation.

Further, the ambiguity in the wording also deprived the letter of the quality of a unilateral commitment. What did it mean that Britain "favored" a national home? That it would be pleased if a national home were to come about? That it would serve high tea to mark the occasion? A later prime minister mocked the Balfour Declaration as "bizarre," a "tragicomically incoherent promise," and "an exquisite masterpiece of Foreign Office fudgerama." "Another way of putting it," wrote Boris Johnson, "might have been that the British government viewed with favour the eating of a piece of cake by the Jewish people, provided nothing should be done to prejudice the rights of the non-Jewish communities to eat the same piece of cake at the same time."[7] The War Cabinet did not define "national home." Nor did it define "Jewish people." That was a category that had no accepted definition, in English law or in international law. In the Eastern Greenland situation, one could tell what commitment was made by Norway. The same was not true of Britain and the Balfour Declaration.

Further still, the statement that the War Cabinet composed was not issued with the level of formality required for a binding obligation. The statement involved no participation by the Crown. It was not an order in council. It was not printed as a command paper. It was not even issued as a public document. It was conveyed as a private letter to the English Zionist Federation, which had lobbied the British Government for it, and which had exchanged drafts with the Government over the preceding months. It was in the nature of a reply to a constituent.

Balfour, as authorized by the War Cabinet, composed a cover note that he addressed to Walter Rothschild, a representative of the English Zionist Federation. Balfour had the document delivered by messenger to Rothschild at his home at 148 Piccadilly in London. Balfour added a sentence, saying, "I should be grateful if you could bring this declaration to the knowledge of the Zionist Federation." The War Cabinet received a deputation from the English Zionist Federation so that they could express thanks.[8]

The Balfour Declaration came to public notice only a week later, because *The Times* obtained a copy, which it printed, explaining, without revealing its source, that "Mr. Balfour has sent the following letter to Lord Rothschild in regard to the establishment in Palestine of a national home for the Jewish people."[9] The Government did not make the letter known, least of all in Palestine, because a negative reaction was to be anticipated.[10] While a unilateral declaration may, in principle, be binding if issued with intent to be bound, it must at least be brought to public attention. As indicated some years later by a United Nations law panel, a unilateral statement, to be binding, must be "publicly made."[11]

These same points distinguish the *Nuclear Tests* cases, on which Dinstein also relied. At the time of those tests, Australia and New Zealand were demanding that France stop detonating nuclear weapons in the atmosphere over the South Pacific Ocean. They sued France in the International Court of Justice. In reaction, France's president said publicly that France would stop testing in the atmosphere. The judges threw the case out of court, saying that France had committed itself not to test. The judges said that this was a binding commitment on France's part. Like the Norwegian Foreign Minister's statement to the Danish ambassador, the French statement was made to the benefit of a state, actually two states, and the nature of the commitment was clearly ascertainable. Any new atmospheric nuclear tests would have been a violation. The International Court of Justice stressed that France's commitment was made to states. The judges explained that "interested States may take cognizance of unilateral declarations and place confidence in them, and are entitled to require that the obligation thus created be respected." "The French Government conveyed to the world at large, including the Applicant [Australia], its intention effectively to terminate these tests. It was bound to assume that other States might take note of these statements and rely on their being effective."[12]

Neither the *Eastern Greenland* case nor the *Nuclear Tests* cases support the proposition that the Balfour Declaration was binding on Britain. The Balfour Declaration was not issued to a state. It did not bespeak an intent to be binding. No clear obligation was described. It was issued informally and was not brought to public notice. Whatever the Balfour Declaration was, it involved no legal commitment.

Chapter 3

THE JEWISH NATIONAL HOME MEANT A JEWISH STATE

By referencing the Balfour Declaration in the 1948 proclamation of Jewish statehood, the founders of Israel took the Balfour Declaration to mean that Britain had promised a state. The meaning of the Balfour Declaration in that regard was a matter of debate all through the period Britain governed Palestine. The Zionist Organization aimed for statehood, and it played a role in implementing British policy in Palestine. The Balfour Declaration itself, however, avoided any definition of "national home."

The context of the adoption and delivery of the statement provides clues. The War Cabinet, in instructing Balfour to convey its statement to the English Zionists, asked him to "take a suitable opportunity of making the following declaration of sympathy with the Zionist aspirations."[1] The Zionists aspired to statehood. In the communications leading up to the issuance of the Balfour Declaration, the English Zionists pressed for a statement that would strongly imply an aim of statehood. Draft language was exchanged that would have recited that the Government "accepts the principle that Palestine should be reconstituted as the National Home of the Jewish people."[2] The War Cabinet's rejection of such phrasing was deliberate. The Balfour Declaration did not by its terms envisage Jewish statehood in Palestine.[3]

In the aftermath of World War I, protection of minority groups was high on the international agenda. New borders were generating new minorities. For example, a German population group who found themselves within Poland as a result of a border shift came to be protected by treaty, so that they could continue to develop in a German cultural environment. Germans inhabiting the sector of Poland in question were guaranteed a right to conduct primary schooling in the German language, in schools funded by the Polish government.[4] In Palestine, the Jews, similarly, were expected to be a minority, hence "national home" might mean something similar. The treaty on Poland did not, to be sure, use the term "national home," but the term served readily as shorthand for what was spelled out in that treaty.

Concern immediately arose on the Arab side in any event about what the War Cabinet had in mind. Hussein bin Ali asked the British Government to clarify. He received a reply in January 1918, in a message delivered by Col. David Hogarth, who headed the British Government's Arab bureau in Cairo. Migration of Jews to Palestine was envisaged, Hussein was told, but migration would not infringe on the political freedom of the Arab population, which made up 90 percent of Palestine's inhabitants. As quoted in 1939 by a British Government committee, the reply to Hussein assured him that "The Entente Powers," meaning Britain and its World War I Allies, "are determined that the Arab race shall be given full opportunity of once again forming a nation in the world." The phrase "once again" referred to the independence that was enjoyed prior to Turkish conquest 400 years earlier. As for the meaning of "national home," the message explained that it would not infringe the economic or political freedom of the existing population:

> Since the Jewish opinion of the world is in favour of a return of Jews to Palestine and inasmuch as this opinion must remain a constant factor, and further as His Majesty's Government view with favour the realisation of this aspiration, His Majesty's Government are determined that in so far as is compatible with the freedom of the existing population both economic and political, no obstacle should be put in the way of the realisation of this ideal.
>
> In this connexion the friendship of world Jewry to the Arab cause is equivalent to support in all States where Jews have a political influence. The leaders of the movement are determined to bring about the success of Zionism by friendship and co-operation with the Arabs, and such an offer is not one to be lightly thrown aside.[5]

The message used the War Cabinet's term "aspiration" and made clear that it did not mean overriding the rights of the existing population. The statement that the Arabs should "form a nation" coupled with the characterization of the role of Jews in various countries signaled that a "national home" did not mean a state. The Balfour Declaration had used the phrase "civil" in regard to the rights of the existing population that were to be protected. Hogarth used the terms "economic and political" to refer to the "freedom" of the existing population to be guaranteed. The Government, through Hogarth, thus took "civil" in the Balfour Declaration to mean "economic and political." Statehood for Jews would be inconsistent with the political freedom of the Palestine population. The Hogarth message meant that the national home was something less than a state.[6] If Jews in Palestine, moreover, were to play a role in Palestine similar to the role they played in other states "where Jews have a political influence," they would not have a state of their own. The mention of "forming a nation" was consistent with a pledge given in 1916 by Britain's High Commissioner in Cairo, Henry McMahon, to Hussein bin Ali for Arab independence if the Arabs rose against Turkey.[7]

The same reading of "national home" came through in a 1919 British Cabinet document that was not made public at the time but that showed, similarly, that the British Government understood "national home" not to mean a Jewish state. The 1919 document was prepared because the British Government wanted its own ranks to be clear on what was meant by "national home." The document clarified that the Balfour Declaration "does not contemplate [...] the government of a majority by a minority."[8]

Concern persisted even after the reply to Hussein, however, because the Zionist Organization was establishing a presence in Palestine under British auspices, and the Zionist aim of statehood was not concealed. To mollify the Arab population, a policy statement was issued in June 1922 over the name of Winston Churchill as Secretary for the Colonies. Churchill explained that the Balfour Declaration did "not contemplate that Palestine as a whole should be converted into a Jewish National Home, but that such a Home should be founded *in Palestine*."[9] Since at the time the possibility of partition had not been raised, this statement negated statehood as the meaning of "national home."

In 1939, in any event, the British Government confirmed that the Balfour Declaration did not envisage a Jewish state. It issued a "white paper" on Palestine in which it stated, "His Majesty's Government declare unequivocally that it is not part of their policy that Palestine should become a Jewish State. They would indeed regard it as contrary to their obligations to the Arabs under the Mandate, as well as to the assurances which have been given to the Arab people in the past, that the Arab population of Palestine should be made the subjects of a Jewish State against their will."[10]

The 1939 white paper was a formal policy statement of the British Government. That same position was repeated by Malcolm MacDonald, who by then was Secretary of State for the Colonies. The League Council had created what it called a Permanent Mandates Commission to take in the reports that states holding mandates were to file with the League.[11] In addressing the Commission, MacDonald said that the phrase "civil and religious rights" that were to be reserved to the broader population of Palestine was intended to include "the normal political rights of a people."[12] A Jewish state set up against the will of the country's majority population would clearly affect "the normal political rights of a people."

The consequence of the view perpetuated by the Narrative that "national home" meant a state is seen in how it led the United Nations General Assembly to recommend a Jewish state. When the Palestine Question was taken up by the United Nations in 1947, its Special Committee on Palestine ignored the meaning Britain gave to "national home," finding in it a basis for a Jewish state. The Special Committee was set up by the UN General Assembly in 1947 after the British Government asked for a recommendation to be made to it about the "future government" of Palestine.[13] The Special Committee said that there remained controversy over "the precise implication" of what the British Government meant by "national home." The Special Committee relied on a 1937 Royal Commission that had said that "there is nothing in it to prohibit the ultimate establishment of a Jewish State."[14] The Special Committee took that negative implication as an indication that the British Government did not exclude the possibility that "national home" might mean a state. The Special Committee, by a majority of its members, then went on to recommend a Jewish state,[15] a recommendation that was soon endorsed by the UN General Assembly.[16]

The Special Committee omitted reference to the statement negativing statehood in the 1939 "white paper" or to MacDonald's similar statement in the Permanent Mandates Commission. Those two statements reflected official British Government policy.[17] The Royal Commission had been set up by the Government only to make recommendations to it. The Special Committee's reliance on the 1937 document while ignoring two contrary official statements in 1939 showed that the Special Committee had not done its homework.

The Special Committee did mention the official statement represented by the Hogarth message but discounted it by saying that it "was not officially made known to the Permanent Mandates Commission until 1939 nor was it acceptable to the Commission as a whole."[18] If the Permanent Mandates Commission, or some of its members, disagreed with the import of the Hogarth message, their dislike is irrelevant to what the British Government intended. Nor is the fact that the message was not communicated to the Permanent Mandates Commission until 1939 relevant to what the message said. The Hogarth message meant what it said, regardless of when it was communicated, and regardless of what some members of the Permanent Mandates Commission thought about it.

Understanding why the Special Committee on Palestine could commit such an error on League procedure requires a comment on how the Special Committee was constituted and how it operated. The Special Committee was made up of representatives of 11 UN member states. Those states were chosen for an absence of self-interest in the Palestine situation, as an assurance of impartiality. But their absence of self-interest meant at the same time that they did not have officials with first-hand knowledge of Palestine.

The Special Committee on Palestine was given only three months by the General Assembly to come up with a recommendation. That time frame left no time for study. Within that time, the Special Committee was expected to travel to the region, consult with relevant parties, hold hearings, and draft a detailed report. The bias in favor of the Zionist perspective was facilitated by the fact that the Arab Higher Committee, the body that represented the Palestine Arabs, considered that the United Nations had no business intruding in their country by making recommendations about its government. As a result, it boycotted the Special Committee. So, the Special Committee heard only from the Zionist side.

The Zionist Organization worked hard to influence the Special Committee to recommend partition, through an entity of its creation called the Jewish Agency for Palestine. The Special Committee was hosted in hearings held in Jerusalem by two young Jewish Agency operatives, David Horowitz and Aubrey (later "Abba") Eban. As Eban later explained, his task was to "fill the minds of committee members with some ideas on a future solution."[19] The pair pushed the committee members to recommend partition, since partition would include a Jewish state.[20] It was not that the Jewish Agency wanted an Arab state, but with Jews numbering less than one-third of Palestine's population a recommendation for a split of the territory was all they could realistically hope to gain from the Special Committee.

The members of the Special Committee were so impressed by the knowledge of Horowitz and Eban that they were invited to travel to Geneva, where the Special Committee planned to draft its report. Ralph Bunche, a UN official assigned to oversee the drafting, realized that he was being lobbied along with the members of the Special Committee. The "Jewish Agency boys," as Bunche referred to Horowitz and Eban, "obviously have it figured out that I will prepare the first draft of the report and are cultivating me steadily."[21] Eban and Horowitz did advise the Special Committee in Geneva on the drafting, in particular on how it would portray what had been done by the League of Nations. As result, the Special Committee's report gave the United Nations General Assembly a distorted picture of the legal situation of Palestine that inclined the General Assembly in the direction of recommending a partition that would include a Jewish state.

"There can be no doubt," Dinstein wrote, "that the [Balfour] Declaration was intended to lay the foundations of some form of a Jewish national entity in Palestine."[22] Whatever may have been intended by some members of the War Cabinet, nothing of the sort was written into the Balfour Declaration. Nor did anything subsequently said by the British Government in explanation of the Balfour Declaration. "National home" did not imply territory for a Jewish state in Palestine.

Chapter 4

THE BALFOUR DECLARATION WAS ISSUED TO AFFIRM JEWISH RIGHTS IN PALESTINE

In 2017, a celebratory event was held in London for the centenary of the Balfour Declaration. Prime Minister Theresa May lauded Balfour. "Lord Balfour," she said, "had the vision and the leadership to make this profound statement about restoring a persecuted people to a safe and secure homeland." As we have seen, of course, it was not Balfour who made the statement. He had a hand in the drafting, but it was the War Cabinet's statement. The aim, May was suggesting in any event, was to protect Jewry. That effort was the more remarkable, she said, because the Government had other matters on its mind. "With Britain still embroiled in the midst of the First World War, the idea of establishing a homeland for the Jewish people would have seemed a distant dream for many."[1]

If the Balfour Declaration was issued to assert Jewish rights, it potentially could serve as a basis for such rights. If the Balfour Declaration was issued for other reasons, then it may not provide such a basis. The 1948 declaration of Jewish statehood, as we just saw, referred to a Jewish right in Palestine and asserted that such a right "was recognized in the Balfour Declaration of the 2nd November, 1917."[2] So the Balfour Declaration was taken by the statehood declarants as a rights-affirming document, issued on the premise that the Jewish people had a legal right to territory in Palestine.

The War Cabinet's statement, however, was not framed in the language of rights. It recited that the War Cabinet "favoured" a Jewish national home, but without saying why. The English Zionist Federation had lobbied for rights-affirming language. One draft it proposed referred to "the right of the Jewish people to build up its national life in Palestine."[3] The War Cabinet avoided such phrasing. The Balfour Declaration as issued contains no hint of legal right. The historical record shows that the War Cabinet issued it not to proclaim Jewish rights, but to promote the War effort.

May said that the statement was issued despite Britain's involvement in the War. May got it wrong. The statement was issued precisely because of the War. Had there been no war, the Cabinet would have had little reason to issue it. In 1917, Britain's military prospects against Germany were uncertain. Germany had the forces of Britain and its allies on the defensive. German submarines were wreaking havoc on Allied shipping. Russia, one of the allies, was beset by internal revolution. The Government that replaced the Russian monarchy in March 1917 was losing on the eastern front, freeing German troops to attack in the west. The United States was just coming on board to support the Allies, but its level of commitment was yet to be tested.

Balfour sailed to the United States to shore up US support. He met with Supreme Court Justice Louis Brandeis, a former President of the Zionist Organization of America, and a confidant of President Woodrow Wilson.[4] According to a retrospective account prepared by the British Foreign Office in 1923, "during this visit the policy of the declaration as a war measure seems to have taken more definite shape. It was supposed that American opinion might be favourably influenced if His Majesty's Government gave an assurance that the return of the Jews to Palestine had become a purpose of British policy."[5]

The Zionist Organization of America made an impression on Britain's policy makers. Robert Cecil, then-Acting Secretary of State for Foreign Affairs, told the War Cabinet "that this was a question on which the Foreign Office had been very strongly pressed for a long time past. There was a very strong and enthusiastic organisation, more particularly in the United States, who were zealous in this matter, and his belief was that it would be of most substantial assistance to the Allies to have the earnestness and enthusiasm of these people enlisted on our side."[6]

The War Cabinet went so far as to ask whether a pro-Zionist statement would please the United States. "The views of President Wilson should be obtained before any declaration was made." Cecil was directed "to inform the Government of the United States that His Majesty's Government were being pressed to make a declaration in sympathy with the Zionist movement, and to ascertain their views as to the advisability of such a declaration being made."[7] The War Cabinet wanted to know if a pro-Zionist statement would solidify US support.

A major concern was that Germany might steal the march on Britain.[8] Germany was thought to be on the verge of making a pro-Zionist declaration.[9] Chaim Weizmann told the British Government that "the German Government were endeavouring by every means at their disposal to work upon the Zionists in Germany, with a view to utilising them for the purposes of a peace agitation."[10] Weizmann warned that Germany sought "to influence Jewish opinion, especially in America and Russia, and to utilise it in the interests of German propaganda against the *Entente*." Weizmann urged the British Government to "give an open expression of their sympathy with and support of Zionist aims."[11]

Intelligence information heightened the War Cabinet's fears.[12] On 2 October, the British consul in Berne sent an account of a meeting said to have taken place in Berlin, involving Foreign Secretary Richard von Kühlmann and German Zionists, "to discuss the Palestine question." Certain unspecified pledges were said to have been given to German Jewry. The Foreign Office commented on the report, "We have already heard that the Germans are frightened of our Zionist propaganda."[13] Balfour, who was not a member of the War Cabinet, was invited to its 4 October meeting.[14] He conveyed intelligence information "that the German Government were making great efforts to capture the sympathy of the Zionist movement."[15]

Jews were fighting as foot soldiers in the armies of Germany and Austria-Hungary, opening the possibility of attracting them to the cause of the Entente. Jews also served in the Russian army. The Foreign Office approached the Russian foreign minister to ask whether a statement of support for Zionism might incline Russian Jews to fight more vigorously for the Entente.[16]

Balfour claimed that the Zionist movement "had behind it the support of a majority of Jews, at all events in Russia and America, and possibly in other countries."[17] Zionism did not enjoy majority support among Jews in any country, but Balfour's information went unchallenged. George Curzon, a member of the War Cabinet, "raised objections" to Balfour "on practical grounds, and urged that to secure for the Jews already in Palestine equal civil and religious rights would be a better policy than to aim at repatriation on a large scale."[18] Curzon asked, "How was it proposed to get rid of the existing majority of Mussulman inhabitants and to introduce the Jews in their place?"[19]

Curzon penned a memorandum to his fellow War Cabinet members to counter what he saw as their inclination to issue a pro-Zionist statement to improve Britain's military prospects. He called these "political reasons." Curzon wrote, "For important as may be the political reasons (and they seem to me almost exclusively political) for adopting such a line of action, we ought at least to consider whether we are encouraging a practical ideal, or preparing the way for disappointment and failure."[20] Alone in the War Cabinet, Curzon queried whether Zionism would be good for Palestine.

Curzon in his memorandum also asked what "national home" meant, and whether such a "national home" in Palestine was feasible. Curzon said that most of the Jewish agricultural colonies had not been successful.[21] He said that the Arabs "have occupied the country for the best part of 1,500 years. [...] They will not be content either to be expropriated for Jewish immigrants, or to act merely as hewers of wood and drawers of water to the latter."[22] The only member of the War Cabinet to have spent time in the Middle East, Curzon tried to convince his colleagues that a European population could not be superimposed on Palestine.[23]

A British Zionist who lobbied for adoption of the Balfour Declaration confirmed that, from the perspective of the War Cabinet, helping Jewry was not the motivating factor. "What the War Cabinet was considering," wrote Leonard Stein, "was not whether, in the eventual peace settlement, Great Britain should try to do something for the Jews in Palestine, but whether the British Government should there and then enter into a public undertaking to the Zionists."[24]

At a War Cabinet meeting on 31 October, Balfour, who again participated, "chose to rest the case for the declaration mainly on its value as propaganda."[25] He related that "the vast majority of Jews in Russia and America" favored Zionism. "If we could make a declaration favourable to such an ideal," he said, "we should be able to carry on extremely useful propaganda both in Russia and America."[26]

Despite his opposition to a pro-Zionist statement, Curzon conceded "that some expression of sympathy with Jewish aspirations would be a valuable adjunct to our propaganda."[27] He cautioned, however, that the War Cabinet "should be guarded in the language used in giving expression to such sympathy." He "did not see how the Jewish people could have a political capital in Palestine."[28] It was at that meeting, on 31 October, that the War Cabinet authorized Balfour to convey the statement.[29]

The War-related rationale for the Balfour Declaration was confirmed in 1923 by Victor Cavendish, who as Secretary of State for the Colonies was responsible for Britain's governance of Palestine. In a confidential memorandum to the British Cabinet, Cavendish described the Balfour Declaration as "a war measure" that was "designed to secure tangible benefits which it was hoped could contribute to the ultimate victory of the Allies."[30] Cavendish explained, "The Declaration was made at a time of extreme peril to the cause of the Allies. Our offensive of the previous summer and autumn had resulted in enormous casualties and had failed to achieve any decisive result. Italy was *in extremis.* Russia had dropped out of the alliance, and the Germans were busily engaged in transferring Army Corps from the Eastern to the Western front in preparation for the grand attack which, in the spring of 1918, was to sweep the British and French armies into the seas. How narrowly the Germans failed in their object is a matter of history."[31]

A confidential memorandum prepared in 1924 by the Colonial Office confirmed the War-related motivation for the Balfour Declaration. The memorandum recited that the Balfour Declaration "had a definite war object. It was designed to enlist on behalf of the Allies the sympathy of influential Jews and Jewish organizations all over the world."[32]

Once Balfour conveyed the statement, the War Cabinet set about exploiting it to win friends. A special office was set up in the Department of Information to disseminate information about it.[33] America was a major target of this information campaign.[34] In Austria and Germany, pamphlets trumpeting the Balfour Declaration were airdropped, aimed at influencing Jewish soldiers there.[35] "Stop fighting the Allies, who are fighting for you, for all the Jews," one message, written in Yiddish, proclaimed. "An Allied victory means the Jewish people's return to Zion," read another.[36]

Britain enlisted its Allies in the endeavor to use the Balfour Declaration for war propaganda.[37] Germany and Austria tried to minimize the damage. Austrian Prime Minister Ernst von Seidler, concerned that Britain had gained the march on the Central Powers by issuing the statement, assured Austrian Jews that a Jewish nationality would soon be officially recognized, a measure that Jewish representatives in Austria at the time were demanding.[38]

A central element of the Narrative is that the Balfour Declaration was issued because the British Government wanted to affirm Jewish rights. Both the wording of the Balfour Declaration and the historical context negate any such implication. The Balfour Declaration was not issued to help Jewry. It was issued to help Britain.

Chapter 5

THE PARIS PEACE CONFERENCE RAISED JEWISH STATEHOOD TO THE INTERNATIONAL LEVEL

The Paris Peace Conference afforded an opportunity for the Zionist Organization to explain its reasons for a Jewish national home. Israeli historian Tom Segev called the peace conference "the pinnacle of Weizmann's diplomatic achievements." Segev wrote that Weizmann "managed to ensure that the British would remain in Palestine." Segev explained Weizmann's success: "Weizmann, at the head of the Zionist delegation, pleaded for the international ratification of the Balfour Declaration. As a result, the League of Nations agreed to grant a mandate to the British, empowering them to govern Palestine, that included an explicit responsibility to help the Jews establish a national home in the country. The mandate was Weizmann's own personal achievement."[1]

Segev's assessment reflects what the Narrative came to reflect, that the Zionist Organization succeeded at the Paris Peace Conference in convincing the world to promote its objectives. The reality was far different. In Paris, the Zionist Organization did not move the international dial on the topic of Zionism. Nor did it ensure that Britain would remain in Palestine. Britain had its own reasons for doing so. Neither did it gain agreement from the League of Nations, which was not yet in existence. And when the League did address Palestine, as we shall see, it did not empower Britain to govern there or to promote a Jewish national home.

Weizmann gave himself less credit than did Segev for his performance in Paris. In his memoir, Weizmann, who was not known for understating his own successes, could find nothing more positive to say about his achievements in Paris than that the Zionist participation resulted in some "good press in France."[2]

The invitation issued to the Zionist Organization to make a statement at the Paris Peace Conference did afford it a chance to state its case in a forum that could shape events. The major powers were gathered to arrange peace with Germany and Turkey and to make decisions about territory being taken from them. The Zionist Organization made both a written and an oral presentation.

In its written plea, the Zionist Organization laid out a plan for Britain to control Palestine, quite a bold move for a non-governmental organization. And it said that Britain should implement a national home there for the Jews. The plan read, "The sovereign possession of Palestine shall be vested in the League of Nations and the Government entrusted to Great Britain as Mandatory of the League." Conditions would be created "as will secure the establishment," the plan continued, "of the Jewish National Home and ultimately render possible the creation of an autonomous Commonwealth." The mandatory power, with Britain as nominee for the role, would be directed to "promote Jewish immigration and close settlement on the land." The mandatory power would also "accept the cooperation in such measures of a Council representative of the Jews of Palestine and of the world." The Zionist Organization plan even defined Palestine territorially by setting out borders for it, something that to date had not been done.[3] For audacity, this projection of borders was the most remarkable feature of the Zionist Organization's plan. Borders are drawn by governments, not by non-governmental organizations.

The document explained a rationale for Jewish statehood, asking for recognition of "the historic title of the Jewish people to Palestine and the right of the Jews to reconstitute in Palestine their National Home."[4] That rationale mirrored what the English Zionist Federation had tried unsuccessfully to get the War Cabinet to insert into the Balfour Declaration. The War Cabinet, as we saw, declined to speak in terms of statehood, or in terms of legal rights.

Weizmann's decision to press this maximalist Zionist position in Paris showed that the Zionist Organization was not content with the wording of the Balfour Declaration. It also showed that the Organization had not given up its effort to push Britain into taking a position in favor of a Jewish state. With Britain providing a path to Zionist aims in Palestine, one might have thought that the Organization would content itself with asking Britain's Allies to endorse the Balfour Declaration. Instead, in what seems a remarkable display of effrontery, the Zionist Organization was asking the Allies to commit to more than had its patron.

A trio of Zionist Organization leaders gave oral testimony in support of the written plan. One reason that the Zionist efforts at the Paris Peace Conference came to be seen, per Segev, as a victory was that they made the Zionist Organization seem to be much more than it actually was. Delegate Nahum Sokolow, claiming to represent "the Jewish population of Palestine," said that the Zionist team "had come to claim their historic rights to Palestine, the land of Israel."[5] What Sokolow's interlocutors did not know was that Sokolow, who was from Russia, had no connection to Palestine's Jewish population. The Zionist Organization enjoyed little following among Palestine's Jews, who, with the addition of agriculturalists from Russia migrating in the late nineteenth century, numbered perhaps 10 percent of Palestine's population.

Among Palestine's Jews, many feared that they would suffer in public opinion in Palestine because of the Zionist Organization's aim of taking over the country.[6] Many of Palestine's Jews followed a strain of Judaism that opposed secular Jewish territorial autonomy.[7] Many lived outside the Palestine economy, subsisting by praying for Jews in Europe, who sent contributions.[8] Weizmann had disparaged Palestine's Jews after a 1907 visit to the country. More than half the Jewish population of Palestine, Weizmann wrote, were "pious European Jews" who engaged in no "gainful occupations" but "were supported by a system of collections in the European communities." Weizmann called them a "useless and retarding element."[9] These Palestine Jews were hardly part of a Zionist Organization constituency.

As for Jews in Western countries, Sokolow had to acknowledge that migration to Palestine was not on their agenda. Perhaps fearful of offending the men who sat before him, representing the major Western powers, Sokolow ticked off France, Britain, Italy, and the United States. "Undoubtedly, happy groups of Jews lived in the countries of Western Europe and in the United States of America," he said.[10]

Most of the world's Jews, however, resided in Eastern Europe, Sokolow said, and they needed protection. "For the great suffering majority of the Jews, living in Eastern Europe, a place would have to be prepared where they would be at home and among their own kind."[11] To show why the Jews of Eastern Europe were deserving of Palestine, he said they had helped the Allied cause. "During the late terrible war the Allies had promised to help the Jews to found a Jewish national centre, where the real home of the Jewish people had always been." He said, "Sustained by that promise, the Jews had been able to organise and to support the Great Powers loyally by creating an entente of all the Jewish parties within the Entente of the Great Powers."[12] Sokolow gave no detail. Britain, as we saw, had hoped for help from Jews in Eastern Europe, but any tangible assistance was hard to identify.

"Now, a victory of great ideals and of justice having been gained," Sokolow averred, "the hour of deliverance of his unhappy people had struck, and the old Jewish traditions could again be introduced in the land of their ancestors, combined with the ideals of New Europe, thus leading to a reconstitution of a people and the transformation of a country."[13]

Menachem Ussishkin, also from Russia, took up the Eastern European theme.[14] Ussishkin introduced himself as "President of the National Assembly representing 3,000,000 Jews of South Russia, an Assembly which, in the month of November last adopted a resolution proclaiming the historic rights of the Jewish people to Palestine."[15] Ussishkin thus was claiming that three million Jews in his National Assembly favored Zionism. The National Assembly was a group of Ukrainian Jews that first appeared only a few months earlier, in 1918, in the city of Kiev.[16] Zionist activity in Russia had, indeed, picked up following the overthrow of the tsar in 1917.[17] But Jews in Ukraine numbered only two million by one estimate,[18] 1.5 million by another.[19] Ussishkin's claim of three million supporting Zionism was a mathematical impossibility, even if all supported Zionism, which most did not.[20]

Like his colleagues, Weizmann gave figures on Jewish support for Zionism that should have raised eyebrows. "In making his statement," Weizmann said, "he spoke for 96% of the Jews of the world, who shared the views which he had endeavoured to express that afternoon."[21] He gave no evidence. Most Jews, in fact, did not support Zionism, which remained in the early twentieth century "a feeble and insignificant movement in the world's Jewish communities."[22]

Weizmann reminded the Western leaders that Russia was in turmoil following the overthrow of the tsar and the advent of Bolshevism. Jewish emigration out of Eastern Europe had been high even before the war, and now it would increase, with most heading westward.[23] Weizmann's not so subtle message was that if the Western governments did not want Eastern Europe's Jews knocking on their own doors, they should open Palestine to them. Dramatizing the threat of large numbers of Jews heading West, Weizmann claimed that "he spoke in the name of a million Jews who, staff in hand were waiting the signal to move."[24]

The Zionist Organization speakers did not mention the Arabs of Palestine. Weizmann did say that Jews would settle in the "empty spaces" of Palestine.[25] After hearing Weizmann, US Secretary of State Robert Lansing asked him whether "Jewish national home" meant "an autonomous Jewish Government." Knowing Lansing to be wary of Zionism, Weizmann began cautiously. Weizmann said he must reply "in the negative. The Zionist organization," he continued, "did not want an autonomous Jewish Government, but merely to establish in Palestine, under a mandatory Power, an administration, not necessarily Jewish, which would render it possible to send into Palestine 70 to 80,000 Jews annually. The Association would require to have permission at the same time to build Jewish schools, where Hebrew would be taught, and in that way to build up gradually a nationality which would be as Jewish as the French nation was French and the British nation British. Later on, when the Jews formed the large majority, they would be ripe to establish such a Government as would answer to the state of the development of the country and to their ideals."[26] Thus, Weizmann's reply to Lansing began as negative but by its end was positive.

Weizmann's assertion that he anticipated a Palestine in which Arabs would be reduced to a minority drew a protest cable to the peace conference from the Muslim and Christian Committee of Jaffa.[27] Foreign Office officials worried that Weizmann's evident aim for Jewish statehood would result in conflict in the region.[28]

The Zionists' efforts in Paris were aided by a lack of serious opposition. On the Arab side came Emir Feisal, son of Hussein bin Ali. Emir Feisal had led the Arab forces that worked with Britain against Turkey. Anxious to collaborate with Britain in the postwar order, Emir Feisal could be counted upon by Britain not to assume a strong anti-Zionist posture. In Palestine, Arabs were organizing to oppose Zionism. A Muslim–Christian Association formed in Palestine early in 1919 and drew up a resolution to take to the Paris Peace Conference, advocating for immediate independence in union with Syria.[29] A delegation was selected to go to Paris. The British authorities, however, were concerned that the Association was not willing to accept British oversight and thus would speak at cross purposes to Britain, which planned to say it would govern Palestine. At the last minute, they prevented the Muslim–Christian Association delegation from departing Palestine for Paris.[30]

Early on at the Paris Peace Conference, the British Government announced its aim of dismembering the Turkish empire. After a war, victorious powers do not necessarily try to take the territory they are occupying. At a meeting of the Allies just as the conference was getting under way, however, they agreed that Turkey should not be allowed to keep its Arab provinces.[31] The mandate idea was already being discussed, and David Lloyd George said that Britain had decided "to accept the doctrine of a mandatory for all conquests in the late Turkish Empire and in the German Colonies."[32] The Turkish delegation made a plea to retain the Arab provinces.[33] Lloyd George, however, tabled a "Scheme for settlement in the Turkish Empire" that showed Britain taking a mandate for Palestine and Mesopotamia (Iraq), and France for Syria, with a notation that these designations were "provisional," dependent on the results of an opinion survey that France, Britain, and the United States were planning.[34] The most Lloyd George was able to pry out of his Allies for Britain taking Palestine was a statement by French Prime Minister Georges Clemenceau, who said, "If his colleagues really wished to induce him to believe that Mesopotamia and Palestine should go to Britain and Asia Minor to America, he was quite ready to think the matter over."[35] Clemenceau's reference to "Asia Minor" was to Britain's idea that the United States would take a mandate over Armenia that would have involved territory in eastern Anatolia, in the Asian part of Turkey. In proposing to take Palestine, Britain did not mention the Balfour Declaration or a Jewish national home.

The Paris Peace Conference managed to forge a peace treaty with Germany, but it made no headway on one with Turkey. Palestine was not discussed during the Paris meetings. Weizmann and his colleagues made no immediate gains in Paris.[36] They did secure a platform that allowed them to make their pitch for Jewish territory in Palestine, but the assembled powers were not ready to discuss Turkey's Arab provinces. What the Conference did do that would have implications for Palestine was to approve a "Covenant" for an international organization called the League of Nations. The document set up a framework for control of German and Turkish territory that the victorious powers planned to keep. This was the Covenant's Article 22.[37] Its opening two paragraphs read,

> To those colonies and territories which as a consequence of the late war have ceased to be under the sovereignty of the States which formerly governed them and which are inhabited by peoples not yet able to stand by themselves under the strenuous conditions of the modern world, there should be applied the principle that the well-being and development of such peoples form a sacred trust of civilisation and that securities for the performance of this trust should be embodied in this Covenant.
>
> The best method of giving practical effect to this principle is that the tutelage of such peoples should be entrusted to advanced nations who by reason of their resources, their experience or their geographical position can best undertake this responsibility, and who are willing to accept it, and that this tutelage should be exercised by them as Mandatories on behalf of the League.

The Covenant was adopted as part of the Treaty of Versailles, a treaty named for the town outside Paris where it was signed in June 1919. This was the peace treaty with Germany, in which Germany renounced sovereignty over its overseas colonies. So as of the date of the Covenant, Germany's "colonies and territories" had ceased to be under its sovereignty. Two paragraphs in Article 22 dealt with colonies in Africa, which meant Germany's. One paragraph dealt with Turkey's holdings, which included its Arab provinces:

> Certain communities formerly belonging to the Turkish Empire have reached a stage of development where their existence as independent nations can be provisionally recognised subject to the rendering of administrative advice and assistance by a Mandatory until such time as they are able to stand alone. The wishes of these communities must be a principal consideration in the selection of the Mandatory.

Since no peace treaty was signed in Paris with Turkey, Turkey still held sovereignty. That being the case, the statement in Article 22 about territories that "have ceased to be under the sovereignty of the States which formerly governed them" seemed not to apply to Turkey's Arab provinces. Article 22 did not purport, in any event, to require that states taking Germany's or Turkey's territories subject them to the mandate system. The choice was left to them. During the Paris Peace Conference, the Allies did parcel out Germany's territories, but not Turkey's. That task they would take up shortly, however, with Britain taking the lead.

Chapter 6

BRITAIN'S ALLIES MADE THE BALFOUR DECLARATION AN INTERNATIONAL COMMITMENT

According to the Narrative, the powers that allied with Britain turned the Balfour Declaration from a commitment by Britain alone into a commitment from the international community. This transformation, it is said, occurred in 1920. One hundred years later, this element of the Narrative gained new attention, when it was spelled out as part of a campaign to explain the legitimacy of Israel. The campaign was timed to the centenary of a meeting of the Principal Allied Powers in 1920, held in Italy. The Jerusalem Center for Public Affairs produced a video about that meeting featuring Center director, Dore Gold, a former Israeli ambassador to the United Nations. Gold was asked about "the signing of the San Remo resolution," and what could be done to make that event better known. Gold replied that the need was to "get a photocopy of it and make sure it's on the desk of every UN delegate."[1]

San Remo was the town on the Italian Riviera where the meeting was held. What occurred at the San Remo meeting that was so momentous? "San Remo converted the Balfour Declaration into a binding international treaty," Gold wrote in the *Jerusalem Post*, "setting the stage for the League of Nations Mandate that was approved in 1922."[2] "British prime minister Lloyd George and his foreign affairs minister Lord Curzon, attended along with the prime ministers of France and Italy," Gold explained. "Representatives of Belgium, Greece, and Japan also took part. Together they constituted what was called the Supreme Council of the Principal Allied and Associated Powers."

A meeting as described by Gold did take place in San Remo in April 1920. And there would be activity in the League of Nations two years later, as we shall see in coming chapters, though not exactly what Gold described. The purpose of the meeting at San Remo was to agree on a text to propose to Turkey as a peace treaty. Britain and France had their sights on Turkey's Arab provinces. They were agreed on demanding that Turkey give up the Arab provinces and renounce sovereignty in favor of the Principal Allied Powers.

They also sought, at the San Remo meeting, to gain agreement, in advance of the anticipated peace treaty, that the Principal Allied Powers would re-convey the Arab provinces to Britain and France. These two had agreed in 1916, as mentioned in our introductory chapter, that each would take a share. In December 1919, they concretized a division. France would take Syria, and Britain would take Palestine and Iraq.[3] The next month, Britain called Japan, France, and Italy to London.[4] The four countries met there over the following weeks as the Principal Allied Powers.[5] There, they charted the outlines of a peace treaty with Turkey in which the Allies would divide up the Turkish Empire, and principally its Arab territories. Italy had no designs on those territories but wanted resource rights within Turkey itself.[6] Japan had no issues to settle with Turkey. Japan had not declared war on Turkey, nor Turkey on it.

During the meetings in London, Lloyd George reminded the others that Britain and France had already agreed during the war about the disposition of Turkey's Arab provinces.[7] That the initiative for a Jewish national home in Palestine was Britain's came through in the reluctant reaction of Philippe Berthelot for the French Foreign Ministry. Berthelot, the meeting notes show, averred that the French would "do their best to favour the development of a Jewish home in Palestine, so long as this development did not run counter to the wishes of the original inhabitants."[8]

France tried to accommodate Britain, whose help France sought on what France wanted itself out of a peace treaty with Turkey. "France would make every endeavour to satisfy the British point of view," Berthelot said.[9] Lloyd George stressed a need for the Allies to forge an agreed position before approaching Turkey. "It was essential," he told the others, "that before peace with Turkey was concluded, the Allies should come to some clear agreement among themselves."[10] "Whatever settlement was reached," Lloyd George said, must "have regard" for "the interests of Great Britain and France."[11] As for Palestine, Berthelot said that "France agreed to Great Britain accepting the mandate."[12] Lloyd George proposed "to assemble the Drafting Committee of the Peace Conference in London in order to commence drafting the Treaty of Peace with Turkey," and the other three agreed.[13]

As plans for a peace treaty with Turkey took shape, the Zionist Organization lobbied the British Government, in private and in public.[14] Chaim Weizmann told the press that "he had been assured that the settlement would satisfy Zionist claims, namely, the allocation of Palestine to Great Britain under a mandate to maintain and develop it into a Jewish National Home."[15] After meeting in London through February, the Allies set a date in mid-April to continue.

The planned venue was San Remo. The meeting was held in a coastal mansion owned by the Earl of Mexborough, who during service in India was attracted to Buddhist philosophy. He named the mansion "Villa Devachan," meaning "dwelling of the Gods."

Gold wrote that the delegates convened as the Supreme Council of the Allied and Associated Powers. The Allied and Associated Powers was a wartime grouping of 27 states. In addition to Britain, France, Italy, and Japan, who were the "principal" allied powers, there were 23 "associated" powers." They were the United States, Belgium, Bolivia, Brazil, China, Cuba, Ecuador, Greece, Guatemala, Haiti, the Hedjaz, Honduras, Liberia, Nicaragua, Panama, Peru, Poland, Portugal, Romania, the Serb-Croat-Slovene State, Siam, Czechoslovakia, and Uruguay. These states had all been parties to the peace with Germany.[16] They did not participate in the discussion of Palestine at the London or San Remo sessions. The United States had a representative sit in on the meetings, but only as an observer.[17]

The states participating in the discussion of Palestine at San Remo numbered only four: Britain, France, Italy, and Japan. Britain, France, and Italy were represented by their prime ministers. David Lloyd George attended for Britain, along with Earl Curzon, who had replaced Balfour as Foreign Secretary. Italian Prime Minister Francesco Nitti came with Foreign Secretary Vittorio Scialoja. France was represented by Prime Minister Alexandre Millerand, who had just replaced Clemenceau in that post, and he brought Berthelot.

Japan was not represented by a prime minister or even a foreign minister. Kishiro Matsui was Japan's ambassador to France. This lower level of representation reflected Japan's lesser role in the decision-making.[18] Not being at war with Turkey, Japan had no need to make peace with it.

An opening session was held at San Remo to set the agenda. Only Britain, France, and Italy participated.[19] Once meetings started to discuss Turkey's Arab territories, Matsui mostly kept to himself. Japan's role at San Remo was described as being "to leave the Middle East to Britain and France."[20] Having emerged as a player only a few years earlier by virtue of its defeat of Russia in the 1905 Russo-Japanese war, Japan was happy to have a place at the table with the Europeans.

The decision-making on who would take which territory was less than high-minded. France and Britain were each keen to get Arab territory that could do them some good. At the Paris Peace Conference, Armenia was on the table, as we saw in Lloyd George's scheme. However, no one wanted Armenia, which lay in ruins and was seen as a financial liability. A British report called Armenia a "derelict region," offering no strategic or economic advantage.[21] Curzon wanted to foist Armenia off on the United States as a mandate.[22] An American lawyer called the Europeans hypocrites for lusting after Syria and Palestine while letting Armenia suffer. "The chief concern of the European Powers, apparently, is not for the welfare of the oppressed nationalities of the Near East," the lawyer wrote, "but the attainment of selfish materialistic ends."[23] Press commentators pilloried France and Britain for refusing to take Armenia.[24] Wilson supported an American mandate over Armenia,[25] but the U.S. Senate killed the idea.[26]

As for Turkey's Arab provinces, Italy and Japan rubber-stamped what Britain and France had already decided. Under the anticipated peace treaty, Syria was to go to France, while Palestine would go to Britain, each to govern by mandate.[27] Gold wanted a "photocopy" of the "San Remo resolution" to be sent to UN delegates, so that they would understand Jewish legal rights. All that exists in writing from San Remo is meeting notes in which, to be sure, one finds the phrase "It was agreed," followed by statements that Britain should get a mandate for Palestine and that the Balfour Declaration should be included. These notes were published by the British and French governments.[28] In a notation about that agreement, the Italian delegation referred to it as a "resolution,"[29] but what the Allies were discussing was only what they planned to demand from Turkey. They were not purporting to make any decision with operative effect. They had no legal standing, moreover, to give Palestine to Britain. The Arab provinces still belonged to Turkey.

Gold said that what was agreed at San Remo amounted to more than a resolution. He said it was a treaty. There was no treaty, however. A treaty would have required a procedure of publication that was not followed. The League Covenant required League members to register their treaties, on penalty of nullity. "Every treaty or international engagement entered into hereafter by any Member of the League," read Covenant Article 18, "shall be forthwith registered with the Secretariat and shall as soon as possible be published by it. No such treaty or international engagement shall be binding until so registered."[30] Treaties after being registered were published by the Secretariat in the *League of Nations Treaty Series*. For example, a British-French treaty concluded at San Remo to give France a share of oil revenues Britain anticipated from Iraq was registered by them with the Secretariat.[31] That act of registration showed that the San Remo participants understood the requirement of registration for anything amounting to a treaty.

Eugene Kontorovich, a lawyer affiliated with Gold's Jerusalem Center for Public Affairs, said in a video lecture, "The international community met at Paris and at San Remo to establish a postimperial world order founded on independent nation-states." "At San Remo," Kontorovich said, "the Jews were promised a national home in Palestine."[32]

There was, however, hardly any "international community" represented at San Remo. The League of Nations did not participate. It was only four states. And their aim, far from being to chart a new world order was to haggle over the spoils of war. Even the four states did not know exactly what territory they were discussing. Since Turkey was still sovereign, no borders had been drawn to define Palestine, Syria, and Iraq. The day after the meeting ended, Prime Minister Millerand composed a memorandum for France's diplomatic bureaucracy, to explain what was done at San Remo. In addition to saying what was done, Millerand listed issues that had not been addressed. One issue on the omission list was "the setting of the respective borders" in Turkey's Arab territories, which, he said was "put off to later decision."[33]

The Balfour Declaration was raised by Britain at San Remo. One element in the Narrative is that at San Remo the Balfour Declaration was endorsed by Britain's Allies. Hersch Lauterpacht, a Jewish Agency consultant on Palestine, and professor at the University of Cambridge, wrote in a 1948 treatise on international law that the Balfour Declaration was "accepted by the other Principal Allied Powers."[34] Lauterpacht did not specify when that occurred, but the major interaction on the issue was at San Remo. The UN Special Committee on Palestine made the same claim, specifying the San Remo meeting as the venue. It took the claim one step farther, asserting that the Principal Allied Powers made Britain's status as mandatory conditional on its implementation of the Balfour Declaration. "On 25 April 1920," wrote the Special Committee in its report to the UN General Assembly, "the Supreme Council of the Allied Powers agreed to assign the Mandate for Palestine to Great Britain on the understanding that the Balfour Declaration would be put into effect."[35]

Italy consented to Britain applying the Balfour Declaration in Palestine but entered a stipulation that its consent was conditional on the satisfaction of a demand it was making for access to coal from mines in Turkey. The minutes recite, and this is where the Italians used the term "resolution," "The Italian delegation, in consideration of the major economic interests that Italy, as an exclusively Mediterranean Power possesses in Asia Minor, reserves its approval to the present resolution, pending satisfaction of Italian interests in Asiatic Turkey."[36] In the event, Italy never got access to coal in Turkey, so its condition for accepting Britain as mandatory in Palestine was never satisfied. The fact, moreover, that Italy conditioned its consent showed that it was not going along because it thought there should be a Jewish national home, rather, it was acceding to a British demand in exchange for gaining something for itself.

Japan had no business being at the San Remo meeting at all, since it was not at war with Turkey. If one takes Italy out of the picture for its unrealized condition, and if one takes Japan out of the picture for not having a legitimate role in peace-making with Turkey, the only effective participants at San Remo were Britain and France.

It was they who finally drew borders. Later in 1920, they drafted a boundary treaty to divide up Turkey's Arab provinces between them, haggling in particular over where to draw a line between Syria and Palestine.[37] This border-drawing exercise was questionable, since neither France nor Britain held sovereignty in Turkey's Arab provinces. Borders are drawn by states holding title.[38] The two powers, nonetheless, finalized and signed a boundary treaty by the end of the year.[39]

What was agreed at the San Remo meeting was nothing more than a common negotiating position to propose to Turkey. The assumption—and the Allies were already writing this point into their draft of a peace treaty—was that Turkey would cede sovereignty to them, and only then would Palestine go to Britain. It was understood, in other words, that Britain could hold Palestine only if it gained sovereignty.

To that extent, the San Remo meeting did not give Britain anything. Only if Turkey were to comply would Britain take Palestine and the Balfour Declaration along with it. As we shall shortly see, this plan would misfire. Turkey would refuse to cede sovereignty, leaving the Allies' assumption unrealized and whatever they had agreed to meaningless. But this aspect of the story must await the next few chapters.

Moreover, although the Balfour Declaration was discussed at San Remo, Britain's Allies did not accept an interpretation of the Balfour Declaration that included Jewish legal rights for Palestine. It is to that matter that we now turn.

Chapter 7

BRITAIN'S ALLIES ENDORSED JEWISH RIGHTS

Even if the San Remo meeting had been the major international event portrayed in the Narrative, the main claim in the Narrative—that at San Remo the Allies endorsed Jewish rights in Palestine—was far from obvious. "At San Remo," Dore Gold wrote, "Jewish historic rights became Jewish legal rights."[1]

The Balfour Declaration was on the table at San Remo, but Jewish legal rights did not figure in what was said. Discussion of the Balfour Declaration was initiated at the 24 April 1920 session at San Remo by Britain, which asked that the Balfour Declaration be mentioned in the peace treaty with Turkey. The others seemed puzzled, because end-of-war provisions on the cession of territory do not normally include detail on how a new sovereign will govern. Curzon opened his plea for inclusion of the Balfour Declaration by saying, "His Britannic Majesty's Government had, two years previously, promulgated a formal declaration which had been accepted by the Allied Powers, that Palestine was in future to be the National Home of the Jews throughout the world."[2] In a hint that Britain was being influenced by the Zionist Organization's lobbying, Curzon added that "the Jews themselves attached a passionate importance to the terms of this declaration," and that "they would not only be disappointed, but deeply incensed if the pledge given in Mr. Balfour's declaration were not renewed in the terms of the treaty."[3] Tellingly, in his entreaty to the Allies, Curzon said nothing about Jewish rights.

Nonetheless, the way in which Curzon depicted the Balfour Declaration rattled the Allies. The Balfour Declaration did not say that "Palestine" was to be "the national home." It said that Britain favored a national home "in" Palestine. Curzon's alteration, whether intentional or not, gave the appearance that a territorial entity was contemplated. The Allies knew what the Balfour Declaration said and what it did not say.

Curzon's statement that the Allies had "accepted" the Balfour Declaration was apparently a reference to statements made by Italy and France that were solicited by the Zionist Organization in 1918. As soon as the Balfour Declaration was delivered to Lord Rothschild, Nahum Sokolow began soliciting statements favorable to Zionism from the Allies.[4] Sokolow reported on his efforts, saying that he approached Italy and France. He did not report any approach to Japan. Italy's foreign ministry replied on 9 May 1918, that it would use its "best endeavors" to facilitate a "national Hebrew center" in Palestine.[5] France's foreign ministry, under the previous government headed by Clemenceau, posted on 9 February 1918, that France agreed with Britain "as concerns the question of Jewish settlement in Palestine."[6] Neither statement mentioned the Balfour Declaration by name or a Jewish national home. The French ministry, in a letter to Sokolow, lauded him for his efforts towards a national home but without endorsing that aim. The French letter referred to Sokolow's efforts to achieve "the wishes of your co-religionists."[7] By using that term, rather than the "Jewish people," the French ministry was declining to endorse the Zionist Organization's claim that Jewry constituted a "people" that might be entitled to self-determination.

Curzon's claim of Allied endorsement evoked no response from the Italians, but the French were incensed.[8] Berthelot responded that he "could not recall that general acceptance had even [*ever?*] been given to Mr. Balfour's declaration by the Allied Powers." Berthelot said that "there had never been any official acceptance of Mr. Balfour's declaration by the Allies of the British Government."[9] Millerand said that if the French Government had previously shown support for the Balfour Declaration, it was on the understanding that a Jewish national home was simply a cultural community within Palestine, but not "that this mandate should carry with it the renunciation of the traditional rights of the inhabitants of Palestine."[10]

In 1919, Japan had expressed support for a national home, but Matsui said as regarded the Balfour Declaration, that he "could not remember that his own Government had ever actually endorsed it." Matsui said that he wanted to "place on record that, so far as he knew, his own government had never accepted the declaration."[11]

The French went further in challenging Curzon. Here mention must be made that at San Remo, there was no stenographer recording verbatim. Notes were taken separately in English by a British secretary and in French by an Italian secretary. The British secretary's notes were published in the British Foreign Office's *Documents of British Foreign Policy 1919–1939*. The Italian secretary's notes were published in the French Foreign Ministry's *Documents diplomatiques français*.[12] The two sets of notes reflect significant variations. Some passages that appear in one are absent in the other. Even where the same passage appears, the wording differs, particularly because the British secretary tended to paraphrase, while the Italian secretary gave quotations verbatim.

The notes for the exchange in which the French challenged Curzon on the Balfour Declaration differ in the English and French versions. The British note-taker had Millerand saying that Britain should not "neglect the traditional rights of the inhabitants generally."[13] The Italian note-taker rendered the same statement as Millerand saying that Britain should "respect the civil, political, and religious rights of the non-Jewish communities and not neglect existing, traditional rights."[14] The British secretary omitted Millerand's mention of political rights. This was a critical difference, because the Balfour Declaration referred to civil rights without clarifying whether governance rights were included in that term.

Berthelot said that since the Allies had not accepted the Balfour Declaration, it could not be written into the peace treaty with Turkey.[15] A draft the French were proposing for the peace treaty, rather than mentioning the Balfour Declaration, averted to a Jewish national home but stipulated that it should not impair the political rights of the Palestine population.[16] Berthelot insisted, "There is no reason the Jews should have rights superior to those of the Muslims and Christians."[17]

The French were getting no satisfaction from Curzon on the issue of whether Britain intended to protect the political rights of the existing Palestine population. Millerand demanded an answer on the record. The British secretary paraphrased Millerand as saying

> that he would ask formally, with a view to having it recorded in the *procès-verbal*, that it should be understood that provision should be made for the safeguarding of the civil and religious rights of the existing non-Jewish communities in Palestine.[18]

Procès-verbal is the French term for the record of a meeting. This same statement of Millerand was rendered by the Italian secretary as a direct quotation:

> I ask that it be formally understood and written into the *procès-verbal* that the phrase "civil and religious rights of non-Jewish communities" includes, in the understanding of the British Government as of ours, political, civil, and religious rights.[19]

As can be seen, the British secretary omitted the term "political." The British notes made no sense on this point. Millerand would have had no reason to demand a commitment to protect only the civil and religious rights, because those were the terms used in the Balfour Declaration. Millerand wanted clarification that Britain understood "civil" rights to include rights relating to the political structure of the country. Curzon's response—even in the English notes—made clear that Millerand had, indeed, asked about political rights. According to a paraphrase by the British secretary, Curzon "enquired what was understood by 'political' as apart from 'civil' rights."[20]

Curzon's response was given verbatim by the Italian secretary as, "I don't see a difference between civil and political rights. In English, the word 'civil' refers to political rights."[21] Thus, per the Italian notes, but not per the British notes, Curzon made a crucial concession that the term "civil" rights as used in the Balfour Declaration encompassed the "political" rights of Palestine's population. To the extent the Allies agreed to put the Balfour Declaration into the peace treaty with Turkey, it was on the understanding that political rights not be impaired.

Italy raised demands of its own on unrelated issues to be resolved with Turkey, making clear that if Britain wanted Italy's consent on the Balfour Declaration, an Italian back would have to be scratched. Italy, which had no particular stake in the war when it broke out, had been promised Turkish booty to attract it to the Allied cause.[22] During the San Remo meeting, France and Britain quietly agreed, without informing Italy, to the bilateral treaty referenced in Chapter 6, to divide Iraqi oil between them.[23] When the Italian government learned of the deal some months later, it was outraged for being excluded, complaining to Curzon that "Italy has no fuel of her own."[24] Italy also wanted access to coal reserves in Turkey as part of a peace arrangement.[25] As well, it wanted a role in ensuring the Vatican's control of holy sites in Jerusalem.[26] France too demanded a role in guaranteeing Roman Catholic access to Jerusalem's holy sites. Prime Minister Lloyd George later conceded that he made concessions to France at San Remo on the holy site issue to get France to let Britain pursue the Jewish national home.[27]

Britain did have benefits it could dispense to the others. Japan was seeking diplomatic support from Britain on several issues. Before the War, Germany held an archipelago called Yap in the Caroline Islands in the western reaches of the Pacific Ocean, using it as a communication center and as a hub for undersea cables. Like Germany's other overseas territories, it was being taken away under the Treaty of Versailles.[28] The United States wanted to put Yap under international administration. But Japan was angling to get the Principal Allied Powers to give it a mandate.[29] Japan needed counter-pressure against the United States.[30] Japan did succeed in gaining a Yap mandate. The United States settled for a treaty with Japan giving it the right to erect communications facilities.[31]

Japan was also concerned about how its people might fare if they were to travel or work in territories being taken from Germany and Turkey, given existing European attitudes towards the Japanese. At the Paris Peace Conference, Japan proposed a clause for the Covenant of the League of Nations, to read:

> The equality of nations being a basic principle of the League of Nations, the High Contracting Parties agree to accord, as soon as possible, to all aliens nationals of States Members of the League equal and just treatment in every respect making no distinction, either in law or in fact, on account of their race or nationality.[32]

The clause was not incorporated into the Covenant, much to the chagrin of Japan's delegation. After that defeat, Japan was hoping at least for a nondiscrimination commitment from Britain. By a diplomatic note, sent shortly after the San Remo meeting, Japan requested an assurance of fair treatment for its own subjects in territories that Britain was taking under mandate.[33]

France, of course, wanted Syria, which had been captured by Britain. Despite their need for Britain's support on Syria, the French mounted a frontal attack on Zionism, repudiating Curzon's pleas. Within French Jewry, Zionism enjoyed only a modest following. In France, one found Zionism written off as an idea promoted in Britain and the United States that would only cause conflict in Palestine.[34] In an apparent reference to the Balfour Declaration as a wartime ploy, Berthelot told Curzon that it "had long been a dead letter."[35] Curzon tried to make the position he was pushing on the Allies seem to be a middle ground. Sheepishly, he explained, "The British Foreign Office had been pressed very closely by the Zionists in order to have the terms of that pledge expanded and improved." The Zionists wanted the Palestine Mandate to call explicitly for a Jewish state. "He himself," Curzon assured the Allies, "as head of the British Foreign Office, had absolutely refused to go beyond the original declaration, and had said that the fairest thing was to adhere strictly to the original terms."[36] This was a remarkable acknowledgment for a diplomat to make. Curzon was admitting to the Allies that the position he was taking with them was one he had had to negotiate with the Zionist Organization.

The plea for sympathy did not succeed. The more Curzon begged, the more hostile the Allies became. They knew that even among Jews, Zionism was supported only by a minority. Berthelot told Curzon sharply that Jews in France were anti-Zionist and had no intention of moving to Palestine.[37]

The Allies did in the end go along with writing into the projected peace treaty an article stating that the Balfour Declaration should be included in the obligations of the mandatory state that would govern Palestine. The meeting notes recorded, however, that the Balfour Declaration could be mentioned in the peace treaty only on the basis of "an undertaking by the mandatory Power that this would not involve the surrender of the rights hitherto enjoyed by the non-Jewish communities in Palestine."[38] Britain had resisted giving this assurance to its Allies. Lloyd George later admitted that he was forced to do so in order to get the Allies' consent to mentioning the Balfour Declaration in the peace treaty.[39]

Each day during the San Remo meeting, the Supreme Council put out a press announcement to explain what had been done that day. After the meeting at which Palestine was discussed, the press announcement barely mentioned mandates, reciting only, "The Supreme Council met this morning at the Villa Devachan. Premiers Nitti, Millerand and Lloyd George, Ambassador Johnson, Signor Sclaloin [Scialoja], M. Berthelot and Earl Curzon were present and discussed the question of mandates over Palestine, Syria and Mesopotamia."[40] Robert Johnson was the US Ambassador to Italy, who attended as an observer. The announcement made no mention of who would take which mandate, or of whether the Balfour Declaration was discussed. The following day, *The New York Times* lifted the curtain on why the official press announcement had been so cryptic. The item was headed "Denies San Remo rumors." It explained that Curzon had telegraphed to London from San Remo to protest newspaper reports of "serious disagreements in the Supreme Council." Curzon was quoted as saying that "there had been unanimity on all portions of the Turkish treaty."[41] But it was precisely the inclusion of the Balfour Declaration in the peace treaty that saw the Allies at each other's throats.

The French Government could not have been clearer at San Remo that it did not consent to Jewish rights in Palestine if that meant a Jewish territorial entity over the objection of Palestine's Arab majority. Two weeks after the meeting, Millerand got a message from France's High Commissioner in Beirut. The Roman Catholic authorities in Jerusalem, seeing that Zionists thought they were given a state at the San Remo meeting, worried about control by Zionists of the holy sites. Millerand assured the High Commissioner that France had not agreed to a Zionist government. "The French Government and its delegates at various conferences have never accepted that Palestine could become a *Zionist state*, or that a *Zionist regime* could be installed in Palestine. There has never been a question of anything other than a *Jewish national home*, that is, to facilitate the establishment and prosperous development of Jewish settlements, agricultural, industrial, at given locations in Palestinian territory, to which Jews could come from various parts of the world to find a home in their ancient native land."[42]

Millerand told the High Commissioner that he had made clear to Curzon that Jews were not to have political control. "It has always been specified in the most explicit way that the Israelite groups," as Millerand called them, would have "no kind of political, civil, or religious rights above those of other populations, whether Christian or Muslim, and that they would not be put in a position that they could restrict the free development or diminish the guarantees given to all the populations living in Palestine. Most recently, at the San Remo conference, the explanations exchanged between Lord Curzon and me have left no doubt on these matters."[43]

Claims that the Allies at San Remo approved Jewish rights in respect of territory find no reflection in the notes of the San Remo meeting.

Chapter 8

BRITAIN TOOK ON PALESTINE BECAUSE OF THE LEAGUE'S MANDATE SYSTEM

"After the victory of the Allied Powers in World War I—and pursuant to Article 22 of the Covenant of the League of Nations," wrote Yoram Dinstein, "the former Turkish territories in the Middle East were placed under the Mandates system. Palestine was assigned as a Mandate to Britain."[1] Per the Narrative, in line with Dinstein's claim, Britain's assumption of a governance role in Palestine came about because of the League's mandate system and through an assignment of Palestine to Britain.

Dinstein's statement conflated two separate issues. One is Britain's right to rule Palestine. The other is the mandate system. The mandate system was not a route to gaining a right to rule territory. It could be used only by a state that held sovereignty over the territory it wanted to place under mandate. Dinstein's wording, however, implied that Britain gained the right to govern through the mandate system.

The League Covenant did, to be sure, suggest that it was desirable that Turkey's Arab provinces, once under new sovereignty, should be administered as mandates rather than as colonies. But the League did not "place" territories under the mandate system. The League had no power to require any state that was holding territory to opt for the mandate system. The League of Nations had no role in determining which states would take on mandates. Nor, as we saw in Chapters 6 and 7, did the Allies have standing to "place" Palestine under Britain's control.

The decision to bring the mandate system into play for Palestine was made by Britain alone. As the San Remo meeting ended, Britain finished a draft of a peace treaty under which it would gain sovereignty from Turkey. The Supreme Council handed the draft to Turkey on May 11, hoping for an immediate signature.[2] Turkey asked for time to respond. Britain was being pressed by the Zionist Organization to "regularize" its tenure in Palestine. From the time the guns of war fell silent, the Zionist Organization lobbied

Britain to take practical steps in Palestine that would lead to Jewish statehood. From April 1918, Britain sponsored what was called the Zionist Commission, made up of Zionists from Europe.[3] This was an advance party of Zionists, hoping to ensure that Britain would give effect to the Balfour Declaration. A Government directive to the military authorities in Palestine explained that the Zionist Commission aimed to take "steps required to give effect to the Government's declaration in favour of the establishment in Palestine of a national home for the Jewish people."[4]

The Zionist Organization and Zionist Commission pushed the Government to declare that Britain was in Palestine to stay. They were unhappy with Britain's status as belligerent occupant, a status that comes into play automatically when an army comes into control of foreign territory. Military control did not take away Turkey's sovereignty.[5] In keeping with its situation as belligerent occupant, the Government in 1918 set up what it called the Occupied Enemy Territory Administration (O.E.T.A.).[6]

The law of belligerent occupation requires an occupant to apply the law of the sovereign, pending a peace treaty that might determine sovereignty going forward. Both Britain and Turkey had recently signed up to a multilateral treaty on the law of war that said precisely that.[7] Britain had even written this treaty into its guidance to the British military. The British Army's 1914 manual on the law of war, in its instructions on belligerent occupation, said that "altering the existing form of government" was not permitted, nor was "upsetting the constitution and the domestic law, and ignoring the rights of the inhabitants."[8] A belligerent occupant must apply the existing law and may enact new regulations only as they relate to protecting itself as an occupant.

Britain's military officials in Palestine understood this international obligation.[9] As indicated, however, they were under pressure from the Zionist Commission to introduce pro-Zionist measures.[10] The military staff broadly sympathized with Arab opposition to Zionism, fearing that the infusion of a Zionist-backed population would make Palestine ungovernable. The Zionist Commission pressured the military administration to adopt regulations to facilitate land purchases by the Jewish National Fund and other Zionist entities seeking to buy land as a base for Jewish statehood.[11]

The military command began to issue enactments on topics for which only a sovereign would be competent. In 1919, it adopted ordinances on the licensing of veterinarians,[12] on business partnerships,[13] and on registration of marriages.[14] Norman Bentwich, the man who would shortly be appointed Attorney-General of Palestine, claimed that the military administration was only "supplementing the Ottoman law where necessary,"[15] and that "the substance of the law of the country has been amended only in a very slight measure."[16] These enactments, however, by their subject matter went beyond what is permitted to a belligerent occupant. For court proceedings and criminal investigation, Bentwich acknowledged that major change was introduced by the military administration. Bentwich said that the changes were an improvement over Ottoman law.[17] Bentwich as much as admitted violation of the law of belligerent occupation as he lauded the changes. "Some essential changes have been brought about," he wrote, "and the ground has been prepared for laying the foundation of British Justice."[18]

Bentwich understood that the role the Government was allowing the Zionist Commission was questionable for Britain as a belligerent occupant. He put it delicately that "the exact status of the Commission was obscure under the international rules concerning military occupation."[19] Bentwich's understatement concealed the obvious illegality of giving a role in governance to a non-governmental organization dedicated to changing the complexion of the country.

The Zionist Commission quickly developed a "full blown Administration." "Every department of the official administration," a Government report stated, "is duplicated in the Zionist Commission." It served as a shadow government, consisting of "no less than a hundred individuals" forming "a complete administrative machine" that was "in active operation."[20]

The Zionist Commission was able to exert pressure on the Government in London with help from the Zionist Organization of America. Bentwich related an incident from 1919, during a visit to Jerusalem by Louis Brandeis, Justice of the US Supreme Court and formerly President of the Zionist Organization of America. In Jerusalem to bolster the work of the Zionist Commission, Brandeis became angry at a social gathering when a British officer expressed sentiments against Zionism. Brandeis, according to Bentwich, complained to the British Government in London and the officer was removed.[21] The Zionist Commission was frequently able to go over the head of the military administration to gain what it wanted from the Government in London.

Immediately after the San Remo meeting, in any event, the wheels were set in motion to proclaim Britain's intent to hold onto Palestine, and to declare rule under the mandate system, even in absence of a peace treaty that might have given Britain sovereignty. Thought was given, though fleetingly, to first gaining approval for a mandate from the League of Nations.[22] Even that would not have given sovereignty, however. Curzon asked former Home Secretary Herbert Samuel to serve as "Governor" (a term used for colonies), and Samuel, who had been advocating for Zionism, accepted.[23]

As the Government's plan become known to institute rule under the League's mandate system, the illegality of claiming a right to govern while still a belligerent occupant became the topic of public discussion in Britain. In June 1920, one member of the House of Lords pointed out that "in occupied enemy territory (which, of course, it is, because we have not made peace with the Turk) it is not permissible to alter the existing form of administration, to upset the constitutional and domestic laws, or to ignore the rights of the inhabitants. That is what we are doing now."[24]

In July, the Crown took the step. It issued a message headed "To the People of Palestine," announcing that "the Allied Powers whose arms were victorious in the late war have entrusted to my country a mandate to watch over the interests of Palestine."[25] This statement was a reference to the San Remo meeting but with a significant distortion of what was said there. The Allies, as we saw, had agreed to put language about mandates into a peace treaty, but they had not authorized Britain to initiate a mandate on its own. And in any event, the Allies had no power to authorize Britain. A belligerent occupant cannot claim a right to govern because states with which it is allied purport to give permission.

The Crown's lack of concern for veracity in characterizing the situation went further. "The Allied and Associated Powers," its public message continued, "have decided that measures shall be adopted to secure the gradual establishment in Palestine of a national home for the Jewish people. These measures will not in any way affect the civil or religious rights or diminish the prosperity of the general population of Palestine."[26] As we saw, it was only the Principal Allied Powers, numbering four, who participated in the discussion of Palestine at San Remo, not the twenty-seven member Allied and Associated Powers.

Britain's unilateral assumption of power, with an added declaration of mandate rule, played well with the English Zionist Federation. Balfour accepted an invitation to mark the King's announcement as a victory for Zionism. "Mr. Balfour will speak next Monday at the Royal Albert Hall," *The Times* reported, "at the demonstration organized by the English Zionist Federation in celebration of the acceptance by Great Britain of the mandate for Palestine as the Jewish National Home."[27] Britain, of course, had "accepted" the mandate from the Allies only after arm-twisting the Allies to offer it. *The Times*, however, was already solidly on board to promote the Government's agenda. *The Times* dispatches from Jerusalem were being run under a by-line "our Zionist correspondent."

1 July 1920, in any event, was the date on which the British Government purported to end its belligerent occupation of Palestine. Herbert Samuel was inaugurated, not as "Governor," but as "High Commissioner."[28] Later in the year, the King confirmed that Britain was undertaking mandate rule. In the House of Lords, he reiterated that he had "accepted" a mandate for Palestine.[29] He repeated that confirmation in the Commons.[30]

The British Government portrayed the July 1 move as lawful on the basis of the San Remo meeting. It would explain some years later, "On the 25th April, 1920, the Supreme Council at San Remo allotted the Mandate for Palestine to Great Britain and on the 1st July, 1920, the military government of O.E.T.A. was replaced by a British civil administration headed by Sir Herbert Samuel, the first High Commissioner for Palestine."[31]

The new "civil" administration announced new enactments unrelated to military administration. Saturday would be observed as the weekly day of rest, rather than Friday as observed by Palestine's Muslims, or Sunday as observed by Palestine's Christians.[32] An ordinance on the sale of land let the Jewish National Fund buy land that would form a nucleus for a Jewish state.[33] An Immigration Ordinance facilitated large-scale immigration of Jews.[34] As deviations from Turkish law, these measures violated the law of belligerent occupation. "Largely motivated by traditional imperialistic beliefs," wrote one analyst about the British approach to governing Palestine, "His Majesty's government reasoned that having conquered Palestine by force of arms, they could do with it as it wished."[35]

Alfred Hyamson, who was appointed as director of immigration for Palestine, acknowledged that there was "no legal basis" for declaring civilian rule, given the absence of a cession of sovereignty from Turkey.[36] Hyamson attributed the decision to replace the military officers to a desire to put Palestine under officials more sympathetic to Zionism. Hyamson understood the extraordinary character of what Britain was doing. He called the switch to a civilian administration an "unprecedented step" taken "in a country whose status was that of Occupied Enemy Territory."[37]

As Hyamson said, a belligerent occupant may not convert an occupation into lawful governance by changing the name of its administration from "military" to "civilian." That proposition was part of British law. Britain's 1914 military law manual provided, "It is of little consequence whether the government imposed by the invader is called military or civil government, for in either case it is a government imposed by the necessity of war and, so far as it concerns the inhabitants or the rest of the world, the laws of war alone determine the legality of its acts."[38] Until and unless it would gain sovereignty via a peace treaty, Britain's status remained that of a belligerent occupant, no matter what it might call its administration. Calling it a mandate administration, as Britain began to do in July 1920, would not suffice.

Adding insult to injury from the perspective of the Palestine population, Prime Minister Lloyd George put responsibility for Palestine into the colonial portfolio, that is, under the Secretary of State for the Colonies. That move took responsibility for Palestine away from Foreign Secretary Curzon, who opposed the Balfour

Declaration, to Colonial Secretary Winston Churchill, who favored it.[39] Apart from personalities, that shift showed what Britain considered Palestine to be. Palestine was administered under the same framework as Britain's colonies.

The effort by Britain to regularize its rule did not go unnoticed by the Arabs of Palestine. A group that grew out of the Muslim–Christian Association calling itself the Palestine Arab Congress protested the erection of a civilian administration, challenging the assertion by Britain of a "competence to enact laws by itself in the absence of any representative or elected Legislative Assembly."[40] The Congress challenged the British Government's aim to set up its own governing apparatus for Palestine and appealed to it "for the justice of immediately proceeding to form a native Government to be responsible towards a Legislative Assembly."[41] The Congress noted that Britain was still a belligerent occupant and therefore lacked legal capacity to adopt legislation for Palestine: "The present provisional Administration in Palestine, which has no right to enact laws before the future status of the country has been defined, but which should govern according to the laws of the past regime, has framed laws and regulations connected with personal liberty and individual appropriation of land and other matters, and has already started putting these into execution."[42] The Congress demanded that "laws and regulations before the war be still carried out and all others framed after the British occupation be annulled."[43]

The Crown's lofty sentiments about Palestine's future as expressed in its announcement of mandate rule were contradicted by the report of a British military court of enquiry appointed to assess the discontent that the Zionist project was engendering. Two weeks before the San Remo meeting, riots broke out in Palestine in which Arabs and Jews were killed.[44] The court of enquiry was convened, and during 50 days of hearings, it heard 152 witnesses. Its report, dated 1 July 1920, found the Arab population "exasperated beyond endurance by the aggressive attitude of the Zionists, and despairing of redress at the hands of an Administration which seems to them powerless before the Zionist organization."[45]

The court of enquiry found the Zionists a disruptive element. "Whatever may be alleged against Turkish rule," read its report, "one fact stands out quite clearly from the evidence. Up to a very recent date the three sects, Moslem, Christians and Jews lived together in a state of complete amity. The Moslem was no doubt, dominant, but such intolerance as there was, seemed rather to be directed against the Christian than the Jew. The Christian could be occasionally troublesome with his appeals to foreign powers. The Orthodox Jew of Palestine was a humble, inoffensive creature, largely dependent on charity for his livelihood in the city of Jerusalem, elsewhere hardly distinguishable from the rest of the peasant population. No serious attack on the Jewish population is recorded since the time of Ibrahim Pasha in 1840."[46]

The Zionists, the report said, differed from the Palestine Jews. "The Orthodox Jew born in the country has never inspired the Arab or Christian with any particular feelings of distrust," but "they already notice that the latest immigrants from Eastern Europe are men of a very different type."[47] The Zionists, the report said, "are ready to use their powerful foreign and home influence to force the hand of this or any future Administration. If not carefully checked they may easily precipitate a catastrophe, the end of which it is difficult to forecast."[48] The Government did not want to have to square this dark picture with the Crown's prediction of a bright future, so it kept the court of enquiry report confidential. In any event, the mandate rule declared by the Crown on 1 July 1920 came not as a result of a requirement of the League Covenant or any decision by any League organ.

Chapter 9

THE LEAGUE OF NATIONS PROTECTED PALESTINE'S ARAB POPULATION

The Crown, in its announcement of Britain's intentions, promised fairness to Palestine's population. "I desire to ensure you of the absolute impartiality with which the duties of the Mandatory Power will be carried out and of the determination of my Government to respect the rights of every race and creed represented among you, both in the period which has still to elapse before the terms of the mandate can be finally approved by the League of Nations and in the future when the mandate has become an accomplished fact."[1] King George did not explain why there was a time period that "has still to elapse" before approval of terms by the League of Nations. His statement was apparently aimed at rationalizing the onset of a mandate without consultation with the League of Nations.

The phrasing about League approval was likely lost on most listeners. The Crown did not say that approval would be sought for the mandate, but only for its "terms." The mandate itself would not be up before the League for approval. Britain had already been appointed, by its lights, by the Allies. So the League could not keep Britain from claiming to govern by a mandate. If the mandate was not conferred by the League, a listener might have wondered, did the League have any control over how Britain might choose to govern?

Even the "terms," however, would not depend on the League. Britain did plan to seek the League Council's approval of a mandate document it was drawing up that would recite "terms." The Covenant did not require approval of the "terms." Members of Parliament who opposed the Balfour Declaration put uncomfortable questions to the Government. One question posed in 1920 was, "Will the League of Nations have anything to say to these terms; can they disregard them after they are decided by the Government?" Cecil Harmsworth, Under-Secretary of State for Foreign Affairs, avoided giving an answer.[2] As we shall see shortly, the Foreign Office would not let the League second-guess the "terms." Under the Covenant's Article 22, paragraph 8, the prerogative of the League Council ran only to terms that related to the degree of authority a mandatory expected to wield, and then only if the mandatory itself failed to explain the degree of authority.

Norman Bentwich set in motion the aspect of the Narrative that claimed that the League would protect the Arab population. Bentwich called Palestine, Syria, and Iraq "infant nations" or "wards" for whom Britain and France would serve as "tutors." "The League delegates the care of the minor to a Power who is termed the Mandatory; and lays down the terms of his charge in a Mandate; and the Mandatory is then responsible to the League as to a Court for the carrying out of the trust."[3] That description painted the mandate arrangement as one of benevolence with oversight. It was inaccurate, however. The League did not "delegate" to Britain. It was Britain who took and kept control of Palestine. The League did not "lay down the terms." Britain wrote the terms. Britain as mandatory was not responsible to the League in the way a guardian is responsible to a court. The League had no control over Britain.

The League had only two organs that even potentially might have exercised control. One was the Assembly, but it had little operative power under the Covenant and none under Article 22 in regard to mandate territories. It decided that a sub-committee would keep track of mandate issues.[4] The Assembly, however, was limited to being able to discuss and express an opinion.[5]

The other organ was the Council, but it too had no control over mandatories. Covenant Article 22 was silent on any power of the Council to supervise a mandatory, or to instruct it in any way. The only role envisaged for the Council in Article 22 was the receipt of information to be supplied by a mandatory, who, it was stated, "shall render to the Council an annual report in reference to the territory committed to its charge," but with no requirement that a report be more than a perfunctory statement. Covenant Article 22 called for a commission to which states taking mandates would give these reports: "A permanent Commission shall be constituted to receive and examine the annual reports of the Mandatories and to advise the Council on all matters relating to the observance of the mandates." That provision did not say who was to appoint such a commission. It was similarly silent on what the Council was to do with any advice given it by such a commission.

In a major policy paper on mandates dated 5 August 1920, titled "Obligations falling upon the League of Nations under the terms of Article 22 of the Covenant (mandates)," the Council in any event took it upon itself to "constitute" a commission.[6] The Council viewed itself as taking a role to ascertain "whether the Mandatory Power has made a good use of these powers and whether its administration has conformed to the interests of the native population." League Covenant Article 22, said the Council in its policy paper, "indicated the spirit which should inspire those who are entrusted with administering those not capable of governing themselves."[7]

Either the Assembly or the Council could seek an advisory opinion of the Permanent Court of International Justice, since they had the right to do so over any issues arising in the course of their work.[8] A mandatory, however, would not be bound to comply with an advisory opinion.

The Crown's references to the League of Nations were aimed at giving the Palestine population assurance that their rights would be protected. Members of Parliament were skeptical. In the House of Lords, A. J. Balfour was challenged by a member who feared that Britain would let the rights of the Arabs be overridden. Balfour answered that the PMC would be up to the task. "It is surely a very poor compliment to the British Government," Balfour replied, "to a Governor of Palestine appointed by the British Government, to the Mandates Commission under the League of Nations, whose business it will be to see that the spirit of the Mandate, as well as the letter, is carried out, and beyond them to the Council of the League of Nations, to suppose that all these bodies will so violate every pledge that they have ever given, and every principle to which they have ever subscribed, as to use the power given to them by the Peace Treaty to enable one section of the community in Palestine to oppress and dominate any other."[9] Balfour's reference to "the Peace Treaty" was to the fact that the Covenant was part of the peace treaty with Germany.

As Balfour explained, however, the task of the PMC would be to inquire whether the terms of the mandate were being carried out. If Britain planned in its mandate to promote a Jewish national home, as the Crown was saying, the task of the PMC would be to ensure that this was being done. So, the PMC's obligation to protect the Arab population would run up against an obligation to promote a Jewish national home.[10]

The fact that the PMC could provide little protection became clear two years later when the Palestine Arab Congress tried to challenge the implementation of the Balfour Declaration as a violation of Arab rights. The PMC reported to the League Council that the "petitioners protest against the terms of the mandate itself, as established by the Council of the League of Nations on July 24th, 1922." The PMC explained to the Council that the terms could not be challenged:

> As regards the protests of the petitioners against the terms of the mandate itself, and more especially as regards the desire for the establishment in Palestine of a fundamentally different regime from that of the mandate at present in force, the Commission, considering that its task is confined to supervising the execution of the mandate in the terms prescribed by the Council, is of opinion that it is not competent to discuss the matter.[11]

The Council approved the PMC's refusal to consider the challenge to the mandate document.[12] The PMC's response, unfortunately for the Palestine Arab Congress, was quite appropriate in light of the limited role of the PMC. Its task was to implement mandate documents. It had no power to override them. The Covenant, moreover, gave the PMC no power to take the mandate away. The most it could do was to report malfeasance to the Council. But even then, no protection for the population could be expected. The PMC had no power even to make proposals to a mandatory power to alter the way it was administering a mandate territory.[13] It could make proposals only by way of a report to the Council.

Even the Council could not revoke a mandate. Nothing in Article 22 gave it such a power.[14] Any proposed resolution to revoke a mandate could be vetoed by the mandatory as a member of the Council. Council resolutions required a unanimous vote, so long as they were not on matters of procedure.[15] The requirement of unanimity applied to mandate issues, with the result that the League had no control over Britain.[16] Some years later, the International Court of Justice acknowledged this veto right on the part of a mandatory power to keep the Council from revoking a mandate.[17] Britain could keep the mandate no matter how badly it behaved. Had Britain turned over the entire administration of Palestine to the Zionist Organization, the League could have done nothing but fume. Bentwich acknowledged that the League could do little against Britain for any violation of the mandate.[18] Britain could be sued over mandate issues by other League members, but only if their own rights were violated.[19] In brief, the Article 22 system for mandates left the Palestine population to the tender mercies of the Crown.

The Article 22 mandate system was seen by some as an expression of idealism fulfilling the obligations of international society.[20] As viewed by others, as we have already seen, Article 22 moved the dial only slightly away from colonial rule. Given that the German and Turkish territories were being taken by the leading colonial powers, one analyst questioned the logic in requiring them to account to the League of Nations only for them, and not for the rest of their colonies.[21] Another analyst said that the mandate system was hard to explain in terms of its logic, that it "was not a product of disinterested juristic thought nor of detached scientific investigation but was a compromise invented by the Versailles statesmen to meet an immediate political dilemma."[22] That dilemma was that Woodrow Wilson was pushing for international administration that would have precluded exploitation of resources, but Britain and France wanted something out of Turkey's Arab territories. Oil was beginning to be an important commodity, and Britain wanted recompense for having defeated Turkey. Lloyd George told

Millerand in a private conversation that the military campaign "cost a good deal of money," and that "the only chance to recoup is oil."[23] The mandate system was, therefore, a "compromise."

The term "mandate" was chosen for public relations reasons, not legal reasons. "Mandate" as used in Article 22 did not reflect the legal meaning of the term.[24] Article 22 borrowed the term from French law, where a mandate (*mandat* in French) is an act whereby "one person gives to another the power to do something." According to France's Civil Code, a mandate is a "contract" that comes into effect upon "acceptance by the mandatory."[25] The person who gives a mandate is always free to revoke it.[26] As applied to Turkey's Arab provinces, if the true meaning of the term were to be followed, some state, Britain for example, would be asked by Palestine's population to act on its behalf, and if Britain did not act in ways that the population found beneficial, the population could revoke the mandate.

Under Article 22, however, it was clearly not a territory's population who would make a request to a potential mandatory to take on a mandate. Article 22 said that the "wishes" of the population were to "be a principal consideration in the selection of the Mandatory." Logically, it would be some other party that would be considering their "wishes." But Article 22 did not say who that would be.

Article 22 said that a mandatory would act "on behalf of the League." If that was true, perhaps the League should have taken applications from states seeking to serve as mandatories. "Without doubt," wrote a Belgian lawyer, "one might think at first blush that the mandatories should be selected by the League of Nations, in whose name they exercised power."[27] But that was not done. The absence of an instruction on who was to select mandatories left it to the victorious powers holding territory. That allowed Britain and France, at the San Remo meeting, to take Turkey's Arab provinces for themselves.[28]

A further variance from the true concept of "mandate" was that no one could revoke it. The population could not do so, and as we saw, not even the League could do so. Had the Covenant's drafters been more straightforward, they would have found a term other than "mandate" to describe what they were creating.

Article 22 did, in a concession to a territory's population, say, as just indicated, that its "wishes" were to be considered. The Crown in the King's message of 1 July 1920, however, did not mention the "wishes" of Palestine's population. Those "wishes" had not been considered. The Crown simply declared a mandate for itself by fiat. So, the mandate was not actually being taken pursuant to the Covenant of the League of Nations. It was being taken in spite of the Covenant.

The term "mandate" created an appearance of limitation on the powers of the administering state that had little to do with reality. Mandatories were self-selected and were subject to no effective outside control. As applied to Palestine, the term "mandate" was doubly pernicious, because of Britain's aim of inserting an outside population group without consulting the existing population. There would have been little chance that the Palestine population would "mandate" Britain to bring in outsiders who openly declared that they wanted to take over the country. They would not have requested their own political extinction.

In a clause that seemed to give some protection, Article 22 said that the Turkish territories were "provisionally recognized" as "independent nations," and that the role of the outside state was to be limited "to the rendering of administrative advice and assistance." But Britain, per the King's announcement, was setting up its own governing apparatus. Its "civil" administration was in total charge. There would be no indigenous governing authority to which Britain would give "advice" or "assistance."

The drafting of a mandate document, which was finalized in the months following the Crown's proclamation of mandate rule, did not bode well for protection. In Chapter 15 below, we shall see that the document was the work less of Britain than of the Zionist Organization. When the British drafters shared a draft with the Allies, the French expressed alarm at the lack of protection for the population of Palestine. One Curzon aide reported to him "that the French are even now convinced that the terms of this mandate go much too far and contain the certainty of trouble." That concern was consistent with the reservations France had expressed at San Remo. The aide described the French as "uneasy" about the document.[29]

In preamble clauses, the British Government recited the steps it planned to take to gain sovereignty in Palestine, as a basis for a right to govern. Turkey was supposedly renouncing sovereignty in favor of the Allies, and the Allies were designating Britain to take Palestine with the Balfour Declaration. One preamble clause said that "the Principal Allied Powers" had agreed that Britain "should be responsible for putting into effect the declaration originally made on November 2nd, 1917, by the Government of His Britannic Majesty." That was at best a half-truth, since the Allies had insisted on a restricted reading of the Balfour Declaration. But then the British Government added a clause that turned the Balfour Declaration on its head. Immediately after a clause on the Balfour Declaration, Britain added, "Whereas recognition has thereby been given to the historical connection of the Jewish people with Palestine and to the grounds for reconstituting their national home in that country."[30]

This clause made it appear that the Balfour Declaration had contemplated a reconstitution of an ancient Hebrew state, and, moreover, that the Allies so construed the Balfour Declaration. The Balfour Declaration spoke only about a Jewish national home. At San Remo, as we saw, the Allies were adamant that they did not authorize Britain to derogate from the traditional, or national, rights of Palestine's population. Yet this clause seemed to do precisely that.

Immediately after the San Remo meeting, as we saw in Chapter 8, Italy, France, and Britain gave Turkey a draft of a peace treaty. Japan played no role. The three Allies worried that the treaty's terms, which included the taking of Turkey's Arab territories, were so harsh that Turkey might balk.[31] On 10 August 1920, at the Paris suburb of Sèvres, Turkey did sign, however. Turkey was to cede sovereignty of its Arab territories to the Allies, allowing Britain to take sovereignty over Iraq and Palestine, and France over Syria, and to govern them as mandates, whose documentation was to be approved by the Council of the League.[32] The Treaty of Sèvres was signed subject to subsequent ratification, so the signing did not put it into effect.[33] Until a cession of sovereignty that would come with ratification, Britain had no legal basis for governing Palestine. Renunciation of sovereignty in favor of the Allies "had indeed to be secured before any definite *régime* could legally be established."[34]

Without awaiting ratification, however, Britain sent to the League Council, on 7 December 1920, its document for the governance of Palestine under the mandate system.[35] The document included the degree of authority Britain planned to exercise. That meant that there were no terms for the Council to define. Norman Bentwich tried to make it appear that the Council had the authority to change the terms of the mandate document that Britain submitted. The terms are "liable to modification," he wrote, "by the Council."[36] That was untrue. Article 22, paragraph 8, gave a mandatory full control of the terms of a mandate document.

When pressed in Parliament, where members were concerned about Britain giving up powers to the League, Lloyd George made clear that it was Britain calling the shots. He was asked whether the League could "alter, amend, and reject a mandate."[37] Lloyd George said that the mandate documents would, yes, be submitted to the Council. However, he continued, "It will require the unanimous consent of the Council of the League to reject them."[38] So were a vote to be taken, the question posed to the Council would not be to approve a mandate document, but to reject it. Britain would not need the votes of other members. So, while Britain was conceding a Council role, that role would have no substance. There would be no procedure that could legitimately be termed "approval" of Britain's mandate document.

Britain was attributing authority to itself, both to take control of Palestine and to implement the Balfour Declaration there. Covenant Article 22 gave the League little control over the terms of a mandate, or how it would be carried out. Protection of the population was ephemeral. Britain could do as it pleased.

Chapter 10

BRITAIN WAS GIVEN PALESTINE BY THE LEAGUE OF NATIONS

On 24 July 1922, the Council of the League of Nations approved what was called in the Council's minutes a "declaration" about Britain's document for mandate rule in Palestine.[1] Jerusalem Center lawyer Eugene Kontorovich took that declaration to mean that Palestine was given to Britain by the League. In a journal article coauthored with Abraham Bell, the two men wrote, "Palestine was awarded to Britain with the charge of reconstituting a national home for the Jewish people."[2]

"Award" implied that Palestine was somehow bestowed upon Britain. One element of the Narrative is that the League Council declaration gave Palestine to Britain. Legal scholar Elihu Lauterpacht, son of Hersch Lauterpacht, has it that on 24 July 1922, the League "granted a mandate in respect of Palestine to the British Government."[3]

Even analysts critical of the Palestine mandate accepted the claim that Palestine was given to Britain by the League. "The Mandate for Palestine issued by the League of Nations in July 1922," wrote historian Rashid Khalidi, "was an internationally recognized document representing the consensus of the great powers of the day as to the disposition of the former Ottoman territory of Palestine."[4]

The League Council, however, never purported to give Palestine to Britain, either in the sense of giving a right to govern the territory, or a right to use the mandate system. The Allies, as we saw from the San Remo meeting, acquiesced in Britain's refusal to evacuate Palestine, but with the British Army firmly in place, there was nothing they could have done to displace it.

The League Council, moreover, had only the powers given it by the Covenant. The League had no rights over Palestine that it could bestow. The League had no authority over the territory that had been Turkey's in the Arab world. The League had no sovereignty there.[5] Covenant Article 22, to repeat, did not give the Council a power to distribute territory. As a result, it could not give sovereignty to Britain. Nor could it "award" a mandate, in the sense of a grant of authority to govern, because, similarly, it had no authority to give.[6]

Nor did the Council have a role under Article 22 in regard to mandate documents. Britain decided to seek approval of the document's terms, apparently as a concession to the procedure suggested by the Council in its 5 August 1920 policy paper on mandates. Article 22 did not require it to do so.

In any event, the Council's 24 July 1922 "declaration" related only to the "articles" of the mandate document, not to the mandate itself. On that date, the Council did not purport to "award" a mandate to Britain. It was only approving the terms of the document, and then only in a conditional manner. No formal resolution was proposed on that date for the Council to adopt. Rather, the "declaration" was read aloud by the Council President, reciting, "In view of the declarations which have just been made, and of the agreement reached by all the Members of the Council, the articles of the mandates for Palestine and Syria are approved. The mandates will enter into force automatically and at the same time, as soon as the Governments of France and Italy have notified the President of the Council of the League of Nations that they have reached an agreement on certain particular points in regard to the latter of these mandates."[7] A notation in the minutes followed, reading, "The Council approved this declaration."[8]

The "declarations which have just been made" referred to matters we will recount in a moment that had been impediments. The Council was making clear in any event that it was not purporting to confer authority on Britain. That was in keeping with an explanation Curzon gave in the House of Lords shortly after the San Remo meeting in 1920, when he was asked about the role of the League of Nations. "It is quite a mistake to suppose," Curzon said, "that under the Covenant of the League, or under any instrument, the gift of the Mandate rests with the League of Nations. It does not do so. It rests with the Powers who have conquered the territories which it then falls to them to distribute, and," in an evident reference to the San Remo discussion, "it was in these circumstances that the Mandate for Palestine and Mesopotamia was conferred upon and accepted by us."[9] It was only one week after Curzon spoke these words that the Crown made its announcement that it was initiating mandate rule—without any action by the League.

The limited nature of what the Council was doing regarding the mandate document came through in a characterization the British Government gave in 1945 of what the Council had done on 24 July 1922. The Government explained that on that date "an agreed text was confirmed by the Council."[10] The terms, in other words, had been agreed to, namely, between Britain and the other members of the Principal Allied Powers. The Council did not purport to assess its articles in light of the Covenant. It merely confirmed a text that had already been "agreed" by the Principal Allied Powers.[11]

The mandate document, in any event, was a separate matter from a right to govern. The Council's "declaration" of 24 July 1922 had no significance for Britain in gaining a right to govern Palestine. Britain's plan for gaining territorial rights ran along the lines it sketched out in the Treaty of Sèvres. Britain would get Palestine from Turkey, not from the League. The states that took German colonies got their titles this way. In the peace treaty with Germany, a section titled "Germany's colonies" contained Article 119, which read, "Germany renounces in favour of the Principal Allied and Associated Powers all her rights and titles over her oversea possessions."[12] The biggest prize was German East Africa, which the Allies, still assembled in Paris as their Supreme Council, "gave" to Britain. The process, to be sure, had an air of unreality about it. The British Army, not coincidentally, was sitting in East Africa, having wrested it from Germany. Anyone who might have tried to "give" East Africa to anyone else would have had to drive the British Army out.

So for Germany's colonies, at any rate, Germany ceded the territory to the Allies, who re-ceded to one or another of themselves. At the San Remo meeting, Britain and France set in motion a plan to achieve the same with Turkey's Arab territories. As we saw, they convinced Italy and Japan to designate Palestine, Iraq, and Syria as falling under French and British control, in the event that Turkey would cede these territories to the four Allies.

The peace treaty that Turkey and the Allies signed at Sèvres incorporated this plan.[13] It contained a provision similar to Article 119 of the peace treaty with Germany, namely, a cession of sovereignty to the Principal Allied Powers. More specific than the peace treaty with Germany, this peace treaty with Turkey named the territories at issue—Syria, Palestine, and Iraq—and said that they were to be governed as mandate territories under the provisions of Article 22 of the League Covenant. So, Turkey would be agreeing not only to cede the territories but also would be agreeing to their being governed as mandate territories. The cession appeared in Article 132, which read, "Outside her frontiers as fixed by the present Treaty Turkey hereby renounces in favour of the Principal Allied Powers all rights and title which she could claim on any ground over or concerning any territories outside Europe which are not otherwise disposed of by the present Treaty."

The important consequence Britain sought was that it would get three things from Turkey—sovereignty (via the Principal Allied Powers), a right to take a mandate, and a right to implement the Balfour Declaration. Britain wanted it to be clear that Turkey as sovereign was not only ceding the territory but was authorizing that it be used to bring in a population of Jews from elsewhere to implement the national home.

While Article 132 gave sovereignty to the Allies, two other articles dealt with these other matters. Article 94 covered Syria and Iraq, reading,

"The High Contracting Parties agree that Syria and Mesopotamia shall, in accordance with the fourth paragraph of Article 22, be provisionally recognised as independent States subject to the rendering of administrative advice and assistance by a Mandatory until such time as they are able to stand alone." That fourth paragraph of Article 22 of the League Covenant said that Turkey's Arab territories were to be provisionally recognized as independent, subject to the rendering of administrative advice and assistance.

Article 95 dealt with Palestine, reading,

> The High Contracting Parties agree to entrust, by application of the provisions of Article 22, the administration of Palestine, within such boundaries as may be determined by the Principal Allied Powers, to a Mandatory to be selected by the said Powers. The Mandatory will be responsible for putting into effect the declaration originally made on November 2, 1917, by the British Government, and adopted by the other Allied Powers, in favour of the establishment in Palestine of a national home for the Jewish people, it being clearly understood that nothing shall be done which may prejudice the civil and religious rights of existing non-Jewish communities in Palestine, or the rights and political status enjoyed by Jews in any other country.

"High contracting parties" is a term used in treaty law to refer to the states that are concluding a treaty. "Principal Allied Powers" meant Britain, France, Italy, and Japan. The preamble to the Treaty of Sèvres specifically defined the term "Principal Allied Powers" to mean these four. The inclusion of Japan made little sense, because Japan and Turkey were not at war with one another. There was no reason for Japan to be making peace with Turkey, much less to be taking sovereignty to some of Turkey's territory.

Article 95 ceded Palestine to the Principal Allied Powers and authorized them to recede it to whomever they liked, but that unnamed state would be required to implement the Balfour Declaration. That level of specificity showed that Britain knew it was on shifting sand as it sought a right to govern Palestine and to bring in an outside population. It was anxious to get the Balfour Declaration written into the treaty, since such a reference in the treaty would bolster Britain's Narrative that its implementation of a Jewish national home rested on an international obligation, rather than being a unilateral policy.

Article 96 recited, "The terms of the mandates in respect of the above territories will be formulated by the Principal Allied Powers and submitted to the Council of the League of Nations for approval."

The Zionist Organization had pushed for the reference to the Balfour Declaration in the Treaty of Sèvres. Weizmann wrote to Curzon's secretary in March 1920, just prior to the San Remo meeting, saying that it was "essential that the dedication of Palestine as the Jewish National Home should find explicit recognition in the Turkish treaty."[14] Weizmann wrote that "it is highly desirable, if not actually necessary from a legal point of view that the League of Nations receive special instructions regarding the objects of the mandate to be issued for Palestine."[15] Weizmann understood, correctly, that a mandate would not come to Britain from the League, hence his injunction that the League should be given "instructions" as to its "objects." Inclusion of the Balfour Declaration in the peace treaty would give Britain a legal obligation to implement a Jewish national home, in the nature of a servitude on Britain's sovereignty. If Britain gained sovereignty without such a proviso, it could abandon the Jewish national home.

In his plea to Curzon's secretary, Weizmann pointed out that other peoples had gained a "national home" in recent peace treaties. "The Jewish people," he wrote, "expect it [the national home] to find a place in the Turkish treaty just as, under somewhat different circumstances to be sure, the national homeland of the Czecho-slavs, the Jugo-slavs and the Poles were recognized in the German and Austrian treaties. If the Jewish National Home were not mentioned in the Turkish treaty, great consternation and resentment would be felt by the Jewish people all over the world. Nothing less than a pronouncement from the Peace Conference would remove the misapprehension."[16] Weizmann feared that "the political status" would be "unsettled" without a provision in the peace treaty giving rights to Britain.[17]

The sovereignty issue had already been addressed by the League Council. In its 5 August 1920 policy paper, the Council said that for a valid mandate, an administering state must hold legal title to the given territory. "It is not enough," the Council said, "that the Mandatory Powers should be appointed; it is important that they should also possess a legal title."[18] Britain, as a Council member, voted in favor of this report. Balfour, in his remarks in Parliament, said that the power to be exercised by British authorities would be "given to them by the Peace Treaty."[19] Consistent with the Council report, Balfour was acknowledging that Britain would have no legal rights in Palestine until and unless it gained sovereignty from Turkey. In absence of a peace treaty, Britain was only a belligerent occupant. But Turkey had signed the Treaty of Sèvres only four days earlier, with its clause ceding sovereignty to the Principal Allied Powers, and the Council expected Turkey to ratify. The Council's 5 August statement on sovereignty, in any event, was hardly more than a truism. A state could not govern without holding sovereignty, or, failing sovereignty, by gaining the consent of the sovereign.

The issue of sovereignty as a precondition for holding a mandate was not long in causing a headache for Britain. When Britain filed its draft mandate document with the League Council in December 1920, Italy immediately objected. It told Curzon that the League Council, of which Italy was a member, could not approve any mandates for the former Turkish provinces until the Treaty of Sèvres was ratified and entered into force. Only then would Britain or France have the requisite status to govern on the basis of a mandate. Curzon responded that Italy was raising "a purely technical point." But acknowledging that the ratification was needed for the mandate to be valid, Curzon said it was the "hope" of his Government that its "position in these territories may be definitely legalized without delay, so that administration and finance can at last be placed on a proper footing and order maintained in the name of duly constituted authority." Curzon said that Britain was "accordingly most anxious to secure the definite issue of the mandates."[20]

Italy was not alone in finding Britain's request for League Council approval premature. The League Assembly at its next annual gathering said that it was pointless for the Council to approve a mandate's terms before a mandatory had sovereignty. The Assembly had formed a sub-committee on mandates within its standing committee on legal matters. "With regard to the A Mandates," the sub-committee opined in a 1921 report, referring to Palestine, Syria, and Iraq, it would be "premature to press for immediate action by the Council." The sub-committee, the report continued, "takes note of the fact that the Treaty of Sèvres has not yet been ratified by the Powers."[21] The Assembly adopted the report of the sub-committee.[22] The Assembly's rationale was the same as Italy's. It made no sense for the Council to approve a mandate's terms before the mandate could be valid.

Britain, however, pushed ahead, seeking Council approval of the terms even if the mandate itself would not be valid. The Foreign Office explained in December 1921 that Britain intended to request approval in 1922 by the Council of the "the terms of the mandate for Palestine as drafted in spite of the dependence of the final legalization of the status of the mandatory upon the entry into force of a treaty of peace with Turkey."[23] By "entry into force," the Foreign Office had in mind the ratification of the Treaty of Sèvres.

Another obstacle for Britain was an objection by the United States that it wanted assurance of market access to Palestine before the Council approved the mandate document. The two contemplated a bilateral treaty that would give the United States the same access rights that Britain was offering to League members. Britain explained to the United States that it wanted to get the terms of the mandate "definitively settled before the [bilateral] treaty can be negotiated and signed."[24]

Britain informed the United States that it hoped to gain approval of the terms at a Council meeting scheduled for 11 May.[25] On that day the Foreign Office posted a notice in *The Times* explaining that the Council would be asked. The notice began by saying that "some uncertainty exists with reference to the position of Great Britain in Palestine." The "uncertainty," of course, related to the fact that Britain had yet to gain sovereignty. The notice continued, "Approval by the League of Nations will not, however, mean that the mandate has actually been granted to Great Britain, as it would be difficult to fulfil that technicality until the Treaty of Sèvres has been properly ratified by Turkey." Explaining its reason for pressing ahead, the Foreign Office ended the notice by saying, "Assuming that the Council of the League of Nations approves of the mandate, the Government will presumably proceed to draft the Treaty with the United States, safeguarding American rights."[26]

Balfour did raise its request in the League Council on 11 May. He made clear that it was only the terms for which he sought approval. He acknowledged that "while the Treaty of Sèvres remained unratified, the Mandate could not legally be in force."[27] Italy re-raised its objection. Italy was not willing to vote on the mandate's terms before Britain gained sovereignty. Italy, like the other Council members, knew that Britain was likely going to have to agree to modify certain terms of the Treaty of Sèvres to get Turkey to ratify. Italy told the Council that the mandates over Turkey's Arab territories "could not be approved so long as the question of the revision of that Treaty was pending."[28] Given the non-ratification of the Treaty of Sèvres, Italy called it "a practical impossibility for the Council to take a decision on the question during the present session."[29]

Undeterred, Britain got the mandate on the Council's agenda a week later, insisting on a vote on its terms despite the non-ratification of the Treaty of Sèvres. Balfour again acknowledged, however, that this vote would have no legal effect. He told the Council, "The final juridical date on which the mandates for the Middle East would become a part of a fixed and authoritative law of nations could only be when the Treaty of Sèvres was finally ratified." Balfour did, however, give himself one other option. He said that the Treaty of Sèvres might need "re-modelling."[30] Balfour was hoping that a revised peace treaty with Turkey would include provisions like Articles 95 and 132.

At the same time, however, and a bit incongruously, Balfour told the Council that the Council had little power in relation to mandates. "The public mind," he said, "might have misunderstood the powers of the League of Nations and of its Council regarding mandates. Mandates were not the creation of the League, and they could not in substance be altered by the League."[31] Balfour was correct. Under Covenant Article 22, as we have seen, the League had no control over the terms of a mandate. Defiantly, Balfour told the Council that a mandate arrangement was "a self-imposed limitation by the conquerors on the sovereignty which they exercised over the conquered territory."[32]

From an advocacy perspective, this was a strange approach for Balfour to take. He wanted approval but was telling the Council that the mandate was Britain's affair and its alone. The Council had no power, he was saying, to "alter" the terms on which Britain was governing Palestine, including whether Britain chose to implement the Balfour Declaration. Balfour was seeking approval of the terms while at the same time telling the Council that it had no role with regard to them.

No Council member objected to Balfour's explanation of the Council's lack of authority. Council members evidently understood that the terms of the mandate document rested within Britain's sole discretion. They knew that Covenant Article 22 had been drafted to let the conquering states decide whether to use the mandate system, who should get the mandates, and how they would govern them. Balfour's outburst highlighted the fact that the exercise of submission of a mandate document had no basis in the Covenant. League Council "approval" had no legal significance.

The League Covenant did not require the submission of a document by a state choosing to undertake a mandate. Article 22 mentioned no such document. Nor did it give the Council a role in approving such a document. In its eighth paragraph, Article 22 did state, "The degree of authority, control, or administration to be exercised by the Mandatory shall, if not previously agreed upon by the Members of the League, be explicitly defined in each case by the Council." Hence, only if a state declaring a mandate could not, perhaps in conjunction with Allies, decide on its "degree of authority, control, or administration" would the Council have a role.

The phrase "Members of the League" was not defined in the Covenant. In theory, that might mean "all" members, which would be another way of saying the League Assembly. But the Covenant's drafters knew full well what the Assembly would be, and if the idea were to give it that role, the Assembly would have been mentioned by name. The Council, in its 5 August 1920 policy paper on mandates, noted that the drafting of mandate documents was undertaken by the Allies even before the Covenant was finalized.[33] The expectation was that a mandate document would be written by the Allies.

The Covenant left it to whichever state was assuming control to decide how to rule. As far as the Covenant required, that rule did not have to be based on a written document. The Covenant did not require a written document. In the case of Iraq, Britain submitted a written mandate document, but Britain then concluded a treaty with Iraq providing for "advice and assistance."[34] Britain withdrew its mandate document.[35] It sent a communication explaining the treaty, and the Council said that Britain was achieving the aims of a mandate and that it would consider there to be a mandate arrangement even in absence of a mandate document.[36] But even this alternative document was not required by the Covenant. Britain decided to submit it for reasons of its own, and the Council, perhaps anxious to show that it was not a useless institution, acted as if Britain should submit something. Britain was clear on that point. It submitted draft documents for Iraq and Palestine out of grace, not out of legal necessity.

Since the Principal Allied Powers were distributing German colonies to themselves just as they were putting the finishing touches on the Covenant, one analyst surmised that the assumption behind Article 22 was that the terms of a mandate would be agreed between a mandatory and them. The Principal Allied Powers would select a mandatory and would determine "by mutual agreement with it" the "precise conditions of the mandate."[37]

Another analyst explained how the Council inserted itself into the mandate-writing process. The Peace Conference formed a Mandates Commission (not to be confused with the Permanent Mandates Commission formed the next year) that, in July 1919, set about drafting documents for mandate control of Germany's colonies. The Council, once it was formed in 1920, asked for these drafts, claimed that they were required, and said that it would check them for their conformity to Article 22.[38] In its 5 August 1920 policy paper on mandates, the Council claimed this power for itself.[39] "The terms of the Mandates according to which the Mandatory Powers should exercise their government," the Council pontificated in the policy paper, "must be especially defined in distinct charters applicable to each Mandatory area."[40] The Council set out a procedure for mandate documents:

1. The Council decides to request the principal Powers to be so good as to (a) name the Powers to whom they have decided to allocate the Mandates provided for in Article 22; (b) to inform it as to the frontiers of the territories to come under these Mandates; (c) to communicate to it the terms and the conditions of the Mandates that they propose should be adopted by the Council from following the prescriptions of Article 22.
2. The Council will take cognisance of the Mandatory Powers appointed, and will examine the draft Mandates communicated to it, in order to ascertain that they conform to the prescriptions of Article 22 of the Covenant.
3. The Council will notify to each Power appointed that it is invested with the Mandate, and will, at the same time, communicate to it the terms and conditions.[41]

League Council members may have thought that an exertion of control was justified in order to keep the mandatories in line, but it was a clear over-reach beyond the limited power given to the Council by Article 22. A French newspaper noted that the Council was giving an "expansive" reading to Article 22 by claiming a power over the "degree of authority" a mandatory would exercise, and not only if the mandatory was unable to agree with its Allies on the "degree of authority."[42] Nor did Article 22 give the Council a power to examine draft mandates for conformity to Article 22.

Britain did not oppose the Council's report but did not abandon its position—one well-grounded in the Covenant—that the terms of a mandate were for a mandatory to determine.[43] Britain on the one hand wanted to keep the League from telling it what to do in Palestine, but at the same time League approval would help politically, given that Britain planned to govern Palestine in ways that violated the Covenant. A blessing from the League would blunt charges that the Government was overriding the rights of Palestine's population.

Even on the "degree of authority, control, or administration," Britain closed the door on the Council. In Article 1 of its mandate document, Britain gave an explicit definition of its "degree of authority, control, or administration," writing, "The Mandatory," by which it meant itself, "shall have full powers of legislation and of administration."[44] That clause excluded the Council from any role in regard to that term of the mandate document, and the Covenant gave the Council no role in regard to any other term.

Italy remained an obstacle to Britain in gaining approval of the mandate's terms, however. Italy, along with Japan and France, had consented at San Remo to proposing a mandate for Britain in Palestine, as we saw, only in the context of a peace treaty with Turkey that would give sovereignty to the Allies. In its note to Britain in December 1920, Italy had said that it did "not accept conferment of mandates at San Remo as definitive pending entry into force of the Turkish treaty."[45] Now Italy was saying that it meant what it said. Italy was not prepared to acquiesce in a League Council approval of the mandate's terms absent acquisition by Britain of sovereignty.

The impasse, however, was resolved by behind-the-scenes political bargaining. Italy's Foreign Minister Carlo Schanzer quietly sent a memorandum demanding a number of concessions from Britain on unrelated matters. In return, Schanzer said that Italy could acquiesce in the League Council to approval of the terms of the Palestine mandate document, even without a peace treaty with Turkey. "The Italian Government," Schanzer wrote, "in order to facilitate the return to normal conditions of the Arab countries detached from the Turkish empire and entrusted to the British mandate, are willing to consent that the Draft Mandates of Palestine and Iraq should be discussed by the League of Nations before the coming into force of the peace Treaty with Turkey and are also disposed to give their approval to the said Drafts, subject to some explanations which are separately dealt with."[46] Britain agreed to Italian demands on a variety of economic and territorial issues of concern to Italy.[47] Italy also had demands about what prerogatives Britain would grant it in Palestine. The Foreign Office passed on to the United States for its information its "assurances to be given to Italy in respect of Palestine."[48]

The British Government accepted Schanzer's commitment, though with some nervousness as to whether Schanzer's statement that Italy was "disposed" to acquiesce was a firm promise.[49] The Colonial Office prepared notes for Balfour to use at the Council's 19 July 1922 meeting, when the matter would again be on the table. The Colonial Office suggested to Balfour that he ask the Council "to signify your approval of the terms of the draft Mandate and to intimate your readiness to issue a Mandate in these terms as soon as the position has been regularised."[50] The Colonial Office, hence, was clear that the mandate was dependent on Britain's status becoming "regularised" through a peace treaty with Turkey. The approval Balfour was seeking in July 1922 would not be an "issuance" of a mandate, the Colonial Office understood. The mandate could be valid only after Britain gained sovereignty.

As it turned out, the British Government was right to be nervous about Italy. At the 19 July Council meeting, Italy balked at approving the Syria and Palestine mandate documents. It again raised the non-ratification of the Treaty of Sèvres as a reason.[51] France, moreover, was unwilling to approve the Palestine mandate without simultaneous approval of the Syria mandate. Balfour made a pitch to decouple the Palestine mandate from the Syria mandate,[52] but France refused.[53]

A few days later, however, Italy indicated that it would honor Schanzer's commitment.[54] Britain returned to the Council on 24 July. In addition to the problem of an absence of British sovereignty in Palestine, there remained the issues that Italy still had with France over the Syria mandate,[55] as Italy's delegate explained to the Council.[56]

Italy even proposed to France that the two conclude a bilateral treaty regulating Italy's rights in Syria before a Council vote on the terms of the Syria mandate.[57] Italy relented to the extent of allowing the Council to deal with the terms, but with the understanding that the Syria mandate would gain the Council's definitive approval only once Italy and France resolved their differences over the Syria mandate. On 24 July, then, the Council approved the "declaration" we quoted above.[58] To repeat, this act of approving, even provisionally, the terms of the mandate document was an act that lawyers would call *ultra vires*, or outside the Council's powers, since Article 22 gave the Council no such role.

The fact that the Palestine mandate could not be approved because of a deal between France and Britain, and that the Syria mandate could not be approved until Italy and France came to terms, bespoke the political rather than legal character of the role the Council was playing. The Council was not assessing the mandate documents for their conformity to the Covenant. It was not playing an adjudicatory role to assure respect for the rights of the populations of these territories.

Beyond having to wait for Italy and France to agree on Syria, Britain still needed to overcome the "technicality" that it had no sovereignty. This shortcoming was a stumbling block as Britain negotiated with the United States in October 1922 over a treaty to define US commercial access rights in Palestine. Curzon was at pains to assure the United States that sovereignty would be forthcoming. Addressing the US ambassador in London, Curzon referred to "the conclusion of peace between the Allied powers and Turkey and the consequent formal issue of the mandate."[59] In so saying, Curzon was acknowledging that Britain could not have a mandate until it had sovereignty. So even if Britain could gain the approval of the League Council not just for the mandate document's terms, but for the mandate itself, it would still be one step away from having a mandate. Legal title was an additional prerequisite and one that in the latter months of 1922 was proving elusive.

Britain never asked for sovereignty from the League of Nations, because the League had no sovereignty to give. Sovereignty could come only from the sovereign-holder, namely, Turkey, as Balfour acknowledged. The proposition in the Narrative that Britain was awarded Palestine by the League of Nations finds no affirmance in the League Covenant or in the way Britain interacted with the League Council.

Chapter 11

THE LEAGUE OF NATIONS PUT THE PALESTINE MANDATE INTO LEGAL FORCE

In 1947, when it approached the United Nations for advice about Palestine, the British Government felt constrained to explain its status there, and how the Palestine mandate could be seen as a lawful exercise of authority. In a memorandum it prepared for the United Nations about the mandate, the Government wrote:

> The terms of the draft Mandate for Palestine were approved by the Council of the League of Nations on the 24th July, 1922. At that time peace had not been concluded between the Allied Powers and Turkey. It was not until the 29th September, 1923, after the Treaty of Lausanne had entered into force, that the Council of the League was able formally to give effect to the Palestine Mandate.[1]

Britain here confirmed that the League Council action of 24 July 1922 related only to the mandate's terms, but that it was not an action that held legal significance for Britain having a mandate, since peace with Turkey was yet to be concluded. That distinction has been missed by many analysts, including Shabtai Rosenne, the first Legal Adviser to Israel's Foreign Ministry. Rosenne wrote that "the Mandate for Palestine was confirmed by the Council of the League of Nations and entered into force on 24 July 1922."[2] As the 1947 British document correctly stated, however, the Council did not purport to confirm a mandate to Britain on 24 July 1922, or to give it any legal effect on that date.

Fourteen months later, on 29 September 1923, the Council did purport to give "effect" to the mandate itself. In 1945, on another occasion when the British Government was explaining its status in Palestine, it said that on 29 September 1923 the mandate "came formally into operation."[3] The British Government never clarified what this characterization meant. The Crown had, as we saw, announced a mandate on 1 July 1920. Was the mandate "provisional" in some sense for three years? Was it only an "informal" mandate, if such a term had any legal meaning? If the mandate lacked "effect" prior to 29 September 1923, did Britain regard itself as a belligerent occupant until that date, despite what it said on 1 July 1920?

The Narrative in any event followed these less than precise statements of the British Government. Before we see what was actually said and done by the League Council on 29 September 1923, an explanation of what occurred after 24 July 1922 is required. By Autumn 1922, it was obvious that Turkey would not ratify the Treaty of Sèvres, which had a number of terms that Turkey found too onerous. Unlike the situation in 1920, Turkey had bargaining power. Turkey was enjoying a military resurgence, and the Allies were not prepared to go to war again to impose the Treaty of Sèvres. To remove an obstacle to the legalization of the Palestine mandate, however, Britain still needed language in a peace treaty that would give it sovereignty.

New negotiations opened in Autumn 1922, this time in Lausanne, Switzerland, for a "re-modelled" treaty. Britain, France, and Italy were the convenors. They invited the United States, but it replied that it would not take part in peace negotiations since it had not been at war with Turkey. "The United States was neither at war with Turkey nor a party to the Armistice of 1918 and does not desire to participate in the final peace negotiations."[4] The three Allies also invited Japan, which accepted, even though it too, as we already saw, was not at war with Turkey.[5] The fact that Japan was not a convenor reflected the marginality of its role.

The Treaty of Sèvres had been drafted by the Allies and presented to Turkey to sign, but now the Allies could not simply hand Turkey a *diktat*. A new, more self-confident, government had replaced the Sultan and had pushed back successfully against Italian and French forces that remained in Anatolia under the 1918 armistice. For the replacement treaty, the conference at Lausanne had Turkey's full participation. Turkey's new government, moreover, stood up for Turkey's Arab populations. In a policy document of 1920, the movement that was in process of forming this new government proclaimed that "the destinies of the portions of the Turkish Empire which are populated exclusively by an Arab majority [...] should be determined in accordance with the votes which shall be freely given by the inhabitants."[6]

The Lausanne conference attracted international attention. A young American news reporter named Ernest Hemingway covered the proceedings and in his off hours wrote scandalous poetry about the principals.[7] A new leader on the Allied side, Benito Mussolini, speechified for Italy. Turkey's Ismet Pasha, partially deaf, famously pretended not to hear when Curzon expounded at length on Britain's demands.[8]

Curzon wrote the text for the Allies, and he evidently calculated that Turkey would not cede sovereignty to the Allies, or endorse the Balfour Declaration, in the manner of Articles 95 and 132 of the Treaty of Sèvres. In place of those provisions, Curzon drafted the following:

> Turkey renounces all rights and titles of whatever kind over or concerning all territories or islands other than those over which Turkish sovereignty is recognised by the present treaty. Turkey recognises and accepts dispositions which have been made or may be taken concerning the attribution, independence or any other settlement of these territories or islands.[9]

Turkey's hope of keeping its Arab provinces, as expressed at the Paris Peace Conference, was being abandoned. In the negotiations, wrote one analyst, that much was taken as assumed.[10] However, the key elements in Britain's strategy for gaining legal status and for a requirement on itself to implement a Jewish national home were lacking in the draft provision. Britain's legal strategy was collapsing. Curzon was dropping a cession of sovereignty to the Allies. He was dropping mention of the Balfour Declaration. After some editing, Curzon's draft provision, by then numbered Article 16 in the proposed treaty, was presented to Turkey. It read:

> Turkey hereby renounces all rights and title whatsoever over or respecting all territories situated outside the frontiers provided for in the present Treaty and the islands other than those over which her sovereignty is recognised by the said Treaty. Turkey recognises and accepts the measures which have been or will be taken respecting the attribution, independence or any other *régime* of these territories or islands.[11]

The Lausanne negotiations, in any event, resulted in signatures on a new peace treaty, on 24 July 1923. Article 16 remained the only provision dealing with Turkey's Arab provinces. In its final form, it read,

> Turkey hereby renounces all rights and title whatsoever over or respecting the territories situated outside the frontiers laid down in the present Treaty and the islands other than those over which her sovereignty is recognised by the said Treaty, the future of these territories and islands being settled or to be settled by the parties concerned.[12]

What was left instead of a cession of sovereignty to the Allies, or to Britain, was this phrase about the "future of these territories."

Ratification, it was specified in the treaty itself, would be required.[13] Without waiting for ratification, however, Britain went back to the League of Nations Council to ask it to say that the Palestine mandate would go "into effect" as soon as that ratification occurred. It said ratification would come quickly. This request was made by Curzon as Foreign Secretary in a 16 August 1923 note to the League Secretariat. Curzon recited that at the next Council meeting, Britain would ask for "the simultaneous entry into force of the British mandate for Palestine and the Treaty of Lausanne." In an effort to explain why this could now legally be done, Curzon explained in the note that by Article 16, "Turkey has agreed to accept the disposal of Palestine by the parties concerned."[14] If this was a reference to San Remo, or to the Council's action of 24 July 1922, neither amounted to a "disposal." Curzon could no longer claim the sovereignty that the League Council said would be necessary before a mandate could be valid.

By suggesting that the Council should say that the mandate would be effective on the day the Treaty of Lausanne became effective, Curzon was asking the Council to say that the territorial disposition outlined in the Treaty of Lausanne would suffice to validate the mandate. He was not asking the Council to attribute sovereignty to Britain. That, he knew, was not a possibility. He was asking the Council to confirm that Britain was gaining a status on its own, via the Treaty of Lausanne.

As for the Council's stipulation that the mandates for Syria and Palestine should go into effect simultaneously, Curzon asked the Council to ignore it. He said that Italy and France had had enough time to work out their differences over Syria, so the Council should wait no longer. It should let the Palestine mandate enter into force upon the entry into force of the Treaty of Lausanne.[15]

Even if Britain could decouple the Palestine mandate from the Syria mandate, it still needed sovereignty. The Lausanne treaty represented the "remodeling" of the Treaty of Sèvres that Balfour had said would be necessary, but it contained nothing similar to the Article 132 devolution of sovereignty to the Principal Allied Powers, or the Article 95 conferment of authority on the Principal Allied Powers to designate a mandatory. In his note to the Secretariat, Curzon mis-construed Article 16 in a last-ditch effort to find sovereignty for Britain in Palestine.[16] Curzon's strategy for gaining a legal status to support a mandate had collapsed.

The Council did not act on Curzon's request to say that the Palestine mandate would "enter into force" once the Lausanne treaty was ratified. France made a new proposal to Italy to overcome Italy's objections to the Syria mandate.[17] Over the next several weeks, Italy worked out its differences with France relating to the Syria mandate.

France and Italy approached the Council on 29 September 1923 and said that they had agreed on the text of the Syria mandate document, hence that the condition that the Council set on 24 July 1922 was met. Britain's delegate expressed "his satisfaction that this question has finally been settled." The Council adopted no resolution, but the minutes for 29 September 1923 reflect the following: "The Council noted that, in view of the agreement between the Governments of France and Italy in respect of the mandate for Syria, the mandates for Palestine and Syria would now enter into force automatically and at the same time."[18]

The import of that notation was far from clear. If the Council was saying that the two mandates actually entered into force on 29 September 1923, this was odd phrasing, since saying that something "would" enter into force automatically contemplates a future event. Tellingly, the Council did not say in a straightforward way that it, the Council, was putting the two mandates into force. Nor did it say that other requisites for effectiveness had been achieved and that as a result the two mandates could enter into force on that day. Instead, the Council said that the two mandates would both enter into force "automatically" upon apparently future events it did not detail.

The Council did use the word "now," but in the context of the sentence, that did not necessarily mean entry into force on 29 September 1923. It seemed, rather, that "now" was being used in the sense that now that Italy and France have come to terms, the mandate could enter into force automatically (that is, without further Council action) when and if Britain gained sovereignty. The Council had said in its 5 August 1920 policy paper, as we saw in Chapter 10, "It is not enough that the Mandatory Powers should be appointed; it is important that they should also possess a legal title."[19] Given the Council's understanding that a mandate required sovereignty, the Council could not have meant that the two mandates entered into force on 29 September 1923.

The Council minutes were kept in both French and English. Where the English reads "would," namely, that the two mandates "would" enter into force, the French text reads "will" enter into force ("*entreront en vigeur*").[20] So the future tense. The use of the future tense is even more inconsistent than the English text for immediate effectiveness of the two mandates, but again with some ambiguity. As of 29 September 1923, Britain was not claiming immediate sovereignty. Curzon's note of 16 August asking for entry into force when the Treaty of Lausanne achieved ratification showed that Britain understood that the mandate could not enter into effect prior to that ratification, even if the Treaty of Lausanne gave it sovereignty. As of 29 September 1923, the Treaty of Lausanne awaited ratification, as the members of the League Council well knew. Ratification would not occur until 6 August 1924, the date on which Britain, Italy, and Japan deposited instruments of ratification.[21] Britain would acknowledge as late as 15 July 1924, that "no peace settlement has yet actually come into force with Turkey."[22]

Yet in 1947, as we saw at the beginning of this chapter, the British Government told the United Nations, "It was not until the 29th September, 1923, *after the Treaty of Lausanne had entered into force*, that the Council of the League was able formally to give effect to the Palestine Mandate."[23] (Emphasis supplied.)

Just one week later, on 4 October 1923, Victor Cavendish, the Secretary of State for the Colonies, gave a speech to the Imperial Conference on the situation in all of Britain's colonies. He included Palestine in his speech. He did not mention the Council statement of 29 September.[24] An odd omission, if 29 September was the date on which the Palestine mandate acquired legal effect, since Britain strongly wanted Council approval.

Secretary-General Eric Drummond, however, informed the British Government a few days later that the Palestine mandate had, indeed, entered into force on 29 September.[25] Britain, of course, had its representative that the 29 September meeting. The fact that Drummond saw a need to give Britain that information reflected a concern on his part as to what was actually done. Beyond the ambiguity of what was said on 29 September lay the fact that Britain lacked sovereignty, and that under the Covenant the Council had no power to confer a mandate.

Ignoring these issues, Britain portrayed the 29 September statement as putting the Palestine mandate into effect as of that date. The Colonial Office termed it that the mandate "was brought into operation by resolution of the Council on 29th September, 1923."[26] In Palestine, High Commissioner Herbert Samuel called together a group of prominent Arab families and informed them that the mandate had entered into force, in order to dissuade them from opposing the mandate and the Balfour Declaration.[27] When Samuel gave Britain's annual report to the Permanent Mandates Commission, he again referred to 29 September as the date on which the mandate became effective.[28] The "fact" that the Palestine mandate took legal effect on 29 September 1923 became part of the Narrative. Even Henry Cattan, one of the Arab Higher Committee representatives at the United Nations, did not challenge Britain on the point despite his strong assertion that the Palestine mandate document was invalid for inconsistency with Covenant Article 22.[29]

Britain never explained the inconsistency between an entry of the mandate into effect on 29 September 1923 and Curzon's 16 August 1923 communication that asked for the mandate to become effective only when the Treaty of Lausanne might enter into effect. In its 1924 report to the Permanent

Mandates Commission, prepared after the Treaty of Lausanne was ratified and in effect, Britain tried to use the Treaty of Lausanne to rationalize its status in Palestine. The report read:

> The ratification of the Treaty of Lausanne in August, 1924, finally regularised the international status of Palestine as a territory detached from Turkey and administered under a Mandate entrusted to His Majesty's Government.
>
> The terms of the Mandate had been approved in anticipation by the Council of the League of Nations in 1922, and the Mandate had been brought into operation by resolution of the Council in 1923.[30]

In Chapter 12, we shall see that Britain gained no status in Palestine from the Treaty of Lausanne. The statement that the Treaty of Lausanne "regularized" Britain's status was simply inaccurate. This 1924 statement, in any event, was evidently not regarded as a sufficient explanation by Britain when it wrote up its 1947 statement, in which it claimed, falsely, that the Treaty of Lausanne had entered into force prior to 29 September 1923. To repeat the words of the British Government in the 1947 statement, "It was not until the 29th September, 1923, after the Treaty of Lausanne had entered into force, that the Council of the League was able formally to give effect to the Palestine Mandate."[31] As we have just seen, however, the Treaty of Lausanne had not entered into force by 29 September 1923. The Treaty of Lausanne entered into force on 6 August 1924, as anyone could have seen by checking the *League of Nations Treaty Series*, where one finds a notation to that effect. The 1924 and 1947 statements, both inaccurate, were inconsistent in their inaccuracies.

Beyond all these defects, the Council's statement of 29 September 1923 could not give "legal effect" to the Palestine mandate because the Covenant gave the Council no role to confer a mandate, the Council's August 1920 report notwithstanding. Britain and the Council were engaging all along in an exercise outside a legal framework but in which each saw an advantage. Just as Britain was in a symbiotic with the Zionist Organization, so too did it develop such a relationship with the Council. Britain had no legal obligation under the Covenant to submit its mandate document to the Council, but it did so in order to gain an aura of legitimacy to its assumption of a mandate on terms wildly at odds with the Covenant's concept of a mandate. For the Council, its assertion of a power to approve mandate documents absent any such role for it under the Covenant enhanced its standing as an institution with a purpose in the world.

There was one legal theory that might have left the Council with a legitimate role. The Principal Allied Powers could have transferred the sovereignty they were gaining from Germany, and the sovereignty they hoped to gain from

Turkey, to the League.[32] Article 22 was drafted in a way, however, that did not allow for this approach.[33] As we have seen, there was no attempt to have the League take sovereignty over the territories of Germany or Turkey. The theory was particularly inapposite for Turkey's Arab provinces, since the Principal Allied Powers never gained sovereignty.

Britain's false statement to the United Nations in 1947 was aimed at concealing the fact that the Palestine mandate never entered into force. Britain was able to fashion an argument for the mandate's entry into legal force only by prevaricating. It said that the Treaty of Lausanne—which it further claimed gave it territorial rights—was in force prior to 29 September 1923. Britain was conceding that the Council statement of 29 September 1923 could put the Palestine mandate into force only if, by that date, Britain had territorial rights. But even if the Treaty of Lausanne gave Britain territorial rights, it was not yet in force. Hence, the Council statement of 29 September 1923 did not put the Palestine mandate into force. After that date, the Council never revisited the question of the entry into force of the Palestine mandate. The only logical conclusion is that the Council never put the Palestine mandate into force.

Britain's prevarication should have been evident to the UN Special Committee on Palestine, recipient of Britain's 1947 memorandum. The Special Committee apparently did not check the *League of Nations Treaty Series* to find a ratification date for the Treaty of Lausanne. Nor did the Special Committee give a careful reading to what the Council actually said on 29 September 1923. The Special Committee accepted and repeated Britain's falsehood, writing in its report to the General Assembly, "The draft mandate was confirmed by the Council of the League of Nations on 24 July 1922, and entered into force formally on 29 September 1923."[34] The Special Committee then used the mandate and its supposed confirmation of Jewish self-determination as a legal basis on which to recommend a partition of Palestine.

In 1946, the British Government gave yet a different story about how it gained sovereignty. In that year, it issued a report on its role in Palestine to a committee set up between it and the United States to make recommendations. After explaining that it set up a supposedly civil administration on 1 July 1920, the British Government recited,

> Turkish sovereignty over Palestine was not, however, formally renounced by Treaty until the signature on the 10th August, 1920, of the Treaty of Sèvres. Under Article 95 of that Treaty it was agreed to entrust, by application of the provisions of Article 22 of the Covenant, the administration of Palestine to a Mandatory who would be responsible for putting into effect the declaration originally made on the 2nd November, 1917, by the British Government and adopted by the other Allied Powers.[35]

Incredibly, the British Government omitted the fact that the Treaty of Sèvres was never ratified, hence a renunciation of sovereignty by Turkey did not in fact occur on the basis of the Treaty of Sèvres, and nothing came to Britain under the Treaty of Sèvres. The 1946 statement also claimed that the Balfour Declaration was "adopted," by the Allies. We have seen that at San Remo, the Allies vigorously denied adopting the Balfour Declaration.

So the 1946 explanation and the 1947 explanation were inconsistent with one another, and neither was accurate. Moreover, neither reflected what Curzon told the League of Nations at the time as to how Britain was supposedly gaining a status under the Treaty of Lausanne that would allow it to govern Palestine. We now turn to the validity of Curzon's claim that Britain gained rights under the Treaty of Lausanne.

Chapter 12

THE PEACE TREATY WITH TURKEY LEGALIZED BRITAIN'S STATUS IN PALESTINE

An element of the Narrative, as we have just seen, was that Britain was lawfully in Palestine. Had Britain gained sovereignty by the Treaty of Lausanne, it would have had status in Palestine sufficient to exercise a mandate. The Treaty of Lausanne, however, gave Britain nothing.

As events unfolded in 1923, Britain did not try to tell the League of Nations what it would later say in the 1947 explanation. League Council members knew that the Treaty of Sèvres was dead. They knew that the Treaty of Lausanne was not yet ratified, so they would have seen through an explanation like the one devised for the report to the United Nations in 1947.

Once the Treaty of Lausanne was signed, however, the British Government tried to fashion an argument that, were it to be ratified, it would give Britain legal status in Palestine. This was Curzon's argument to the League Council in his16 August 1923 communication that we saw in Chapter 11. The defunct Treaty of Sèvres had specified sovereignty to the Principal Allied Powers and had recited that the Balfour Declaration was to be applied. The Treaty of Lausanne had nothing of that. All Curzon had was its Article 16, whose text bears repeating. It read:

> Turkey hereby renounces all rights and title whatsoever over or respecting the territories situated outside the frontiers laid down in the present Treaty and the islands other than those over which her sovereignty is recognised by the said Treaty, the future of these territories and islands being settled or to be settled by the parties concerned.[1]

It was the final clause of Article 16 that Curzon recited to the League Council in August 1923. To repeat, in his communication to the League Council, Curzon interpreted this phrase to mean, "Turkey has agreed to accept the disposal of Palestine effected by the parties concerned." Article 16, however, did not identify those parties. Nor did it specify what may have already been "settled." At San Remo, the Principal Allied Powers had "settled" nothing but had only anticipated that Britain would keep Palestine and implement the Balfour Declaration if that would be agreed by Turkey in a peace treaty.

With no mention of the Principal Allied Powers or the Balfour Declaration, Curzon was implying that the final clause of Article 16 was a reference to the San Remo arrangement. But that arrangement had been premised on Britain gaining sovereignty through a peace treaty. And now any such claim to sovereignty was gone.

Curzon's suggestion that the "parties concerned" included Britain is not borne out by the text of Article 16. As it happens, although Curzon prepared drafts in English, the text of the Treaty of Lausanne was authenticated in French, and in French only.[2] The English text quoted above is a translation produced by the British Government after the fact, hence a text that has no standing. In the authentic French text, the term for "parties concerned" clearly excludes Britain. Article 16 read:

> La Turquie déclare renoncer à tous droits et titres, de quelque nature que ce soit, sur ou concernant les territoires situés au dela des frontières prévues par le présent Traité et sur les îles autres que celles sur lesquelles la souveraineté lui est reconnue par ledit Traité, le sort de ces territoires et îles étant réglé ou à régler par les intéressés.

The critical difference in the French original is in the final word. Where the English text reads: "by the parties concerned," the French text reads "*par les intéressés*." In legal French, the term *l'intéressé* refers to a party with a legal interest in a matter.[3] One could say that Britain, or even the League, was "concerned" about Palestine's status, but neither had a legal interest in the sense of title or sovereignty. The League never claimed a legal interest. Britain could gain a legal interest only from Turkey, but Article 16 gave it none. Curzon was claiming that Britain had an interest when it could only have gotten one from the Treaty of Lausanne itself.

The only states with legal capacity to determine sovereignty would be those holding it, and under the Treaty of Lausanne, those holding it were the states being formed out of Turkey's Arab provinces. Britain, as a state lacking sovereignty, had no legal capacity to give these provinces to anyone, hence was not included among "*les intéressés*." Once Turkey renounced sovereignty, without renouncing in favor of Britain or the Allies, there was nothing Britain could do to gain sovereignty. Britain was left without status in Palestine.

Some years later, an argument based on Lausanne Article 16 was made in support of Britain's status in Palestine by Elihu Lauterpacht, who worked from Turkey's renunciation of sovereignty in Article 16. Unlike Curzon, Lauterpacht speculated on who the "parties concerned" might be as regarded Palestine. He wrote that "'the parties concerned' had already settled its future," saying, "On 24th July, 1922, the League of Nations with the assent of the Principal Allied and Associated Powers, had granted a mandate in respect of Palestine to the British Government. We thus have the situation," Lauterpacht continued, "in which Turkey's title to Palestine devolved upon the Principal Allied and Associated Powers who, in their turn, had in effect already conveyed their rights to the League of Nations."[4]

Lauterpacht misfired in more than one way. First, the "Associated" Powers played no role in relation to the Palestine mandate. The mandate document recited that it was the "Principal Allied Powers" who had selected Britain. Second, the Council action of 24 July 1922 was not a "grant" of a mandate to Britain but merely an approval of the mandate document's terms, and even that only on a conditional basis. Third, Turkey's title had not devolved upon the Allies, because the Treaty of Sèvres had not been ratified (and never would be). Fourth, the Allies had no rights to convey. Fifth, the Allies never purported to convey rights to the League of Nations. Sixth, the League of Nations never claimed to hold any right conveyed to it by the Allies.

The League, being a creature of its Covenant, was not in any event a potential bearer of sovereignty. It did exercise an administrative role in regard to a few pieces of territory in Europe, but that was by delegation from a particular peace treaty.[5] Nothing of the sort applied to Palestine. The League had nothing to do with sovereignty in Palestine.

Lauterpacht took the phrase that, in the English translation, reads "the future of these territories and islands being settled or to be settled by the parties concerned" to relate to what the Allies had done or might do. That phrase, however, was included to explain the consequence of Turkey's renunciation of sovereignty. The phrase referred not to the Allies, but to the territories, to underline their prerogatives now that they were becoming states. As will be seen shortly, the Treaty of Lausanne made these territories into states.

A different rationale for a supposed legal status for Britain in Palestine coming out of Article 16 was offered by a former Legal Advisor to the Foreign Ministry of Israel. Robbie Sabel explained his theory at a 2015 symposium at Hebrew University titled Legalities and Legacies: The Past, Present, and Future of the Palestine Mandate in International Law. "Under international law, certainly as it was at the time," Sabel was recorded to say, "Britain and France were entitled to sovereignty over those parts of the Ottoman Empire they had occupied during the war; in the Treaties of Sèvres and Lausanne Turkey renounced, in favour of Britain and France, any claims it had over the Ottoman Empire. It was thus Britain and France who had the power to dispose of the Ottoman Empire, including Palestine."[6]

Sabel elsewhere argued that though Turkey never ratified the Treaty of Sèvres, the sovereignty renunciation in it was effective since Turkey declined to ratify for reasons unrelated to Palestine. As for the Treaty of Lausanne, Sabel said that Britain did not need to be mentioned in light of the League Council 1922 action.[7] Neither point is valid. Turkey's motivation for not ratifying the Treaty of Sèvres is irrelevant. The non-ratification meant that the treaty's terms never gained effect. As for Sabel's point about the Treaty of Lausanne, the League Council in 1922 did not purport to give territorial rights to Britain.

Sabel's argument that Britain gained rights in the Treaty of Lausanne also runs up against provisions of the Treaty of Lausanne that leave sovereignty elsewhere. The territorial entities formed out of Turkey's Arab provinces, not Britain or the Allies, were the successors to Turkey in sovereignty. International lawyers who analyzed the Treaty of Lausanne at the time understood that it made the Arab territories into states.[8] They were referred to in the Treaty of Lausanne as "states" being "detached" from Turkey. Article 46 dealt with responsibility to pay off the Ottoman public debt. Territories that were being separated from Turkey were to be responsible to pay a portion of the debt. One group of them that was to be responsible for paying a share was identified as "the states newly created on the Asian territories detached from the Ottoman Empire by virtue of this treaty."[9] The Arab territories were located in Asia, hence this reference included Palestine. Palestine was being "detached" from Turkey by Article 16.

The Treaty of Sèvres, to be sure, had its own provision on the Ottoman public debt, and it too referred to the states "detached" from Turkey as being responsible for a portion.[10] Thus, even as early as 1920, the Allies envisaged that the territories that would be subjected to mandate rule were states. In the Treaty of Sèvres, as we saw, "title" was renounced in favor of the Allies, meaning that these states would fall under the sovereignty of the Allies, who were then transferring that sovereignty to France and Britain. In the Treaty of Lausanne, on the other hand, the Allies were not mentioned, hence title went to the detached states themselves. That disposition was recognized when the details of apportioning the Ottoman public debt were submitted to arbitration in 1925. The detached states—Syria, Lebanon, Iraq, Transjordan, and Palestine—were parties to the arbitration, and each of them—not France or Britain—was held responsible for a portion of the Turkish debt.[11] As regarded Palestine, it, not Britain, was viewed by the arbitrator, interpreting the Treaty of Lausanne, as the state holding sovereignty. Whereas by the Treaty of Sèvres, Palestine was to be a state under British sovereignty, by the Treaty of Lausanne, it was a state under no other sovereignty.

Sovereignty in Palestine, rather than in Britain, emerged from two other provisions of the Treaty of Lausanne. One related to concession contracts that had been granted by Turkey to foreign entrepreneurs before the War. "In territories detached from Turkey under the Treaty of Peace signed this day," read Protocol XII, Article 9, of the Treaty of Lausanne, "the State which acquires the territory is fully subrogated as regards the rights and obligations of Turkey towards the nationals of the other Contracting Powers."[12] Litigation ensued over this provision in 1924, when a national of Greece, which was a "contracting power" in the Treaty of Lausanne, was denied rights under a prewar concession granted by Turkey to develop electrical capacity in the Jerusalem area.[13] The *Mavrommatis Palestine Concessions* case went to the Permanent Court of International Justice, which had to decide whether "the State which acquires the territory" was Britain or Palestine. The Court said it was Palestine. "Palestine is subrogated," said the Court, "as regards the rights and obligations of Turkey."[14] "Subrogation" occurs when one party replaces another on a legal obligation. The Court read the Treaty of Lausanne to mean that Palestine was subrogated to Turkey, since sovereignty was held by Palestine.

A provision on the nationality of inhabitants in the Treaty of Lausanne likewise referred to the territories detached from Turkey as "states." "Turkish subjects habitually resident in territory which in accordance with the provisions of the present Treaty is detached from Turkey," read Article 30, "will become ipso facto, in the conditions laid down by the local law, nationals of the State to which such territory is transferred."[15] The territory of Palestine was being transferred to Palestine. Its laws would govern nationality in Palestine. Again, this designation as a "state" for nationality purposes was carried over from the Treaty of Sèvres. It too had provided that nationals of Turkey would become "nationals of the State to which such territory is transferred."[16] That formulation meant the newly constituted states, not the mandatories.[17]

Article 30 of the Treaty of Lausanne was at play in a 1940 case in a British court and was read as having made Palestine a state. The case concerned the nationality status of a man who was a resident of Palestine. He wanted to be considered a national of Britain. He said that, as a resident of Palestine, he was automatically a national of Britain. His lawyer argued that, as applied to Palestine, the phrase "State to which such territory is transferred" in Article 30 meant Britain, and therefore that inhabitants of Palestine became British nationals. The court ruled, however, that "there was no provision" in Article 30 "for the transfer of territory to Great Britain."[18]

The man, therefore, was not a national of Britain. Since the territory had been transferred to Palestine, the man was a national of Palestine.[19]

Britain's 1947 statement that it had attained legal status in Palestine stood in sharp contrast to what the British Government itself said in 1924 about the Treaty of Lausanne. In the *Mavrommatis Palestine Concessions* case, Britain was represented by Cecil Hurst, a Government legal advisor. In a statement to the Permanent Court of International Justice, Hurst undertook to explain Britain's situation in Palestine.

Hurst said that Britain had no lawful status in Palestine, even after the Treaty of Lausanne. Hurst pointed out, as we have seen, that the Treaty of Sèvres would have given Britain a status in Palestine. Hurst said, however, that it "was never ratified and has expired. It has become extinct, as if it had never been drafted at all. It has been replaced by another instrument." "If the terms of this later instrument, known as the Treaty of Lausanne, are studied," he said, "it will be seen that it is not a treaty which creates the British rights of control or government in Palestine."[20] So no rights came to Britain via either treaty, the first treaty because it was never ratified, the second because it gave Britain nothing. Hurst's statement directly refuted Curzon's claim to the League Council that the Treaty of Lausanne gave Britain rights in Palestine.

Hurst used the term "succession," which refers to the assumption of rights by a new sovereign. Referring to what he called "the international law sense of the term," Hurst said, "there has been no succession between Turkey and Great Britain in regard to Palestine." This was a remarkable admission for the British Government to make. Hurst was acknowledging that Britain had no legal standing in Palestine. What, then, was its status there? Hurst continued, "All that has happened is that Palestine as a geographical entity has passed under the control and under the administration of Great Britain. That is not or would not have been the case had the abortive Treaty of Sèvres ever been ratified because in it there was a definite renunciation by Turkey of her rights over the territories outside her borders in favour of the Principal Allied Powers."[21]

Hurst understood full well how Britain was seeking sovereignty via Article 132 of the Treaty of Sèvres. He also understood that Britain had failed, because the Treaty of Lausanne gave Britain nothing similar. Contrary to what Curzon told the League Council, Hurst said, "Under the Lausanne settlement, Turkey merely renounces her rights altogether over the territories outside her borders and disinterests herself in their future."[22] "The British rights, therefore, to-day in Palestine are really an emanation from the occupation which began after the war."[23] Britain, Hurst was saying, was in Palestine solely by dint of controlling it militarily. Hurst did not recite the name of the applicable status, but what he was saying was that Britain, in 1924, was still a belligerent occupant.

Hurst was no junior lawyer who might have spoken out of turn. He was the Principal Legal Advisor to the British Government. A few years later, the British Government nominated him as a judge on the Permanent Court of International Justice, and he spent the rest of his career there, serving for several years as the chief judge. An acknowledged expert in international law, a collection of his writings on the subject was later published.[24]

Hurst, moreover, had been at the center of British policy in Palestine. He was on Britain's delegation at the Paris Peace Conference when Prime Minister Lloyd George outlined what would become Article 22 of the League Covenant.[25] As Legal Advisor, he played a role in the drafting of the Palestine mandate document.[26] Yet now, standing before the Permanent Court of International Justice, Hurst made no mention of the mandate document when explaining Britain's legal situation in Palestine. Hurst understood that Britain derived no rights in Palestine from the mandate document or from the League. The Permanent Court of International Justice agreed with Hurst that Britain lacked territorial rights. It read the Treaty of Lausanne to mean, as we just saw, that Palestine, not Britain, succeeded to the obligations of Turkey towards the Greek entrepreneur.[27]

Despite having no legal basis for being in Palestine, the Crown adopted a sweeping Order in Council immediately following the League Council's July 1922 action. The Order in Council was a kind of constitutional document for British rule in Palestine. Its text purported to explain how it was that Britain might lawfully legislate for Palestine. The Order in Council gave as a reason, "And whereas, by treaty, capitulation, grant, usage, sufferance and other lawful means, His Majesty has power and jurisdiction within Palestine."[28] In 1947, the UN Special Committee on Palestine accepted this and later orders in council as reflecting a "constitutional basis" for the British "Government of Palestine." The "constitutional basis," wrote the Special Committee, "is set out in the Palestine orders-in-council."[29]

The Special Committee failed to ask itself whether the "whereas" clause in the Order in Council made sense. Had it done so, the Special Committee would have seen that none of the bases listed in the "whereas" clause supported the Crown's "power and jurisdiction within Palestine." The items listed bore no relation to Britain's situation in Palestine. They were copied from a colonial-era piece of British legislation called the Foreign Jurisdiction Act of 1890, adopted to explain various possible legal bases on which Britain might exercise jurisdiction "out of Her dominions."[30] None of these bases applied to Britain in Palestine. "Treaty" was listed in the Order in Council, but no specific treaty. "Capitulation" meant extraterritorial rights for British nationals in certain foreign countries, but not to a right to govern an entire foreign territory. "Grant" did not apply, because a grant could have come only from Turkey. "Usage" or "sufferance" might apply if Britain's presence were accepted over time, but those concepts did not apply, since Britain had not been accepted by Palestine's population.

Britain's lack of status in Palestine was raised in Parliament. David Ormsby-Gore, the Under-Secretary of State for the Colonies, was challenged in the House of Commons by a member who asked "by what legal authority is the Government of Palestine entitled to exist or legislate."[31] Ormsby-Gore did not name a basis.

In a 1926 court case, the Judicial Committee of the Privy Council in London faced the question of whether Britain's control of Palestine came within the Foreign Jurisdiction Act. After reciting the list of bases in the Foreign Jurisdiction Act, the judges pontificated, "There can be no question that the jurisdiction exercised by this country under the League of Nations Mandate for Palestine comes within the above description."[32] Like Ormsby-Gore, however, the judges specified no particular base.

The deception reflected in the Order in Council should have been evident to the Special Committee on Palestine, but as we have seen, the Special Committee, coached by the Jewish Agency, did little independent research. At the level of public relations, Britain succeeded in deflecting attention away from its lack of status in Palestine. Its prevarication to the United Nations in 1947 went unnoticed. The Narrative's adherents simply passed over the fact that Britain had no lawful status. That left them free to fashion arguments that Jewish territorial entitlement had been endorsed in some lawful fashion. Even lawyers critical of British policy did not note the defect.[33] In April 1947, just as the United Nations was beginning to deal with the Palestine matter, the Arab Higher Committee published a pamphlet to explain Arab rights. The Committee castigated Britain for violating Arab self-determination and for reneging on its pledges to the Arabs.[34] Yet it did not mention the fact that Britain never acquired a status in Palestine more than that of a belligerent occupant.

Chapter 13

THE PALESTINE MANDATE DOCUMENT WAS A TREATY BETWEEN BRITAIN AND THE LEAGUE

The 1948 declaration of Israeli statehood cited the Palestine mandate document as an affirmation of Jewish legal rights. Moshe Sharett, who would become prime minister of Israel, called the mandate document "an open covenant, openly agreed to by the League of Nations." "With the Balfour Declaration," Sharett said, the Palestine mandate document was "an international instrument guaranteeing to the Jewish people special facilities for immigration and settlement throughout Palestine."[1]

Yoram Dinstein put Sharett's statement into legal terms. "The Mandate for Palestine," wrote Dinstein, "was an international agreement concluded between the League of Nations, on the one hand, and the Mandatory Power (Britain), on the other. It was not only Britain that was bound by the instrument, but also the League of Nations (the international organization in which most of the then-existing states of the world were members)."[2] "International agreement" is another way of saying "treaty."[3]

We have just seen, of course, that the mandate document was never finalized. Since Britain never gained sovereignty in Palestine, it could not hold a mandate. Even if one overlooks that defect, however, the Palestine mandate document would not qualify as a treaty.

Dinstein did not elaborate to explain his characterization of the mandate document. On its face, the document does not bear the appearance of a treaty. Its full text can be found in the Documents Annex. It begins with the phrase "The Council of the League of Nations" and then recites terms. It reads like a document that, as is stated in it a few lines later, "confirms" what has been submitted to it. A treaty, at least one that is memorialized in a single document, would bear the names of the parties as having come to an agreement. Britain's name does not appear as a party to the document.

A treaty is normally signed on behalf of the parties.[4] The Palestine mandate document bore no signatures. Signatures attest that a treaty was negotiated by persons with the authority to do so on behalf of the parties. Treaties on significant matters are normally signed subject to ratification.[5] No ratification was contemplated for the Palestine mandate document.

If the document were a treaty, Britain would have registered it as a treaty with the Secretary-General of the League of Nations, and the Secretary-General would have published it in the League's *League of Nations Treaty Series*. Britain did not register it and it was not published in the *Treaty Series*. That procedure was required for all treaties concluded by members of the League.[6] Britain scrupulously complied with this obligation for treaties it concluded during the era of the League of Nations. The fact that it did not register the Palestine mandate document showed that Britain did not regard it as a treaty.

In the Palestine mandate document, Britain included, in fact, a provision showing that it regarded it as something other than a treaty. It inserted a final clause that read, "The present instrument shall be deposited in original in the archives of the League of Nations and certified copies shall be forwarded by the Secretary-General of the League of Nations to all Members of the League." That was a procedure at odds with treaty procedure, which required publication. Britain, moreover, in explaining that the document should be archived, used the term "instrument" to characterize it. It did not call it a "treaty" or an "agreement."

A treaty involves obligations being assumed by the parties. The Palestine mandate document imposed no obligations on the League of Nations. Two provisions that mentioned a role for the League were Article 27, which dealt with modification of the document, and Article 28, which dealt with its termination. Even the role envisioned for the League in Articles 27 and 28 involved no obligations on its part during the pendency of the document. As to possible modification of the document's terms, Article 27 read, "The consent of the Council of the League of Nations is required for any modification of the terms of this mandate." But no obligation was placed on the League.

As to termination, Article 28 provided, "In the event of the termination of the mandate hereby conferred upon the Mandatory, the Council of the League of Nations shall make such arrangements as may be deemed necessary for safeguarding in perpetuity, under guarantee of the League, the rights secured by Articles 13 and 14, and shall use its influence for securing, under the guarantee of the League, that the Government of Palestine will fully honour the financial obligations legitimately incurred by the Administration of Palestine during the period of the mandate, including the rights of public servants to pensions or gratuities." The League would have this duty only after Britain terminated the mandate. And when Britain did so in 1948, the League, of course, was no longer in existence.

Under Covenant Article 22, to be sure, the Council's Permanent Mandates Commission would, on the Council's behalf, "receive and examine the annual reports." Neither the PMC nor the Council, however, had any role in administering the mandate.

The extinction of a party to a bilateral treaty terminates it.[7] Early on, however, it was accepted that if the League were to go out of existence, mandates would not automatically terminate.[8] When the League of Nations did dissolve in 1946, Britain did not declare the mandate document to be of no effect. Had it been a treaty, the disappearance of that party would have meant a loss of legal force. Despite the disappearance of the PMC, of the Council, and of the League itself, Britain considered the mandate to be in effect until it terminated it in 1948.[9]

The introductory phrase of Article 28 of the mandate document referred to termination but provided no role for the League in the termination process. Britain regarded the document as one it could terminate unilaterally. In 1948, when Britain was contemplating termination, the issue was raised in Parliament. "There is no doubt that we are legally entitled to terminate our Mandate," Attorney-General Hartley Shawcross explained in the House of Commons. "Even if it were the case, as it certainly is not, that the Mandate is a kind of international statute or contract, giving rise to enforceable obligations, the complete frustration of the object contemplated by the Mandate would certainly relieve us of our obligations in the matter."[10] Shawcross did not regard the mandate document as an agreement with the League or with anyone else.

The League Council, for its part, did nothing to suggest that it regarded the mandate document as a treaty. During the years of the League's existence, the Council did not enter into agreements with states. Whether it had the legal capacity to do so was debated. Some of the functions it took on suggested that it might have a legal personality.[11] On the other hand, nothing in the Covenant provided for a legal personality separate from that of its members.[12] In any event, the League's only arrangements with other parties related to the practical functioning of the organization, and these were handled by the Secretariat, not by the Council. For arrangements with Switzerland for the headquarters in Geneva, the Secretariat had what it called a *modus vivendi*.[13] In 1946, the League arranged with the United Nations to transfer physical assets to it, with the Secretariat again taking the lead.[14]

The Palestine mandate document did figure in the *Mavrommatis Palestine Concessions* case, which we saw in Chapter 12. One article in the mandate document, a provision commonly called a "compromissory" clause, said that any member of the League could sue Britain in the Permanent Court of International Justice if its rights under the document were violated.

This was Article 26 of the document. Article 26 read, "The Mandatory agrees that, if any dispute whatever should arise between the Mandatory and another member of the League of Nations relating to the interpretation or the application of the provisions of the mandate, such dispute, if it cannot be settled by negotiation, shall be submitted to the Permanent Court of International Justice provided for by Article 14 of the Covenant of the League of Nations."[15]

Greece was suing to enforce another provision of the mandate document, Article 18, which said that League members were entitled to access to the Palestine market.[16] Greece claimed a violation, because the Greek entrepreneur had a concession agreement with Turkey to construct electrical works in Palestine. The Palestine administration, however, as part of its effort to promote a Jewish national home, began negotiating with a Jewish entrepreneur for the electrical works. Greece filed suit against Britain, saying that the entrepreneur's arrangement with Turkey carried over to the new sovereign.

The Court's statute, by its Article 36, gave it jurisdiction to hear "matters specially provided for in Treaties and Conventions in force."[17] Invoking that article together with the compromissory clause in the mandate document, the Court said that it had jurisdiction to hear Greece's complaint against Britain. The Court reached that conclusion not by its own reasoning, however, but by virtue of the fact that Greece claimed the Court had jurisdiction and that Britain did not contest the point. The Court said only, "The Parties in the present case agree that Article 26 of the Mandate falls within the category of 'matters specially provided for in Treaties and Conventions in force' under the terms of Article 36 of the Statute."[18] The dispute did relate to the mandate, and Covenant Article 14 gave the Court jurisdiction over a "dispute of an international character." By limiting itself to saying that Greece and Britain agreed upon the Court's jurisdiction, the Court avoided giving any characterization of the mandate document.

Greece could not afford to question the mandate document's validity, or it would have no basis for suing Britain. Britain could not object without admitting that the mandate document had no legal standing. As a result, the character of the mandate document was not litigated in *Mavrommatis Palestine Concessions*.

In his effort to establish that mandates were binding documents between the mandatory and the League, Dinstein cited a 1962 case in the International Court of Justice.[19] The case did not concern Palestine. It concerned South-West Africa (later "Namibia"), which had been a German colony but was taken by Britain, which delegated mandatory functions to the Republic of South Africa. Liberia and Ethiopia, as former members of the League of Nations, sued South Africa in 1962, hoping for a ruling that South Africa was violating its obligations as mandatory by policies of racial segregation.[20] The mandate document for South-West Africa arguably allowed League members to sue the mandatory in the Permanent Court of International Justice, and under the rules of the International Court of Justice, a compromissory clause for submission to the Permanent Court of International Justice automatically transferred to the International Court of Justice. The carry-over was available, however, only if the document in which jurisdiction was given to the Permanent Court of International Justice was a treaty.[21]

Unlike the *Mavrommatis Palestine Concessions* case, in which the parties agreed that jurisdiction obtained, South Africa contested jurisdiction. A narrow majority of the judges ruled that the Court did have jurisdiction, because, they said, the mandate document had sufficient status. They said that

> this Mandate, like practically all other similar Mandates, is a special type of instrument composite in nature and instituting a novel international regime. It incorporates a definite agreement consisting in the conferment and acceptance of a Mandate for South West Africa, a provisional or tentative agreement on the terms of this Mandate between the Principal Allied and Associated Powers to be proposed to the Council of the League of Nations and a formal confirmation agreement on the terms therein explicitly defined by the Council and agreed to between the Mandatory and the Council representing the League and its Members. It is an instrument having the character of a treaty or convention and embodying international engagements for the Mandatory as defined by the Council and accepted by the Mandatory.[22]

These judges did not say more about other mandates. They did not explain why they found their reasoning to apply only to "practically all other similar Mandates" but not to all other mandates. They did not explain which mandates in their view did not qualify. They did not clarify whether by "similar Mandates" they meant mandates over territory taken from Germany, since for them the mandatory would have had sovereignty, under the Treaty of Versailles. Britain, as we have seen, never gained sovereignty in Palestine.

Whatever the majority may have meant as to the scope of its reasoning, their statement that the South-West Africa mandate document was tantamount to a treaty rested on uncertain legal footing. The majority was taken to task, in fact, by three of the Court's judges, who said that the mandate document was not a treaty. Judge Basdevant said that the action of the Council approving the South-West Africa mandate document did not make the document a treaty.[23] Judges Spender and Fitzmaurice said the same, that although the Council approved the document, it was not a treaty.[24] These three judges were dealing, of course, with the South-West Africa mandate, but what they wrote about its form would apply equally to the Palestine mandate document. Spender and Fitzmaurice used in the first instance a common-sense test. The South-West Africa mandate document, they wrote, "does not look like a treaty." What it "looks like," they said, is "a Declaration promulgated by a resolution of the Council of the League in the exercise of a power conferred upon it by paragraph 8 of Article 22 of the Covenant." They concluded, "To all appearances therefore, the Mandate was a quasi-legislative act of the League Council."[25]

The Spender-Fitzmaurice analysis mirrors what we have said about the Palestine mandate document on critical aspects. The two jurists pointed out that on its face the South-West Africa mandate document does not appear to be a treaty. They pointed out that the power of the League Council on a mandate document came into play only under Article 22, paragraph 8, which, to repeat, read, "The degree of authority, control, or administration to be exercised by the Mandatory shall, if not previously agreed upon by the Members of the League, be explicitly defined in each case by the Council."[26] The Council was given no role in Article 22 to conclude a treaty with a potential mandatory.

Like the Palestine mandate document, the South-West Africa mandate document had not been registered as a treaty. The absence of registration presented an obstacle for the majority judges. To find the South-West Africa mandate document one having "the character of a treaty or convention," the majority judges had to explain why it was not registered. Covenant Article 18, as we have seen, required registration of treaties entered into by League members. That rule applied, however, only if the treaty was entered into after the coming into force of the League Covenant. The mandate for South-West Africa was seen by the majority judges as an arrangement between Britain (and the Republic of South Africa) on the one side, and the Council on the other, dating from 1919, which was prior to the entry into force of the Covenant in January 1920. Because of that timing, the judges said, the document did not have to be registered.[27] The mandate for Palestine was arranged only after the Covenant entered into force. By the logic of the majority judges, therefore, if the Palestine mandate document was a treaty, it would have been subject to the registration requirement. It, therefore, would have been legally null, since Covenant Article 18 deprived an unregistered treaty of legal force. "No such treaty or international engagement shall be binding until so registered," Article 18 recited. So, under the reasoning of the majority judges in the *South-West Africa Cases*, the Palestine mandate document, even if a treaty, was void.

The majority judges, to be sure, added an additional reason why, in their view, the South-West Africa mandate document did not need to be registered. They said that Covenant Article 18 did not apply to a treaty between the League and a member state, given that a mandate arrangement was an internal matter within the League. Article 18, however, made no exception for a treaty between the League and one of its members. It read, to repeat, "Every treaty or international engagement entered into hereafter by any Member of the League shall be forthwith registered with the Secretariat." Spender and Fitzmaurice, as we just saw, characterized the Council's role in approving a mandate's terms as the performance of "a quasi-legislative act of the Council." That is a more accurate characterization, and one inconsistent with the theory that a mandate document was a treaty. In a 1971 advisory opinion, the Court again characterized the South-West Africa mandate document as a treaty, but only by citing its own 1962 statement to that effect.[28]

The theory that the Palestine mandate document was a treaty became part of the Narrative through Israeli officials like Sharett, as quoted at the outset of this chapter. The British Government never called it a treaty. In the account of the mandate arrangement it gave to the United Nations in 1947, it described its interaction with the Council in some detail but did not call the Palestine mandate document a treaty.[29]

A 1922 assessment by Balfour of the Palestine mandate document showed that Britain did not regard it as a treaty. Balfour explained the document to the League Council by saying that the Council's role with respect to mandates was minimal. He called a mandate, as we saw in Chapter 10, a "self-imposed limitation by the conquerors." It was not a limitation imposed by the League. Balfour said that "the League was not the author." His point was that the mandate system was written into the League Covenant, a document that preceded the League. The Covenant was part of the Treaty of Versailles, hence the "author" of the mandate system was not the League, but the states party to the Treaty of Versailles. "The League of Nations," Balfour said, "is not the author of the policy but its instrument. It is not they who invented the system of the Mandates."[30] The states party to the Treaty of Versailles had, by Covenant Article 22, given the League the role of receiving annual reports from states that might opt into the mandate system. That role hardly made the League a party to a document a mandatory power might compose to describe how it planned to rule.

The Palestine mandate document was not a treaty. It lacked the hallmarks of a treaty. It did not read like a treaty. It was not registered as a treaty. It was terminable by Britain. It was not regarded as a treaty by Britain or by the League of Nations.

Chapter 14

THE LEAGUE OF NATIONS REQUIRED BRITAIN TO IMPLEMENT THE BALFOUR DECLARATION

A key element of the Narrative is that a legal obligation to implement the Jewish national home was imposed on Britain by the League of Nations. The American lawyer Felix Frankfurter, who, as we shall shortly see, helped draft the Palestine mandate document, wrote, "The Mandate explicitly recited the Balfour Declaration and charged the mandatory with putting it into effect."[1]

Even international law writers who denounce Britain for overriding Arab rights concede the point. Jean Allain, for example, in a book that castigates Britain roundly, wrote that as a result of "the willingness of the allied Powers to include the [Balfour] Declaration in the British mandate for Palestine," the Balfour Declaration rose "from a political pledge to a legal obligation."[2]

The same view was expressed by the Special Committee on Palestine, whose report, as we have seen, was key to the UN General Assembly recommending Jewish statehood. In Chapter 6, we saw the Special Committee's statement, "On 25 April 1920, the Supreme Council of the Allied Powers agreed to assign the Mandate for Palestine to Great Britain on the understanding that the Balfour Declaration would be put into effect." The Special Committee immediately followed that statement, saying, "The draft mandate was confirmed by the Council of the League of Nations on 24 July 1922, and entered into force formally on 29 September 1923."[3] In that fashion the Special Committee suggested that a requirement imposed on Britain by the Principal Allied Powers was imposed on it by the League Council as well. However, the League Council never discussed the Balfour Declaration. It did approve, in the conditional fashion we saw, the mandate document that incorporated the Balfour Declaration, but it was never given the opportunity to say what it thought about the Balfour Declaration. And of course, as we saw, Britain never gained the legal status required for a mandate to be lawful.

The idea that Britain was required to implement the Balfour Declaration was espoused in 2015 at the Hebrew University symposium on the Palestine mandate.[4] "The 1922 Mandate for Palestine—a binding resolution of the Council of the League of Nations—required Great Britain to implement the terms of the 1917 Balfour Declaration," wrote Yuval Shany, a professor of law at the University.[5] To prove his point, Shany quoted Article 2 of the mandate document, which read, "The Mandatory shall be responsible for placing the country under such political, administrative and economic conditions as will secure the establishment of the Jewish national home."[6]

Article 2 did, indeed, read as if it required Britain to implement the national home concept. But the appearance was illusory. Article 2 was written not by the Council, but by Britain. From the public record, there is no indication that the Council ever gave voice to the advisability of a Jewish national home. Under Covenant Article 22, the Council's role of defining terms was limited to the "degree of authority, control, or administration to be exercised by the Mandatory," if not defined by the mandatory. That was a reference to the role a mandatory power would take in relation to local authorities since, under Article 22, a mandatory power governing a state in Turkey's former Arab provinces was to provide only "administrative advice and assistance." If a mandatory did not make clear what degree of authority it planned to exercise, the Council could define it. Other aspects of a mandatory's planned policies were not subject to being defined by the Council.

Britain did not leave any terms of the mandate up to the Council. It defined its degree of authority in Article 1, giving itself "full powers of legislation and of administration." So, even on the one issue on which the Council in theory could have defined terms, Britain preempted any power on the part of the Council.

As for the legal character of what the Council did, Shany called its action on the mandate document "a binding resolution of the Council." The term "resolution" implied a deliberative process leading to a consensus that there should be a national home for the Jewish people in Palestine. What the Council did on 24 July 1922 was to endorse a "declaration" that was read aloud by the presiding officer of the Council, in which he stated, "In view of the declarations which have just been made, and of the agreement reached by all the Members of the Council, the articles of the mandates for Palestine and Syria are approved."[7]

As we saw in Chapter 10, the "declarations which have just been made" are seen in the minutes as statements by France and Britain that neither the Palestine nor the Syria mandate should be approved without the other one being approved at the same time. There was so much distrust between France and Britain that neither was willing to vote for the other's mandate until it got its own. The minutes reflect no discussion of the contents of either the Syria or the Palestine mandate. Neither on that date nor previously had the Council discussed provisions other than those relating to holy sites.[8] And even on that issue, the discussion was not aimed at achieving a view of the Council, but rather at getting the parties, namely, France, Italy, and Britain, to agree among themselves.[9]

The fact that Britain and France had agreed between themselves that neither mandate should be approved by the Council before the other reflected the circumstance that it was Britain and France in control of the process, not the Council. As these minutes show, no vote was taken to approve the terms of the two mandates. Nor was a vote even taken framed as a vote to reject the terms. The presiding officer did not explain "the agreement reached by all the Members of the Council." From what can be read between the lines in the Council minutes, the presiding officer apparently meant that no member was demanding a vote. The Council was letting France and Britain have their mandate documents without having to admit publicly that the Council had no power over these documents.

Shany next addressed the question of whether the mandate document left room for political rights for Palestine's Arab population. "The Palestine Mandate has generally been viewed as a strong political endorsement of the objectives of political Zionism," he wrote. Shany endorsed that assessment, saying, "This assessment is borne out by the juxtaposition in Article 2 of the *political* rights of the Jewish community in Palestine (the creation of a Jewish national home) and the *civil and religious* (but not the political) rights of Palestine's non-Jewish inhabitants."[10] So Shany's conclusion was that the League of Nations did not regard Arab political rights as being guaranteed.

In fact, the Council never required Britain to protect anyone. It never discussed the subject. Article 2 did not require Britain to promote the political rights of the Jewish community. Article 2 speaks of "the establishment of the Jewish national home, as laid down in the preamble." Shany is taking that to mean the political rights of the Jewish community. The mandate document did not use the term "political rights." Article 2 referred to the "national home," not to political rights. "National home" in the Balfour Declaration, as we saw, did not include political rights. The Article 2 phrase "as laid down in the preamble" may have been a reference to the third preamble paragraph that spoke of "reconstituting" the national home—a gloss on the Balfour Declaration that, as we have seen, was inaccurate. In any event, Article 2 was written by Britain, and, to repeat, the Council did not give a collective opinion on any provision of the mandate document.

The Council, in theory, could have refused to approve the terms of the mandate document, but a refusal was not a realistic possibility. In Chapter 9, we saw Lloyd George's view that a rejection would require a resolution to reject, and the Council's unanimity rule on resolutions meant that Britain could kill any proposed resolution. Moreover, since Britain and France had decided that the mandates for Syria and Palestine could not be approved without the other, a refusal on the Palestine mandate would have meant a refusal on the Syria mandate as well. The mandate system was the crown jewel of the League of Nations. Had the Council left the appearance that the Palestine mandate was being implemented improperly, the moral standing of the League would have been jeopardized. Britain had backed the Council into a corner.

Shany claimed that the nonexistent 24 July 1922 "resolution" of the Council was "binding." He did not explain on whom it was binding. Of course, since there was no resolution, there was nothing that could be binding. All the Council did on 24 July 1922 was to approve the wording of the document that Britain chose to submit. The Council was not prepared to approve the mandate itself on 24 July 1922, because the Syria document was not ready for approval. The Syria document, as we saw, awaited accommodation between Italy and France. And of course, Balfour had told the Council that the Council could not give approval with immediate effect, because Britain still needed to gain sovereignty from Turkey. So even with the "approval" of 24 July 1922, the document was still two steps removed from even potentially having any status with legal force.

Shany did acknowledge that the mandate document might suffer from legal defects. But if it did, he said, time cured any defect:

> Given the passage of considerable time since the conclusion of the Palestine Mandate, the broad international recognition the Mandate attracted in 1922 and in subsequent years (including the implicit support of the Arab delegation to the Peace Conference), and the dramatic changes in the demographic composition of Palestine since the 1920s, which transformed Jews from a small minority into the majority group in Palestine, one may argue that reversing the consequences of the Mandate is not only politically unrealistic, but would entail grossly unjust consequences. In other words, it is hard to accept that any formal legal defect that the international community would now attach to the Palestine Mandate could prevent reliance on its validity almost a hundred years later, after the lives of generations upon generations of Jews and Arabs who relied on its legal effects have been irreversibly changed.[11]

So Shany's bottom line was that the mandate document provided a basis for Israel's legitimacy even if it did not. Shany did not explain "the implicit support of the Arab delegation to the Peace Conference." At the time of the Peace Conference, the mandate document had not been written, so the Arab delegation could not have supported it. There was a document that Chaim Weizmann solicited from Emir Feisal on the subject. In that document, dated 3 January 1919, Feisal recited that the Balfour Declaration should be implemented in Palestine.[12] In his oral statement at the Paris Peace Conference, however, Feisal said nothing about Zionism or the Balfour Declaration.[13] He did exclude Palestine from the territory in which he sought an Arab state.[14] But in a memorandum he submitted, he said that if a mandate was to be set up for Palestine there would have to be "a representative local administration."[15] An administration representing the population would not have abided Zionist aims.

Feisal's father, it will be recalled, had been told by Col. Hogarth that the national home referenced in the Balfour Declaration was for a cultural community only. So, if Feisal was accepting the Balfour Declaration, it was the Balfour Declaration as it had been explained to his father. Weizmann acknowledged what he called Feisal's "reservation" to his acceptance of Zionism.[16] Britain, as we have seen, refused to allow an indigenous administration in Palestine. Given Feisal's *caveat* or "reservation," there was no agreement that could be taken as "implicit support" for the national home concept, at least in a form that might lead to Jewish statehood. Palestine Arabs, moreover, consistently objected to the Balfour Declaration, both in street protests in various cities of Palestine and in reasoned written representations to the British Government.

Shany also referred to "the broad international recognition the Mandate attracted in 1922." Britain was in control of Palestine, and other states accepted that control as a fact, just as they accepted colonial control by European powers elsewhere in the world. Other than Britain, no state extended anything that could be called "recognition" in the sense of endorsement of the advisability of a Jewish national home, whatever that concept might mean. Balfour made clear to the League Council that the declaration bearing his name was the affair of Britain and of Britain alone. Balfour well understood that the Balfour Declaration had generated opposition. He told the Council in 1922 that it did not matter whether they liked the Balfour Declaration or not. It was Britain's policy and for Britain alone to decide whether to continue with that policy. "Those who hoped and those who feared that the declaration which he had made previously on the British policy with regard to Palestine," he said, referring to the Balfour Declaration, "was going to suffer any modification were mistaken. The fears were not justified, the hopes were not justified. The general line of policy stood, and must continue to stand."[17] This was hardly a statement being made on behalf of a state that was being required, or even pressured, to adopt a policy. Britain was telling the Council what it planned to do and that it was making that determination on its own.

Balfour was telling the Council that it had no say in the matter. The claim that Britain was required by the League of Nations to implement the Balfour Declaration has no basis in fact. Britain decided unilaterally to implement the Balfour Declaration. It was not told to do so by the League of Nations.

The Palestine mandate has political significance in Israel as a claimed underpinning for the legality of Jewish statehood. In 2012, a report titled Commission to Examine the Status of Building in Judea and Samaria was issued. The Government-appointed commission was chaired by retired Supreme Court Judge Edmund Levy. In an excursus on Jewish rights, the commission identified the League Council's action of 24 July 1922 as having "recognized, as a norm enshrined in international law, the right of the Jewish people to determine its home in the Land of Israel, its historic homeland, and establish its state therein."[18] As we have just seen, the Council did not endorse Jewish political rights. And it said nothing about a right of the Jewish people as a norm of international law.

To be sure, Britain wrote the mandate document in a way that gave the impression that the inclusion of the Balfour Declaration was the result of a deliberative process of the Council of the League of Nations. It set the Narrative in motion on this point. The preamble begins with the phrase "Council of the League of Nations" and recites that the Council "confirms" the mandate and "defines its terms as follows." Then the operative articles follow. But as we have seen, the Council did not "define" any of the terms. The Council did not write a single sentence. The Council had little choice but to approve whatever Britain submitted. The thesis that the League of Nations required Britain to implement a Jewish national home has no historical basis.

Chapter 15

THE PALESTINE MANDATE DOCUMENT IMPLEMENTED THE LEAGUE COVENANT

Hersch Lauterpacht wrote that "the legal position" of Palestine as a "mandated territory" was "governed" both by the mandate document and by "the general principles of Article 22."[1] The implication of League Covenant Article 22 was that if a state chose to exercise a mandate, it would do so in a fashion that comported with the requirements for a mandate as elaborated in Article 22. In its mandate document for Palestine, Britain purported to respect the Covenant. The mandate text recited that the Principal Allied Powers had decided that a mandatory should take on Palestine "for the purpose of giving effect to the provisions of Article 22 of the Covenant of the League of Nations." Here the British Government was saying that the document provided for the governance of Palestine in a manner consistent with Article 22.

The next line, however, recited that "the Principal Allied Powers have also agreed that the Mandatory should be responsible for putting into effect the declaration originally made on November 2nd, 1917, by the Government of His Britannic Majesty, and adopted by the said Powers." This provision was problematic, because Article 22 called for protecting "the well-being and development" of the "peoples" of a mandate territory as "a sacred trust of civilization." It was presumably the peoples inhabiting the territory whose well-being and development were to be fostered, not peoples brought in from outside. Even a belligerent occupant was precluded by law from flooding a territory with an outside population.

There was also a factual problem with the statement that the Principal Allied Powers had adopted the Balfour Declaration. At the San Remo meeting, as we saw, Curzon was assailed when he tried to tell the Allies that they had adopted the Balfour Declaration. Curzon had to pull teeth to gain even half-hearted consent to letting Britain include mention of the Balfour Declaration in the anticipated peace treaty with Turkey. And even so, their consent was saddled with the understanding that the traditional rights of Palestine's existing population would be respected. The recitation in the mandate document of "adoption" by the Principal Allied Powers was fiction.

Then Britain compounded the deception by slipping in a follow-up clause to the one claiming that the Principal Allied Powers had adopted the Balfour Declaration, reading, "Whereas recognition has thereby been given to the historical connection of the Jewish people with Palestine and to the grounds for reconstituting their national home in that country." The word "thereby" referred to the claim that the Allies had adopted the Balfour Declaration. Here Britain was saying that the Allies had adopted the Balfour Declaration in an interpretation according to which an "historical connection" warranted a "reconstitution" of a national home. The Balfour Declaration, as we have seen, said nothing of the kind. Britain attributed to the Principal Allied Powers a reading of the Balfour Declaration to which they had never assented.

This clause about "historical connection" and "reconstitution" was not of Britain's making. Its inclusion represented an achievement of the Zionist Organization which, as we have seen, had tried to get comparable language into the Balfour Declaration and then had used the same terms to explain its objectives at the Paris Peace Conference. These terms took the Balfour Declaration a step closer to advocating Jewish statehood. Curzon had even assured the other Principal Allied Powers at San Remo, as we saw, that Britain would not stretch the meaning of the Balfour Declaration. But in this preamble clause, the British Government did precisely that.

By juxtaposing the terms "historical connection" and "reconstitute," Britain created the impression that the League Council not only backed the national home mentioned in the Balfour Declaration but that the League Council thought that a national home was warranted based on history. The preamble, it will be recalled, began with the words "The Council of the League of Nations." So Britain was putting this interpretation into the collective mouth of the League Council. Anyone reading the document would think that the Council took the Balfour Declaration as a commitment to "reconstitute" a Jewish national home in light of the "historical connection" of the Jews to Palestine. The mandate document read as if the Council had studied the history and applicable law and had come to a reasoned conclusion that there was an "historical connection" that merited the "reconstitution" of a national home. Yet the question of whether anything tantamount to a "national home" ever existed for Jews in Palestine, or what it might mean to "reconstitute" it was never put before the Council for evaluation. A British journalist wrote that the mandate document "was issued under cover of the League of nations, as though it were the result of the collected debates of the world's lawgivers."[2] It was not. The League Council engaged in no discussion of what was meant by "reconstitution" or "historical connection."

The 1937 British Royal Commission explained how this phrasing found its way into the mandate document. As a follow-up to the plan the Zionist Organization presented to the Paris Peace Conference, "A more detailed plan, dated the 28th March [1919], was drafted by Mr. Felix Frankfurter, an eminent American Zionist. From these and other documents and records," the Royal Commission said, "it is clear that the Zionist project had already in those early days assumed something like the shape of the Mandate as we know it. The right of the Jews on historic grounds to re-establish their National Home in Palestine was affirmed. Jewish immigration and close settlement on the land were to be promoted. A body representing the Jews of Palestine and the world at large should co-operate with the Mandatory."[3]

Frankfurter was chief drafter for the Zionist Organization at the Paris Peace Conference.[4] He would later relate in a memoir that the mandate was "a legal document and called for lawyers of experience and understanding." The English Zionists, he said, "were very anxious that I should go, to be, as it were the American responsible for working with the British, particularly the British, on the terms of the mandate in doing what one could do to get an appropriately worded, or appropriately formulated mandate issued out of the deliberations of the Paris Peace Conference."[5]

The Zionist Organization did not wait for Britain to draw up a mandate document. It wanted to pin Britain down on promoting a national home and to define the national home in line with the Zionist desire for a state. It drew up a draft, in the form of a document to be issued by the Council of the League of Nations. The document was submitted with a cover letter on Zionist Organization letterhead, signed by Frankfurter, to David Hunter Miller, a US official who was a central figure in the drafting of the Covenant. The document was dated 28 March 1919.[6] It is also reproduced in the Annex to this book.

The document was replete with the Zionist desiderata. The Jewish people would be declared to hold legal title to Palestine, and this by virtue of historical right. Palestine—the entirety of Palestine—would be constituted as the "national home." The "national home" was defined to be a "commonwealth," a code word for "state." Britain would cooperate with "appropriate Jewish agencies" to promote Jewish migration and other aspects of the national home.[7]

The submission of this draft was a significant breach of international protocol. Here was a private organization proposing a document to be issued by an international organization and affecting the governance of territory. One might have expected the British Government to react by telling Miller to pay no heed. President Woodrow Wilson was known to be favorable to Zionism, so the submission of the document to Miller, a US official, was a way of pressuring Britain.

The effrontery was greater because the document outlined a procedure whereby Britain would gain sovereignty over Palestine in order to have a right to govern it. Sovereignty questions are dealt with by states, not by non-governmental organizations. Yet the document recited that the peace treaty between Turkey and what it called "the Signatory Powers," presumably the Allies, would give Palestine to the "Signatory Powers" and that they in turn "hereby constitute Great Britain [as] the Mandatary." This was a road map for Britain, predating the strategy Britain actually followed in the Treaty of Sèvres to try to gain sovereignty.

The document included recitations about the population of Palestine. It said that the population was not capable of self-rule and that it was "the wish of the inhabitants and of the Jews" that Britain should become the "mandatary." The statement that the population was not capable of ruling itself was not explained. It was apparently thought self-evident that a non-European population required European guidance. Nor was the statement about "the wish" of the inhabitants explained.[8] In fact, British military officials were already seeing that the Arab population feared that Britain as ruler would promote a Zionist agenda.

Frankfurter was not working alone. "Informal discussion between representatives of the Zionist Organization and British representatives at Paris on the Mandate for Palestine began in the spring of 1919," a journal of the Zionist Organization of America recounted. "Dr. Weizmann and Mr. Sokolow received much aid from the American Zionist delegation. Later, when the British delegation returned to London and when Dr. Weizmann was absent in Palestine and Mr. Sokolow in Paris, negotiations were conducted by Mr. Herbert Samuel, Dr. Jacobson, Dr. Feiver [Feiwel], Mr. Harry Sacher, Mr. Landman, and Mr. Ben Cohen. Drafts of the Mandate were prepared by Prof. Felix Frankfurter and Mr. [Howard] Gans. The first draft was presented to the British delegation on July 15, 1919."[9] The named individuals were drawn from Britain and America rather than from Palestine.

The interaction continued, carrying over after the conclusion of the Paris Peace Conference. In London in early 1920, the Zionists made certain concessions after getting feedback from British officials.[10] The London Zionist Executive, the British branch of the Zionist Organization, became engaged on the British side.[11] The Foreign Office gradually took over the drafting, particularly after the San Remo meeting.[12]

As explained by the Zionist Organization of America, a draft dated 19 June 1920, "showed the following omissions from the first tentative draft. (1) A paragraph in the preamble recognizing the historical connection of the Jewish people with Palestine. (2) The term 'self-governing commonwealth' was deleted and 'self-governing institutions' substituted. (3) The right given to the Jewish Agency to be consulted in regard to the granting of concessions which it does not take up itself. (4) The recognition of the establishment of the Jewish National Home as the guiding principle in the execution of the Mandate. (5) The entrusting of Jewish education to the Jewish Agency. (6) Mention of Jewish Sabbath and holidays. The Zionists objected strenuously to these proposed changes and entered into negotiations with prominent British officials and with groups in the House of Commons. Finally in December 1920, the Cabinet decided to reincorporate into the Mandate the statement regarding the historical connections of the Jews with Palestine."[13]

Weizmann described the Palestine mandate document as a contract between the Zionist Organization and the British Government. He explained that before Britain submitted the document to the League Council, the Zionist representatives, despite not being entirely happy with the content, signed off on it. The Zionist Organization composed what Weizmann called "our letter of acceptance" to Curzon's draft. The letter was signed by the members of the Zionist Executive.[14]

France and Italy were not pleased with Britain's drafts, which Curzon let them see. "When it was first shown to the French Government," Curzon reported in a confidential memorandum to the Cabinet, "it at once excited their vehement criticisms on the ground of its almost exclusively Zionist complexion and of the manner in which the interests and rights of the Arab majority (amounting to about nine-tenths of the population) were ignored. The Italian Government expressed similar apprehensions."[15] What angered the Allies most was a draft of the "historical connection" clause that had read: "Recognising the historical connection of the Jewish people with Palestine and the claim which this gives them to reconstitute Palestine as their National Home."[16]

The Allies said that what they had been willing to agree to "was far from constituting anything in the nature of a legal claim, and that the use of such words might be, and was, indeed, certain to be, used as the basis of all sorts of political claims by the Zionists for the control of Palestinian administration in the future," and "that, while Mr. Balfour's Declaration had provided for the establishment of a Jewish National Home in Palestine, this was not the same thing as the reconstitution of Palestine as a Jewish National Home."[17]

The Allies did not see the Jews as having "a legal claim" that would let them try to make a political claim. Britain modified the clause. "On the other hand," Curzon said, "the Zionists pleaded for the insertion of some such phrase in the preamble."[18] Curzon personally agreed with France and Italy. He wrote in a note dated 8 August 1920, that he did not "recognise that the connection of the Jews with Palestine, which terminated 1200 years ago, gives them any claim whatsoever."[19] Curzon saw the Zionist Organization's aim as being to set a "foundation" for "the complete government of the country."[20] Curzon's skepticism about a legal claim based on history was shared by Felix Frankfurter, even though the draft mandate document of 1919 that Frankfurter drafted on behalf of the Zionist Organization had based a Jewish national home on what it said was "the historic title of the Jewish People to Palestine."[21] "From the viewpoint of international law," Frankfurter wrote in 1931, "the historic connection of the Jewish people with Palestine may afford a dubious prescriptive right." Frankfurter's reference to "prescriptive right" was to a doctrine that gives title to land based on long-time occupation. The International Court of Justice has said that without occupation, a centuries-old title does not give sovereignty.[22] Frankfurter's acknowledgment of this obvious point was telling since he, as much as any other lawyer, was responsible for convincing Britain to insert in the mandate document the preamble clause about a "historical connection of the Jewish people with Palestine" as a basis for "reconstituting" a Jewish national home.

Weizmann in his memoir quoted Curzon as saying he did not want Weizmann to be able to use such a phrase to make demands of Britain based on a supposed legal entitlement in Palestine.[23] Britain deleted the term "claim" from the clause, so that the clause would not be saying that the Balfour Declaration reflected a legal claim.[24]

That said, the inclusion of the phrase "historical connection" and the word "reconstitute" was a key Zionist victory.[25] Weizmann saw this phrase as "the most important part of the Mandate."[26] At the same time, Curzon's explanation of the reason for deleting the word "claim" removed any hint that the mandate document was taking the Balfour Declaration to mean that the Jews had a legal claim to Palestine.

Other key provisions in the mandate document showed the hand of the Zionist Organization and further inconsistency with Covenant Article 22. The Palestine mandate document's Article 2 recited, "The Mandatory shall be responsible for placing the country under such political, administrative and economic conditions as will secure the establishment of the Jewish national home." Like the preamble clause on the Balfour Declaration, Article 2 of the mandate document subordinated the rights of the existing population to those of the population Britain aimed to insert, at least if the insertion of the outside population were undertaken against the will of the existing population. The language of Article 2, moreover, clearly came from the Zionist Organization, tracking the Zionist Organization proposal at the Paris Peace Conference, which had recited, "Palestine shall be placed under such political, administrative and economic conditions as will secure the establishment there of the Jewish National Home."[27]

Article 4 as well came from the Zionist Organization. It read, "An appropriate Jewish agency shall be recognised as a public body for the purpose of advising and co-operating with the Administration of Palestine in such economic, social and other matters as may affect the establishment of the Jewish national home and the interests of the Jewish population in Palestine." As for how that agency would be constituted, "the Zionist organization," Article 4 continued, "shall be recognised as such agency. It shall take steps in consultation with His Britannic Majesty's Government to secure the co-operation of all Jews who are willing to assist in the establishment of the Jewish national home."[28] Britain had let the Zionist Organization write itself into the mandate document. Article 4 tracked the Zionist proposal at the Paris Peace Conference for "a Council representative of the Jews of Palestine and of the world" that would participate in governing Palestine.

Article 6 said that Britain would "facilitate Jewish immigration" and encourage "close settlement of Jews on the land," and that it would cooperate in this endeavor with "the Jewish agency referred to in Article 4." The phrase "close settlement" came from the Zionist proposal at Paris, which called for Britain to "promote Jewish immigration and close settlement on the land." So too did the injunction to facilitate Jewish immigration.[29]

The Article 6 promotion of Jewish immigration was at odds with the Covenant Article 22 statement that the population was provisionally ready for independence. The aim of the Zionist Organization was to increase the Jewish component of the population over time so that it could take over the country. That aim would require British presence for a substantial period of time. Palestine was declared to be ready for independence, yet independence would not soon be permitted, and only then after a demographic shift that would impair what independence might mean.

Another violation of Covenant Article 22 came in the mandate document's provision on the style of rule.[30] Article 22 said that the Turkish territories were to be administered on the basis of a mandatory providing only "administrative advice and assistance." In Article 1 of the mandate document, however, Britain gave itself complete power in ruling Palestine.[31] Article 1 did not provide for a local administration to which "administrative advice and assistance" could be given.

In Syria, to the contrary, an Arab administration came into being, to which France, as mandatory, could give "advice and assistance." In Syria, local elements were sufficiently strong to force France to accept them as part of the governing structure. A French bureaucrat working in Syria was envious of his British counterparts in Palestine for the control they enjoyed. He urged his home office in Paris to "eliminate" in Syria any "indigenous litigant," his term for a locally constituted administration.[32]

The Zionist Organization had a hand in preventing a local administration in Palestine. The attribution of complete power to Britain was foreseen in the 1919 Zionist Organization draft of a mandate document. In a memorandum written to accompany the draft it gave to Miller, Frankfurter explained that the mandatory should be accorded "flexibility of governmental and administrative means."[33] Frankfurter did not attempt to explain how such "flexibility" comported with the Covenant Article 22 requirement of a local administration.

Covenant Article 22, moreover, required that "the wishes" of the community "must be a principal consideration in the selection of the Mandatory." Britain selected itself without ascertaining "the wishes" of the Palestine population. The British Government ignored the findings of a team that US President Wilson sent in 1919 that found that the population did not want Britain as a mandatory. Britain had been asked by Wilson to participate in the 1919 survey, but it declined. The British Government later explained its refusal by saying, "President Wilson pressed for the dispatch of an inter-Allied Commission to Syria and Palestine to discover the wishes of the peoples of these two areas. This project failed, however, and the President then sent an unofficial American Commission which toured these areas in June and July, 1919, and privately reported that the Arabs wanted complete independence for a united Syria and Palestine."[34] As a joint project, the effort "failed," not of its own weight, but because the British Government pulled out, knowing that the finding would be that it was not wanted in Syria or Palestine. The US commission found that if there was to be a mandatory, the United States was preferred to Britain.[35] Balfour was not apologetic about violating the Covenant by ignoring the wishes of the population. In an August 1919 memorandum to Curzon, Balfour wrote:

> The contradiction between the letters of the Covenant and the policy of the Allies is even more flagrant in the case of the "independent nation" of Palestine than in that of the "independent nation" of Syria. For in Palestine we do not propose even to go through the form of consulting the wishes of the present inhabitants of the country, [...][36]

Britain went ahead proclaiming a mandate in July 1920 against the wishes of the population, in obvious violation of Covenant Article 22. On the ground in Palestine, the assessment of Britain's military officials was in line with the finding of Wilson's commission. The Chief Administrator, Major General A.W. Money, reported that "if the Zionist programme was a necessary adjunct to a mandate," as was then under consideration, "France or the United States would be preferred as the mandatory," because "Great Britain was believed to be more systematically committed to the Zionist programme." General Money's assessment was that "no mandatory power could carry through the Zionist programme save by force, and by suppressing the wishes of the large majority of the people of Palestine."[37]

Then too, the mandate provision calling for the implementation of the Balfour Declaration could not be justified under Article 22. "The British mandate for Palestine," wrote an American legal analyst, "requires the development of a national home for the Jews there, which in view of the widespread Arab opposition is hardly compatible with the covenant's insistence that the well-being and development of the inhabitants is the main object of the mandates" or with the Article 22 statement that Turkey's Arab communities "should be provisionally recognized as independent nations."[38]

One can only wonder how the League Council could approve a mandate document so clearly at odds with the League's Covenant. Lawyer Jean Allain is on the mark when he writes, "The willingness of the Council of the League of Nations to accept the British Mandate for Palestine belies the manifest violations of its own Covenant."[39] The British Government had let a private organization, the Zionist Organization, shape a document that on its face contravened the Covenant in fundamental ways. Balfour told the Council, as he explained the limited character of its role, that "the duty of the League" was confined to "see[ing] that the terms of the mandates were in conformity with the principles of the Covenant."[40] The Council, strongly under the sway of Britain, did not perform even that limited task. Bereft of a legitimate role with respect to mandate documents, the Council could hardly be too demanding of mandatories. The Council's act of approving the Palestine mandate document, far from being an exercise of statecraft, reflected the Council's impotence.

The UN Special Committee on Palestine understood that it would be on thin ice recommending Jewish statehood if the mandate document did not validly envisage at least a "national home." It responded to and rejected the arguments that the Palestine Arabs made against the validity of the mandate. On the self-attribution to Britain of full power of administration, the Special Committee replied by quoting the 1937 Royal Commission that this difference in treatment for Palestine, over and against Syria and Iraq, "was confirmed by the Supreme Council in the Treaty of Sèvres and by the Council of the League in sanctioning the Mandate."[41] That, of course, was no response at all. As we have seen, the Allies had no standing to make such a determination, and the Treaty of Sèvres was never ratified.

The Special Committee gave as another reason to justify full power, again citing the 1937 Royal Commission, that paragraph 8 of Covenant Article 22 "prescribes that the degree of authority to be exercised by the mandatory shall be defined, at need, by the Council of the League."[42] The Special Committee's apparent reasoning was, again, that the Council had approved the mandate document's terms, and that "degree of authority" was a matter on which the Council potentially had a role. This reasoning made little sense, however, since the Arab argument was that the self-attribution to Britain of full powers violated the Covenant. The Special Committee did not explain how the mandate document could be valid given that inconsistency. The Special Committee's statement that the Council could define degree of authority "at need" was a distortion as regards the Palestine mandate document, since Britain itself defined its degree of authority. As a result, the Council had no need to do so.

The Special Committee dismissed the Arab argument that the mandate document was invalid for ignoring the wishes of the population. Against this argument, the Special Committee cited a resolution adopted 2 July 1919 in Damascus by the General Syrian Congress, an institution in which Palestine representatives participated.[43] The Special Committee said that the Congress considered the possibility of a mandate and gave Britain as the second choice for mandatory after the United States.[44] The Special Committee thus implied that the Congress expressed a willingness for Britain to serve as mandatory. The Special Committee omitted, however, the Congress' explicit protest against Covenant Article 22 for its assumption that a mandatory was needed, and the Congress' call for complete independence. The Congress addressed the possibility of a mandate only because its participants knew they might not be able to force the Europeans out. It was in that context that they said they would prefer the United States and only second Britain. Making Britain second choice did not mean that they were willing to have Britain, but the only other state that was a realistic possibility was France, which the participants wanted even less. So putting Britain as second was a way of saying "No" to France. Even if a mandate were imposed on them, the participants stipulated that the "assistance" envisaged by Article 22 should "not infringe the complete independence" of the country.[45]

The Special Committee did not explain how the mandate could be valid given that it was never definitively approved by the League Council, or that Britain never gained sovereignty. The Special Committee accepted the Narrative in all respects. The frailty of its reasoning highlighted the difficulty of rationalizing the Palestine mandate as legally valid.

With the mandate document enjoying the imprimatur of the Special Committee, however, the Zionist Organization was free to exploit it, and particularly the "historical connection" clause, to its advantage. In the 1948 declaration of the establishment of a Jewish state, reference was made to Theodor Herzl proclaiming a right for the Jews of the world to statehood in Palestine.

The declaration then proclaimed, "This right was recognized in the Balfour Declaration of the 2nd November, 1917, and re-affirmed in the Mandate of the League of Nations which, in particular, gave international sanction to the historic connection between the Jewish people and Eretz-Israel and to the right of the Jewish people to rebuild its National Home."[46]

The Palestine mandate document, far from being an implementation of Covenant Article 22, violated it at every important turn. It was nothing short of a travesty that the League Council could give its terms even a conditional approval, and that the UN Special Committee on Palestine could use the document as a reason to recommend Jewish statehood.

Chapter 16

THE PALESTINE MANDATE DOCUMENT RECOGNIZED JEWS AS A NATIONAL GROUP

An element of the Narrative, as we have just seen, is that Jewry was regarded as holding a collective right to territorial entitlement in Palestine. The 1948 declaration of statehood claimed that this right was "re-affirmed" in the Palestine mandate document. The declaration recited that the 1897 Zionist congress called for the "the right of the Jewish people to national rebirth in its own country. This right," the 1948 declaration continued, "was recognized in the Balfour Declaration of 2 November 1917, and reaffirmed in the Mandate of the League of Nations, which, in particular, gave international sanction to the historic connection between the Jewish people and Eretz-Israel and to the right of the Jewish people to rebuild its National Home."

The 1948 declaration's reference to the mandate document as a document "of the League of Nations" was questionable since, as we have seen, the document was written by the British Government, not by the League of Nations. The reference to "the Jewish people" held significance, because only a "people" has a right to self-determination. Further, even a group that is a "people" may not necessarily be entitled to exercise self-determination in a particular territory. As was the case in Palestine, another people may have their own claim. The claim of a right for the Jewish people was particularly problematic since they, in the main, did not inhabit the territory of Palestine. A people making a claim to a territory typically inhabits that territory. This circumstance was lacking for Jewry.[1] One early analyst of the Palestine mandate referred to Jews as "an absent people."[2]

As a minimum, in any event, the collectivity making a territorial claim must be a "people." Ruth Gavison, professor in international law at the Hebrew University, explained in a book published by the Jerusalem Center for Public Affairs, "The claim that Jews are not a nation in the context of our concerns comes from the fact that international law recognizes the right of peoples to self-determination, while only recognizing cultural and religious rights for other cultural groups, with a special sensitivity to the claims of national minorities. If Jews are only a religion, basic elements of their claim to a right to selfdetermination in Zion may be undermined."[3]

This distinction that Gavison mentions between people and minorities was well understood in the League of Nations era. A number of treaties coming out of World War I aimed to protect populations that were minorities in countries in which a different population predominated.[4]

A right to self-determination would later be written into the Charter of the United Nations as "self-determination of peoples,"[5] and into a worldwide treaty, with a statement that similarly limited the right to a people: "All peoples have the right of self-determination."[6] The characterization of Jewry as such a "people," however, was far from obvious. Gavison used the term "nation," which in this context is the equivalent of "people." "It must be conceded," wrote Gavison, "that the existence of Jews before the establishment of the state could indeed raise doubts concerning their status as a nation. The doubts are raised not only by the characteristics of Jews and Judaism, but by the fact that different states treated Judaism and Jewish identity in different ways." The identity, however, of Jewry as a national group, Gavison wrote, was solidified in the mandate document. "Be this as it may, the question of whether Jews had national rights was clearly resolved in international law by the 1922 Mandate for Palestine, in which Britain accepted the Mandate to facilitate the establishment of a 'national home' for Jews in Palestine, explicitly recognizing the historical roots of Jews in the country."[7]

The "national home" written into the Palestine mandate might just as easily be read, however, to mean that Jews were regarded as a minority population in Palestine. If, as Gavison concedes, the identity of Jews as the Jewish people was uncertain, there is little reason to take either the Balfour Declaration or the Palestine mandate document as resolving the issue in favor of peoplehood. Jews resided in many countries. They held the citizenship of those countries. If Jews in a particular country were part of a worldwide "people" or "nation," did that mean they were not part of their countries of nationality? Jews who opposed Zionism feared precisely that if Jews came to be seen as part of a worldwide grouping, their status in countries of residence might be jeopardized.

Gavison, who in 2011 was awarded the prestigious Israel Prize for her work in Legal Research, did not further explain how the mandate document resolved the issue of Jewry as a nation or a people. The mandate document contained no definition of "Jewish people." It merely reproduced the Balfour Declaration, leaving hanging the question of the identity of Jews as being a religion, a people, a series of minority groups, or something else. Gavison's reference to "the historical roots of Jews in the country" was a reference to the preamble clause in the mandate document that recited that the Balfour Declaration reflected an "historical connection" that warranted a "reconstitution" of what existed in ancient times. That preamble clause, however, did not resolve the question of the characterization of Jews any more than did the Balfour Declaration. The League Council never considered the question of how to characterize Jewry.

Gavison said that by the mandate document, "Britain accepted the Mandate to facilitate the establish of a 'national home' for Jews in Palestine." As we have seen, Britain "accepted" nothing. It was Britain, not the League, who put forward the national home concept. The League Council did not question what Britain wrote about the Jewish people or anything else that Britain inserted in the mandate document. Whatever the mandate document might have meant in regard to the identity of Jewry cannot be attributed to the League Council.

Gavison claimed that the mandate document resolved the issue in favor of Jews being a "people." But Britain's inclusion of the concept in that document hardly achieved that result. The mandate document could not convert a "non-nation" into a "nation" or a "non-people" into a "people." The mandate document did not in any respect reflect an understanding shared so widely as to be deemed of significance as a matter of international law. Even if the mandate document had some status as a matter of law—which, as we have seen, it did not—it could hardly be taken as giving an authoritative definition of Jewry.

Gavison's characterization of Jewry as a "nation" has been contradicted by the Supreme Court of Israel, which had occasion to define Jewry in the immigration context. Israel's Law of Return grants an entry right with resultant citizenship to "every Jew."[8] The Law of Return defines "Jew" as "a person who was born of a Jewish mother or has become converted to Judaism and who is not a member of another religion."[9] The criterion for being a Jew thus appeared to have a religious element. If one can become a Jew by conversion into Judaism, and stop being a Jew by adhering to a religion other than Judaism, then religion seems key to the definition.

The Supreme Court of Israel has confirmed this religious criterion. In 1962, it ruled that a person is not a Jew for purposes of the Law of Return though born as a Jew if the person becomes a member of a religion other than Judaism. The issue arose in the case of a Jew who became a Roman Catholic. The Court held that he was not a Jew.[10] Israel, the state founded on the theory that Jews enjoyed self-determination as a people, thus seems to define Jewry as religion-based. The Knesset and the Supreme Court undermined the rationale for Israeli statehood and for a claim to the territory of Palestine.

Chapter 17

THE PALESTINE MANDATE DOCUMENT BOUND BRITAIN TO THE BALFOUR DECLARATION

Moshe Sharett, as we saw, called the Palestine mandate document "an open covenant" and "an international instrument." Whatever other implications Sharett intended, he certainly meant that the document would be binding on Britain, and specifically, that Britain would be bound to implement the Balfour Declaration.[1] Yoram Dinstein said, to show that Britain intended to be bound, that the Balfour Declaration was "formally acknowledged and reiterated by successive British governments."[2] One feature of the Narrative is that the mandate document required Britain to implement a Jewish national home. There could clearly not be any Jewish rights at the international level if the mandate document was not at least binding on Britain.

No sooner had Britain declared mandate rule in 1920, however, than it began to have second thoughts about the feasibility of implementing the Balfour Declaration. Arab opposition in Palestine to the Zionist project forced a reevaluation. Britain faced a population intent on immediate independence. In May 1921, Arabs staged major protests in Jaffa, Palestine's largest city, as they feared that Britain was helping the Zionist Commission, renamed by then as the Palestine Zionist Executive, to take over their country. In a plea to Britain to cancel the Balfour Declaration, the Palestine Arab Congress complained that the British Government "is already carrying out this declaration into effect in spite of our wishes."[3] A commission of enquiry was appointed, and its recitation of Arab grievances mirrored those of the 1920 military court of inquiry we saw in Chapter 8.[4]

Minutes from 1921 meetings of the British Cabinet reveal concern that the Palestine situation might spin out of control:

> The Cabinet were informed that recent reports from Palestine were of a disturbing character. Arabs and Jews were armed, or were arming, and a conflict might shortly ensue, particularly if the Moslem Christian Delegation, now in London, returned without having secured the withdrawal of Mr Balfour's pledge to the Zionists. The latter were naturally anxious as to their position, and wished to be reassured as to the Government's support.[5]

Canceling the Balfour Declaration and ceding power to an Arab-led government was considered:

> Two courses were open to the Cabinet. They could withdraw from their Declaration, refer the Mandate back to the League of Nations, set up an Arab National Government, and slow down or stop the immigration of Jews: or they could carry out the present policy with greater vigour and encourage the arming of the Jews with a view later on of reducing the numbers of the British garrison and cutting down expenses.[6]

Reasons were voiced for continuing to promote a Jewish national home. According to the Cabinet minute-taker, "stress was laid on the following considerations." They were:

1. The honour of the government was involved in the Declaration made by Mr Balfour, and to go back on our pledge would seriously reduce the prestige of this country in the eyes of Jews throughout the world:
2. The Prime Ministers of Canada and South Africa had recently stated that our Zionist policy had proved helpful in those Dominions:
3. It was not expected that the problem could be easily or quickly solved, especially in view of the growing power of the Arabs in the territories bordering on Palestine:
4. On the other hand, it was urged that peace was impossible on the lines of the Balfour Declaration, which involved setting up a National Home for the Jews and respecting the rights of the Arab population. The result of this inconsistency must be to estrange both Arabs and Jews, while involving us in futile military expenditure. Against this position it was argued that the Arabs had no prescriptive right to a country which they had failed to develop to the best advantage.[7]

In October 1922, a new government came to power in Britain under the Conservatives, replacing the Coalition that had presided from the time of the War. Hopes were raised on the Arab side that Britain might abandon the Balfour Declaration. In a report to the Permanent Mandates Commission, however, the new Conservative government gave no hint of change. It reported that "no disturbances of the peace occurred." The report said that the June 1922 Churchill statement on Palestine, which we saw in Chapter 3, made clear that the Balfour Declaration was being implemented in a way that "left no doubt of the determination of His Majesty's Government to preserve the rights and interests of the non-Jewish population."[8]

In 1923, however, the Conservative government took a harder look at Palestine policy, still out of the public eye. Victor Cavendish, Secretary of State for the Colonies, explained his concerns in a lengthy memorandum. Cavendish mentioned the criticism voiced in the House of Lords that we noted in Chapter 9. "It would be idle," Cavendish wrote, "to pretend that the Zionist policy is other than an unpopular one. It has been bitterly attacked in Parliament and is still being fiercely assailed in certain sections of the press." Cavendish recounted three criticisms that were being leveled at the Government: "(1) the alleged violation of the McMahon pledges; (2) the injustice of imposing upon a country a policy to which the great majority of its inhabitants are opposed; and (3) the financial burden upon the British taxpayer."[9]

"There can be no doubt," continued Cavendish, "that the change of Government in England has greatly revived the hopes of the Arab politicians. Their supporters in the late Parliament were mainly drawn from Conservatives who were out of sympathy with the Coalition Government, and who might not unreasonably be expected to carry more weight with the present than with the late Administration."[10] Cavendish went on to assess the negative consequences for Britain were it to change course. If Britain were to repudiate the Balfour Declaration, "We have no alternative but to return the Mandate into the hands of the League of Nations and evacuate Palestine forthwith. We should be placed in an intolerable position if, after breaking a promise made to the Jews in the face of the whole world, we were to retain any connection with Palestine from which we derived, or could be held to derive, any conceivable benefit. We should, indeed, stand convicted of an act of perfidy, from which it is hardly too much to say that our good name would never recover."[11] So Cavendish thought that if Britain renounced the Balfour Declaration it would have to "evacuate Palestine," not because it would have a legal obligation to evacuate, but because remaining would be seen as "an act of perfidy." From a legal or institutional standpoint, as we have seen, there was little the League could do to force Britain out. Cavendish's assertion that Britain would have to evacuate was likely designed to convince his colleagues not to change course, since Britain had reasons of its own to want to stay.

Evacuating Palestine was said to be inadvisable for political or strategic reasons. "If we surrender the Mandate," Cavendish said, "the League of Nations may or may not succeed in finding another Mandatory. If they do not succeed, the Turks will inevitably return. Our position in that event will be an unenviable one. We shall stand for all time as the Christian Power which having rescued the Holy Land from the Turk, lacked the strength or the courage to guard what it had won."[12]

Cavendish recited reasons Britain should stay. "There is the further point," he wrote, "that apart altogether from our pledges to the Zionists or to anybody else, there are Imperial considerations that favour the retention of Palestine by Great Britain. Recent developments have profoundly modified our position in Egypt and circumstances might easily arise, under the new conditions, that would seriously affect our hold upon the Suez Canal. In such a contingency the control of Palestine might be of vital importance to us."[13] By 1922, Britain and Egypt were negotiating the terms of Britain's withdrawal from Egypt, which Britain had more or less occupied since 1882. The Suez Canal provided a vital route to India, the crown jewel of the British Empire. Britain faced the prospect of having no military units in Egypt capable of defending the Suez Canal.

The Cavendish memorandum stirred Cabinet-level action. Conservative Prime Minister Stanley Baldwin secretly appointed a 10-member committee "to advise the Cabinet as to the policy to be adopted by the Government in regard to Palestine." The assumption behind the formation of this committee was that Britain had a free hand, from the legal perspective, to do whatever was in its interests. Cavendish chaired the committee.[14] The committee summoned Palestine High Commissioner Herbert Samuel to London to explain how the Balfour Declaration was being implemented.[15] The committee reported back to the Cabinet four weeks later that it could not achieve consensus.

The committee pointed to the mandate document's provision calling, at once, for a Jewish national home and for the preservation of the rights of all the inhabitants of Palestine. Based on that language in the Palestine mandate document, the committee found it "difficult to blame those who argue... that the entire Mandate is built on the fallacy of attempting to reconcile the irreconcilable, and to combine in the same framework the creation of Jewish privileges with the maintenance of Arab rights."[16]

The Arabs were seen by the committee as having rights, whereas the Jews had only "privileges" given to them under the Balfour Declaration. The committee did not see the Jews as having any rights, hence a repudiation of the Balfour

Declaration would face no legal obstacle. The committee's conclusion, however, was identical to that reached by Cavendish in his memorandum. In a statement reflecting a lack of consensus, the committee nonetheless advised prioritizing Jewish privilege over Arab rights:

> [I]t is no longer pertinent to discuss the policy of the original Declaration of 1917. There are some of our number who think that that Declaration was both unnecessary and unwise, and who hold that our subsequent troubles have sprung in the main from its adoption. But that was nearly six years ago. We cannot ignore the fact that ever since it has been the accepted policy of His Majesty's Government, that it was also accepted, not indeed without some reluctance, by the whole of our Allies, that it met with especial favour in America, that it was officially endorsed at San Remo, that it figured in the original Treaty of Sèvres, and that it was textually reproduced in the Mandate for Palestine, which was officially submitted to and approved by the Council of the League of Nations in July 1922. Further, it has been the basis upon which Zionist co-operation in the development of Palestine has been freely given and upon which very large sums of Jewish money have since been subscribed.[17]

The committee explained that it regarded these considerations as more important than the issue of the soundness of the Balfour Declaration:

> Whether this policy has been wise or unwise, the above considerations, which cannot be disputed, possess a cumulative weight from which it is well-nigh impossible for any Government to extricate itself without a substantial sacrifice of consistency and self-respect, if not of honour. Those of us who have disliked the policy are not prepared to make that sacrifice. Those of us who approved the policy throughout would, of course, speak in much less equivocal terms.[18]

Renunciation would call into question Britain's "honor." Britain would be accused of inconsistency. The upshot of the reconsideration was that Britain would continue with the Balfour Declaration even at the risk of boxing itself farther into a corner.[19] The committee listed four reasons against repudiating the Balfour Declaration:

1. We see no way of reversing the policy without throwing up the Mandate.
2. If we return the Mandate, another claimant would very quickly be forthcoming. Whether that claimant were France or Italy, the result would be equally injurious to British and, as we think, to Palestinian, interests.

3. If no applicant were forthcoming and the Palestinian Arabs were left to work out their own destiny, the sequel could hardly fail to be the return at no distant period, of the Turks. This would be an even more disastrous consequence, and would, indeed, involve the final sacrifice of all for which we fought and won the Eastern war.
4. Although the strategical value of Palestine is rated by the Imperial General Staff less highly than it had been placed by some authorities, yet none of us can contemplate with equanimity the installation in Palestine of another Power.[20]

The Cabinet approved the committee's report.[21] In all this discussion, the Cabinet never worried that it was legally required to implement the Balfour Declaration, whether by the original issuance of it or by anything related to the League of Nations. The Cabinet regarded Palestine policy as entirely within Britain's discretion. The supposed concern about having to give up the mandate if the Balfour Declaration were repudiated was likely included in the report as a scare tactic aimed at Cabinet members who might have been inclined to scrap the Declaration. As we have seen, the League Council could not force Britain to relinquish Palestine. And formal repudiation would not have been necessary. Britain could readily have explained to the Council that it had decided to implement the Balfour Declaration in a way that would not engender Arab opposition.

Chapter 18

THE INTERNATIONAL COMMUNITY COMMITTED ITSELF TO THE BALFOUR DECLARATION

The British Government's efforts to make it appear that an international obligation to implement a Jewish national home was being imposed on it allowed proponents of that concept to argue that the international community had embraced Jewish rights in Palestine. Noting that the mandate document reproduced the Balfour Declaration, Felix Frankfurter wrote, "Thus was the Balfour Declaration made part of the law of nations, and thereby the establishment of a Jewish national home became an international obligation."[1]

It became an element of the Narrative that a Jewish national home was sanctified in a way that neither the Palestine Arabs nor anyone else could oppose. "Virtually the whole international community, as it existed in the era between the two World Wars," Yoram Dinstein claimed, "was legally committed to the Mandate for Palestine, which included the obligation for the establishment in Palestine of a national home for the Jewish people."[2] Dinstein elaborated that an obligation to promote a Jewish national home was undertaken by all states that were members of the League of Nations. "Through the Mandate for Palestine (as an international agreement), the entire membership of the League of Nations became bound by the Balfour Declaration."[3] Dinstein's rationale was that the document was a treaty involving the League as one party, hence it would be binding on all League member states.

Maurice Hirsch, an Israeli lawyer who served as chief prosecutor in Israel's military courts in the Palestine territory that Israel occupied in 1967, argued along the same lines. Hirsch said that the international community backed a Jewish home in Palestine, and he saw this support as the legal underpinning of the Jewish statehood that was declared in 1948. Hirsch started from the San Remo meeting. "The first decision of the international community to support the establishment of 'a national home for the Jewish people' was made in the post-World War I conference held in San Remo, Italy, in April 1920."

From there, Hirsch moved to the Council of the League of Nations. "In 1922," he wrote, "the League of Nations, the predecessor of the United Nations, reconfirmed the international community's support for 'a national home for the Jewish people' and placed responsibility on the British mandate 'for putting into effect'."[4]

In fact, it is hard to make a case that the international community rallied around the idea of a Jewish national home. Advocacy of a Jewish national home came from Britain, and from Britain alone. Britain had its Army in Palestine and there was little that other states could have done—individually or through the collectivity of the League of Nations—to force Britain to forego the idea. The most one can say is that other states acquiesced in what Britain was doing, whether out of inability to get Britain to do otherwise, or because they wanted Britain's backing for their own interests and were willing to concede Palestine policy to Britain. The major powers did not encourage Britain to promote a Jewish national home. France, the only other major power with any potential for opposing Britain, spoke up for Arab rights at the San Remo meeting, but it could not oppose Britain too strongly, because it needed Britain, which had captured Syria from the Turkish army, to withdraw from Syria to let France rule there.

We have seen that nothing done at the San Remo meeting, in any event, could be called a decision of the international community, since it involved only four states, and of these, only one, Britain, promoted the idea of a Jewish national home. As for the League Council, we have seen that it took the mandate document as submitted. Hirsch's suggestion that the Council "placed responsibility" on Britain for a Jewish national home had the matter backward. It was Britain that wanted approval for a mandate document that appeared to impose responsibility on itself. As we saw in Chapter 17, had Britain decided in 1923 that the promotion of the Balfour Declaration was not worth the candle, it was quite ready to scrap it. Even Britain itself did not think it had a legal obligation to promote a Jewish national home.

Dinstein's assertion of a generalized international commitment to a Jewish national home is not borne out. Nor, as we saw in Chapter 13, is his claim that the mandate document was a treaty. As a result, there could be no treaty obligation falling more broadly onto League members. Even if it had been a treaty between Britain and the League, the League's member states would have borne no obligation individually. Obligations would have fallen only on the League itself.

Dinstein did not explain how League members could bear obligations based on an action by the Council. The League of Nations had little power to require action, or inaction, from member states. With the possible exception of situations relating to the outbreak of war, member states were not required to comply with decisions of any League organ, including the Council.[5] The Council's action in approving the terms of the Palestine mandate document could in no fashion create obligations for member states.

As evidence of international support for the Balfour Declaration, Dinstein cited a 1924 bilateral treaty between Britain and the United States relating to Palestine. "It is well known," Dinstein wrote, "that one major power—namely, the United States—never joined the League of Nations. However, Britain went to the length of concluding a special bilateral agreement with the United States on the subject of Palestine. This is the 1924 Anglo-American Convention, in which the United States gave its assent to the administration of Palestine by Britain in accordance with the Mandate."[6]

Britain and the United States did have such a treaty. The 1924 Anglo-American Convention, however, had nothing to do with the propriety or legality of what Britain was doing in Palestine. It had a limited aim, as reflected in its full title, Convention between the United States and Great Britain with respect to rights in Palestine.[7] The object of the treaty was to ensure to the United States the same rights of commercial access as were enjoyed by members of the League of Nations.

The Palestine mandate document, in Article 18, assured all League members of commercial access to Palestine. It provided:

> The Mandatory shall see that there is no discrimination in Palestine against the nationals of any State Member of the League of Nations (including companies incorporated under its laws) as compared with those of the Mandatory or of any foreign State in matters concerning taxation, commerce or navigation, the exercise of industries or professions, or in the treatment of merchant vessels or civil aircraft. Similarly, there shall be no discrimination in Palestine against goods originating in or destined for any of the said States, and there shall be freedom of transit under equitable conditions across the mandated area.[8]

As a nonmember, the United States was not entitled to these rights, hence its desire for the bilateral treaty. In Article 1, as Dinstein correctly stated, this treaty did include an expression of US consent to Britain's mandate control of Palestine. Article 1 reads, "Subject to the provisions of the present convention the United States consents to the administration of Palestine by His Britannic Majesty, pursuant to the mandate recited above."[9] But the following provision, Article 2, gave the United States the same commercial rights Britain was giving to League members. The United States could hardly demand those rights for itself if it did not accept Britain's control of Palestine.

Article 1 was copied, in fact, from a comparable treaty the United States had just concluded with France regarding Syria. The United States had the same commercial access issue with Syria.[10]

In that treaty, similarly, the United States consented to France's administration of Syria. That consent did not extend, however, to whatever France might be doing in its governance of Syria. Nor did US consent in the treaty with Britain extend to whatever Britain was doing in Palestine.

Dinstein wrote that Britain "went to the length" of concluding the treaty with the United States. It was the United States, however, that initiated the treaty. It wanted commercial access. As the two negotiated in 1922, Britain tried to use the US desire for market access to wrest from it an expression of approbation for the Palestine mandate.[11] Given the frailty of its legal status and of the national home concept, Britain was desperate for major-power endorsement. It hoped to use a treaty with the United States that hopefully would include a pro-Balfour Declaration statement to spur action by the Council of the League of Nations to approve the mandate. The United States was not willing to be used in this fashion. It was unwilling to sign a treaty with Britain over Palestine until Britain gained sovereignty in a peace treaty with Turkey.[12]

Britain made a concerted effort to gain provisions that would make it appear that the United States supported the mandate and the Jewish national home. Curzon so said explicitly as the two countries parried. "His Majesty's Government are anxious if possible," wrote Curzon to the United States, "that the convention should contain a specific allusion to the policy of establishing a national home for the Jewish people in Palestine, having regard to the interest taken in this policy in the United States."[13] Curzon referred to the Convention as he was discussing its drafts with the United States as "the treaty for recognition by the United States of America of the British mandate in Palestine."[14]

The United States was having none of it.[15] The Convention was a dollars and cents treaty, not a political treaty. The United States was not politically invested in Britain's status in Palestine, or in the Balfour Declaration.[16] It focused on US rights in Palestine, like preserving the extraterritorial rights for its businesspeople that it had enjoyed during Turkish rule.[17] Those rights let legal matters relating to US business interests in Turkey be decided by a US consul, not by the local courts. The United States insisted that Britain respect those rights, which were based on a treaty with Turkey that was still in effect for Palestine, pending a renunciation of sovereignty by Turkey.[18] The United States did not yield to Curzon's plea to make a pro-mandate or pro-Balfour statement in the treaty. "With respect to the preamble to the convention," replied the US ambassador in London, "I am instructed to express the hope of my Government that objection will not be raised to the formula which has already been adopted in the case of the convention relating to Syria and the Lebanon. If this result would be facilitated by my Government's concurrence in incorporating not only the text of the mandate but also the preamble to the mandate in the preamble to the convention, my Government is prepared to accept this modification."[19]

The language of the Syria treaty would suffice for the Palestine treaty, the US was saying. The Syria treaty similarly reproduced the text of the Syria mandate, albeit without its preamble. The US conceded to let Britain reproduce the text of the Palestine mandate with its preamble. The United States agreed to the inclusion of the preamble as *quid pro quo* for Britain agreeing to language the United States wanted elsewhere in the treaty.[20] The US concession was not made as a show of support for the Balfour Declaration.

The preamble to the Palestine mandate document, of course, included references to the Balfour Declaration and the Jewish national home. Several analysts took that fact to mean that the United States became a "signatory" to the mandate document.[21] Even if the mandate document had some legal validity, however, it was not a document to which other states could formally adhere. The United States in any event did not regard this inclusion as an affirmation, even at a political level, of the Palestine mandate.

When the Convention was signed, the State Department issued a press release that showed the Convention's limited purpose. The release said nothing about a Jewish national home or the Balfour Declaration. It read, "The treaty between the United States and Great Britain in its principal provisions is similar to the treaty already concluded by this Government with France with respect to the Mandate for Syria and the Lebanon, which has already entered into effect. The Palestine Mandate Treaty provides that the United States and its nationals shall enjoy in the mandate territory all the rights and privileges assured to states members of the League of Nations under the terms of the Mandate."[22]

The US refusal to include a statement of support for the mandate or of the national home did not go unnoticed. A pro-Zionist US newspaper bemoaned the fact that the Convention did not have the United States endorsing the Balfour Declaration. "The scope of the treaty," the *American Israelite* accurately reported, "is limited to defining the rights of the American Government and its citizens in Palestine and does not touch further upon the subject of the Jewish national home."[23]

There was no generalized international endorsement of the advisability of a Jewish national home in Palestine. The League of Nations did not endorse a Jewish national home. League member states did not assume any obligation to promote a Jewish national home. Britain alone promoted the concept, and even so, not as a matter of legal obligation.

Chapter 19

BRITAIN HELD LEGAL STATUS IN PALESTINE

Britain was largely successful during the 1920s in escaping criticism that it lacked legal status. Other states focused on their own interests in Palestine. That passivity let Britain operate as if it were in Palestine legitimately. If Britain were merely a belligerent occupant, the infusion of immigrants from Europe and the role the Zionist Organization played in governance were unlawful.

In 1932, however, a situation developed in which Britain could not avoid the issue of its status in Palestine. The British Government found itself in a dilemma from which it could extricate itself only by asking other major powers what they thought Britain's status in Palestine to be. In that year, Britain enacted tariffs for goods entering Britain from foreign countries, imposing, in general, a duty amounting to 10 percent of their value.[1] The dilemma was that the British Government did not want to charge this duty on goods entering Britain from its various possessions around the world. Parliament had provided an exception for this situation in the 1932 legislation, which was called the Import Duties Act., The exception was that the Government was given the option to grant what was called a "colonial preference" to goods entering Britain "from any part of the British Empire." Mandate territories were mentioned specifically in the Act, as Parliament knew they would present a problem. The Import Duties Act authorized the Government to accord a "colonial preference" to "any territory in respect of which a mandate of the League of Nations is being exercised by the Government of the United Kingdom."[2]

The Government issued an order granting a preference to three territories Britain held under mandate in Africa: Tanganyika, Cameroons, and Togoland.[3] These territories fell under Covenant Article 22, paragraph 5. Their status was lower than that of Turkey's Arab territories, which fell under Article 22, paragraph 4, as having attained "a stage of development where their existence as independent nations can be provisionally recognized."

The Government delayed, however, in issuing a comparable order that would have applied to Palestine. The reason for the Government's hesitancy was that if it accorded Palestine a preference, states with which Britain had a bilateral most favored nation treaty might claim that goods entering from their own territories were entitled to the same preference. Under treaties of this type, a pair of states agree to admit goods of the other at a tariff rate no higher than they charge on goods entering from any other state of the world.[4]

Britain had such treaties with several major trading partners. If these states were to demand duty-free entry for their goods, the entire tariff regime of the 1932 Act would crumble. Palestine was the Government's greatest worry. The Cabinet conferred, to devise a way to avoid charging duty on goods from Palestine without inspiring claims for zero tariffs from the treaty partners, who, it feared, might point to Palestine, "due to its Mandatory status."[5]

The Cabinet decided to ask major trading partners with whom Britain had treaties with most favored nation provisions if they would invoke those provisions if Britain extended a preference to Palestine. The Cabinet decided that the states to be approached were the United States, Spain, Italy, Brazil, and France.[6] The Cabinet hoped they would decline, but the Cabinet further agreed that if they were to say they would insist on their treaty rights, Britain would seek their consent to submit the matter to the Permanent Court of International Justice for adjudication.[7] This intent to seek adjudication if the other states insisted on their treaty right was not made known. The Cabinet feared that if other states knew that Britain was prepared to go to that length, "the negotiations with foreign countries would be prejudiced."[8]

The Cabinet set up a committee to study the matter, calling it the Committee on Imperial Preference for Palestine. The Cabinet was concerned that questions about "imperial preference" might be raised in Parliament, thereby giving it publicity, so the Cabinet members agreed "the less said the better." The Cabinet decided that "the proper course" was "in Parliament to play for time." If questions were raised in Parliament, the Government would not mention the most favored nation treaties and its concern that they might be invoked to Britain's detriment, but would say only "that very difficult legal and other complications were involved and that the whole question was being considered carefully in all aspects."[9]

The Government was in fact asked in the House of Commons about a preference for Palestine by a member who wanted Palestine to benefit. The question was "whether His Majesty's Government intends to issue an Order in Council declaring that the mandated area of Palestine shall profit from the preferential treatment accorded to the British Empire in the Import Duties Act." The Government answered in a way that disguised its concern, saying only, "This question is still under consideration."[10]

The League's Permanent Mandates Commission was asking as well. It too wanted Palestine to be granted an "imperial preference," once it saw that a preference was being granted to Tanganyika, Cameroons, and Togoland. It also was aware of the Government's ambiguous response in Parliament.[11]

In keeping with the Cabinet's decision, the Government approached the five trading partners. With the United States, a most favored nation provision was in an 1815 commercial treaty that read, in Article 2:

> No higher or other duties shall be imposed on the importation into the territories of his Britannick majesty in Europe of any articles, the growth, produce, or manufacture of the United States, than are or shall be payable on the like articles being the growth, produce, or manufacture of any other foreign country.[12]

In a note to US Secretary of State Henry Stimson, Britain's ambassador in Washington referred to the 1815 treaty and related that his Government was contemplating "a preference to Palestinian produce imported into the United Kingdom." The ambassador inquired "whether the United States Government feel any objection to this proposal."[13] Stimson replied that if Palestine were granted the preference, the United States would demand it for itself on US exports to Britain. Stimson explained the US view of Britain's relation to Palestine. "The Government of the United States considers that Palestine is a 'foreign country' within the meaning of the term as used in Article 2 of the Convention," Stimson wrote, "and therefore holds that any tariff privileges accorded to Palestine should also accrue to the United States."[14]

The other addressees also responded. Spain's commercial treaty with Britain dated from 1922.[15] Spain's Minister of State replied that the treaty's most favored nation provision would apply. The Minister referred to League Covenant Article 22 and to the Palestine mandate document to say that "the territory in question can in no way be considered as Imperial territory, but only as a foreign country dependent on the League of Nations, which from an economic point of view, is in a similar position as regards the Mandatory Power as it is in regard to other countries and Sovereign States."[16] Palestine, said Spain, "was in a situation with regard to the mandatory power analogous to other sovereign states."[17]

Italy's answer was just as categorical. Its commercial treaty dated from 1893. Italy's Ministry of Foreign Affairs replied that "it does not appear possible that the Italian Government should give up the right to claim in favour of Italian goods, in virtue of the Anglo-Italian commercial treaty of the 15th June, 1893." The Ministry noted "the fact that Palestinian territory, judging by the standard of the other territories under mandate, is to be considered as a foreign country *vis-à-vis* the mandatory nation, and therefore not as forming part of the British Empire."[18]

Brazil had a commercial treaty with Britain, dating only from 1930. Brazil's Ministry of Foreign Affairs replied that it "would have no objection to raise against this assimilation of Palestine to the other territories of the Empire, for the effect of the preferential tariff, if it could have the assurance that the projected concessions would not be extended to oranges, so that the similar product of Brazil exported to Great Britain would not be unfavourably affected."[19] Oranges were a major export to Britain for both Palestine and Brazil.[20] So Brazil was insisting on getting the same preference as Palestine, on the rationale that the most favored nation provision applied.

Of the states queried, only France replied that it would not insist on its most favored nation status.[21] France, of course, had its own status to protect in Syria. It had gained its own mandate only by acceding to Britain's. France was approached less because of its trade with Britain than "because it seems probable that the French Government, owing to their position in Syria, may have an interest in this question somewhat similar to that of His Majesty's Government."[22] In other words, France was approached in the anticipation of a friendly reply.

The Secretary of State for the Colonies reported the replies to the Cabinet.[23] The Foreign Office told the Cabinet that its assessment of the replies was that Britain's partners in the commercial treaties regarded Palestine as a "foreign country" and "would claim for their goods imported into the United Kingdom any preferential rate which might be accorded to goods from Palestine. This attitude," the Foreign Office explained to the Cabinet, "is in accordance with the view of the situation which the Law Officers have taken in the past."[24] The "law officers" were the Attorney General and Solicitor General, the officials who advised the British Government on legal matters.

The law officers had been consulted as to whether the most favored nation treaties could be invoked by Britain's treaty partners if Britain were to grant a preference to Palestine. As the Foreign Secretary related to the Cabinet, "The question of possible damages was referred to the Law Officers in connexion with the Palestine question, and they then took the view that if preferences were granted in a case where His Majesty's Government's treaty obligations did not permit the grant of preference, the risk of a claim for damages for breach of treaty would be a serious one."[25]

As for the possibility of taking the matter to the Permanent Court of International Justice, the Foreign Office thought that Britain would lose.

It said "that the case of His Majesty's Government in this matter must (in view of the series of adverse opinions by successive law officers) be regarded as a weak one and that His Majesty's Government in the United Kingdom would be running a serious risk of losing it if it were referred to a court for a legal decision."[26]

The opinion of the Law Officers matched that of others who held that position previously.[27] It also matched what Cecil Hurst told the Permanent Court of International Justice in 1924. The legal advisors knew that the Permanent Court of International Justice had already said, in the *Mavrommatis* case, that Palestine was its own state.

The following week, the Committee on Imperial Preference for Palestine, citing the negative replies from other governments, advised the Cabinet "that the proposal to extend Imperial Preference to Palestine must be abandoned."[28] The Cabinet heeded that advice. It did not take the matter to the Permanent Court of International Justice. It issued no Imperial preference for Palestine.[29]

The Import Duties Act episode showed that other major powers did not regard Britain as having legal status in Palestine. They were telling Britain that they stood in the same relation to Britain as did Palestine. Britain and Palestine were just as separate from the sovereignty standpoint as were Britain and the United States.

The responses were in line with the Treaty of Lausanne, namely, that Britain and Palestine were entirely separate states. These other powers did not spell out the consequences more than was necessary to insist on their most favored nation rights, but if an entity has the status of a state, another state can exercise rights there only with its consent. It was not unheard of for one state to be administered by another, but the rationale for such an arrangement, called a protectorate, was that the protected state consented. A treaty was typically involved between the protecting and the protected state.[30] France's administration for a time of Morocco is an early twentieth-century example of a protectorate.[31] With Palestine, however, there was no treaty, no consent. Britain had simply come to Palestine and had refused to leave.

Britain decided to keep the issue out of the Permanent Court of International Justice, fearing that judicial clarification would show the frailty of its hold on Palestine. The contretemps over the imperial preference showed that Palestine was regarded as a state. The only basis for Britain to be exercising governance lawfully would have been a request from Palestine. Palestine had not, however, asked Britain to govern it. The logic behind the answers given to Britain by its treaty partners thus was that Britain lacked a legal basis for governing Palestine. Even Britain's own legal advisors could not find a way to rationalize Britain's status in Palestine.

In 1947, when it felt it had to give an explanation of its status, the British Government could find nothing rational to say, and so, as we saw in Chapter 11, it resorted to prevarication. Britain's initial status in Palestine in 1917 was that of a belligerent occupant, and as Hurst told the Permanent Court of International Justice, that status did not change. Britain remained in Palestine on the strength of the British Army, ruling the country despite having no legal basis for doing so.

Chapter 20

THE UNITED NATIONS CHARTER CARRIED FORWARD A JEWISH ENTITLEMENT TO STATEHOOD

The demise of the League of Nations cast even more doubt on the status of Britain in Palestine. The League Council did not meet after 1940. Nor did the Permanent Mandates Commission. The League itself was formally dissolved by the League Assembly in 1946. If Britain's position in Palestine derived from the League, the extinction of the League might have meant extinction of Britain's role in Palestine. If the Palestine mandate document was a treaty between the League and Britain, the League's disappearance would deprive it of whatever legal force it might have had, since one of the two supposed parties no longer existed.[1] Members of the League were concerned about the fate of those mandate territories that had not achieved independence. They addressed the issue as the Assembly closed the League down at its last session. Mandatories were asked to continue to administer until other arrangements were made.[2] Egypt objected. "It is the view of my Government," Egypt's delegate told the Assembly, "that mandates have terminated with the dissolution of the League of Nations."[3] Several mandatories indicated, however, that they planned to continue to administer at least temporarily on the basis of the existing mandates.[4] Britain, as we saw in Chapter 13, purported to govern under the mandate until 1948.

The demise of the League, nevertheless, deprived both Britain and the Zionist Organization and its affiliate Jewish Agency of institutional backing for the Palestine mandate. If it could be shown that the Palestine mandate document was accepted by the United Nations, the rights the Jewish people supposedly had under it could be seen as continuing to be accepted even after the termination by Britain of the mandate.

This theory was spelled out by Paul S. Riebenfeld, who had represented the Jewish Agency before the Permanent Mandates Commission. Noting the liquidation of the League of Nations, Riebenfeld claimed, "The continued validity, however, of rights derived from a Mandate after the expiry of the

League and the Mandate system was spelled out in the Charter of the United Nations, in its Article 80." Riebenfeld quoted from Article 80 the phrase relating to the rights of "any peoples or the terms of existing international instruments to which Members of the United Nations may respectively be parties."[5] Riebenfeld's implication was that Article 80 brought rights based on mandates under the protection of the United Nations.

To understand Riebenfeld's argument, one must understand what Article 80 was and what it was not. It was found in Charter Chapter 12, a chapter on a new trusteeship system being created for non-self-governing territories. Chapter 12, in Articles 77, 79, and 81, gave a state holding a mandate the option to place it under the supervision of a Trusteeship Council that the Charter created. Britain did not choose to put Palestine under the supervision of the Trusteeship Council. Article 80 addressed the question of whether the new Trusteeship Council would apply automatically to mandates. Article 80 said it would not:

> 1. Except as may be agreed upon in individual trusteeship agreements, made under Articles 77, 79, and 81, placing each territory under the trusteeship system, and until such agreements have been concluded, nothing in this Chapter shall be construed in or of itself to alter in any manner the rights whatsoever of any states or any peoples or the terms of existing international instruments to which Members of the United Nations may respectively be parties.
>
> 2. Paragraph 1 of this Article shall not be interpreted as giving grounds for delay or postponement of the negotiation and conclusion of agreements for placing mandated and other territories under the trusteeship system as provided for in Article 77.

Article 80 thus did not provide for the "continued validity" of "existing international instruments," it merely said that the trusteeship system would not apply automatically to them. Article 80 did not purport to bring rights under existing instruments under the protection of the United Nations. Existing rights might continue as valid, but it was not by dint of Article 80. Article 80 did not substitute the United Nations for the League of Nations in regard to existing arrangements.

This limited character of Article 80 was correctly explained by Hersch Lauterpacht in 1946, in a legal opinion he wrote for the Jewish Agency. Article 80 meant only, Lauterpacht pointed out, that "nothing in the provisions and the principles of chapter XII of the Charter relating to the 'International Trusteeship System' shall be construed '*in or of itself*' to alter rights under existing international instruments."[6]

As we have seen, the Palestine mandate was not a document carrying legal force. It could not, therefore, be carried forward by the UN Charter.[7] But even if Jewry could have been said to hold rights under the Palestine mandate, and even if the Palestine mandate was an "existing international instrument," Article 80 did not transport those rights into the UN Charter. Nor did it require UN member states to guarantee those rights.

Article 80 did not enhance the rights of "states" or of "peoples." It simply said that if a state, or if a people, had rights, those rights were not being taken away. A state either had rights, or it did not. A people either had rights, or it did not. Article 80 did not convert prior existing rights of states or peoples into rights under the UN Charter.

At the 1945 San Francisco conference that produced the UN Charter, the Arab states and the Zionist Organization were both heavily invested in the formulation of what became Article 80.[8] Article 80, however, was narrow in its meaning. The phrase beginning "the terms of existing international instruments" was inserted out of concern expressed at the San Francisco drafting conference that the provision might be interpreted to "alter the terms" of mandate documents.[9]

Article 80 was saying that the fact that the UN Charter opened the possibility that a mandatory might conclude a trusteeship agreement with the United Nations did not in and of itself affect whatever obligations the mandatory might have. Charter Chapter 12 was not meant to convert mandates into trusteeships automatically. Article 80 was written as a failsafe measure to acknowledge the *status quo* for mandate territories pending anticipated trusteeship agreements.[10]

Even if Riebenfeld was correct that Article 80 transported rights of states or peoples into the UN Charter, the only clear right of that sort would be the right of Palestine as a state. Palestine was a state under the Treaty of Lausanne and was accepted as such by other states. But that status for Palestine did not depend on Article 80. As for "peoples," and particularly the Jewish people, that would depend on whether they had rights. As we have already seen, they did not. And as for the mandate document itself, we have Shawcross as Attorney-General saying, as we saw in Chapter 13, that it was not "a kind of international statute or contract, giving rise to enforceable obligations."

POSTSCRIPT: WHY HISTORY MATTERS

The mandate system is sometimes described as a waystation between colonialism and independence. The population of Palestine had lived under foreign overlords, but not in classic colonialism. Under Turkey, the Palestine Arabs enjoyed considerable autonomy in local governance. They even held seats in Turkey's parliament. Britain not only assumed full control but, in collaboration with the Zionist Organization, inserted an outside population bent on taking over the country. The League of Nations, more through its weakness than as a matter of its policy, provided cover for Britain, lending an aura of pseudo-legality to its project. When the Arabs staged an armed revolt, as they did in 1936, Britain put it down so harshly that their capacity to protect themselves was severely reduced. As a result, the European settlers who came under Zionist auspices were able, a decade later, to force most of the Arabs out of the country.

The star of self-determination shone briefly at the Paris Peace Conference as Britain felt itself compelled to subject its conquest of Arab territory to a procedure that gave the appearance of limiting Britain's power. That appearance was largely illusory. Britain could decide on its own to remain in Palestine and to govern it. Britain could define the territory of Palestine. The mandate system required Britain to consult the population on the choice of a mandatory, and to allow for an indigenous government. Britain ignored these stipulations, and the League Council did nothing to enforce them. The Covenant, to be sure, gave the Council no enforcement authority, leaving Britain a free hand. The mandate system presupposed that a mandatory would hold legal title to the territory. Britain never gained that title, so even by the Council's standards, Britain had no legal authority over Palestine.

The peace treaty by which Turkey renounced sovereignty, the Treaty of Lausanne, gave no sovereignty to Britain or its Allies. Britain conceded that fact, as we saw, in the Permanent Court of Justice. It acknowledged to the Court that Britain had taken Palestine militarily during World War I and was holding it on that basis and on that basis alone. The Treaty of Lausanne substituted Palestine for Turkey as sovereign, thereby leaving Britain in the position of occupying Palestine instead of occupying Turkey, but with no legal right to be there.

Britain purported to gain rights in Palestine from its Allies, and they had no more right to Palestine than did Britain. Britain also looked to the Allies for approval of the project of inserting a population of Jews from Europe into Palestine, but again, the Allies had no warrant to give such authorization. And they balked when Britain asked, because they did not agree with the justice of Britain's aim. At the 1920 San Remo meeting, the Allies stipulated that the Balfour Declaration had to be construed in a way that would protect the national rights of the existing population of Palestine.

Britain nonetheless wrote a document to govern Palestine, the Palestine mandate document, that asserted that the Balfour Declaration called for "reconstituting" a national home, even though words to that effect did not appear in the Balfour Declaration. That clause, which was included after intense lobbying by the Zionist Organization, gave the Zionist Organization an opening to say that Jewish entitlement was being accepted by the League of Nations.

Britain also wrote into the Palestine mandate a clause saying that it planned to govern Palestine with the advice and cooperation of the Zionist Organization, to ensure the implementation of a Jewish national home. When it tried at the San Remo meeting to convince the Allies to back the Balfour Declaration, it did not tell them that it would give the Zionist Organization a formal role in the governance of Palestine. The League Covenant required a mandatory to let an indigenous governing structure operate, but Britain was doing the opposite by ceding a measure of authority to an outside group. As a belligerent occupant, Britain had no authority to bring in an outside population. An occupant is required to maintain the status quo pending a peace treaty. Instead, Britain set the stage for the country to be taken from its inhabitants.

The League Council never definitively approved the Palestine mandate document, hence never gave its approval to anything Britain was trying to do. The Council's action of 24 July 1922 was stated by the Council to be dependent on the finalization of the Syria mandate, hence was not deemed by the Council to have legal significance. The Council's action of 29 September 1923, stating that the document was to take legal effect because the Syria mandate had been finalized, was dependent on the Council's injunction that Britain must acquire sovereignty. Britain never did. The mandate document remained nothing more than a unilateral statement of intent by a belligerent power that had no right to govern the territory concerned.

At the final session of the League of Nations, the Egyptian delegate who argued that the Palestine mandate should terminate noted that the other

Arab territories that had been under Turkey on mandate had gained independence.[1] When the United Nations was poised, the following year, to initiate a study to make recommendations to Britain, the five Arab states that were UN members suggested that the UN General Assembly should recommend to Britain "the termination of the mandate over Palestine and the declaration of its independence."[2] That was the solution contemplated by the League Covenant for the successful conclusion of a mandate.

The Zionist Organization's insertion of a European population into Palestine brought the situation to such a point by 1947 that many member states of the United Nations could fathom no mutually acceptable solution. Their floor discussion in 1947, as they prepared to vote on partition, reads like a Greek tragedy. They knew they were relegating Palestine to warfare, but they said they could find nothing to do other than split the country. One must examine their dialogue with a magnifying glass to find anyone saying that a division of the country would be fair to the Arab population of Palestine. Britain had driven Palestine into a *cul de sac* in two ways. It had allowed a foreign movement to assume a position of military predominance, and it had given that movement a legal argument, albeit a flawed one, to bolster its claim. Britain's effort to depict its own rights in Palestine as being based on decisions of the international community let the Zionist Organization do the same for Jewish entitlement. As one writer put it, "the Articles of the Mandate were the initial pathways through which the Zionists found legitimacy and developed their national home."[3]

Britain's actions set the stage for a claim of a carryover of Jewish rights from the time of the League of Nations, specifically through the distorted account the UN Special Committee on Palestine gave the UN General Assembly as a basis for recommending the creation of a Jewish state. Norway was one of the countries that voted in favor of the General Assembly resolution to recommend a partition of Palestine into a Jewish and an Arab state. Norway's delegate clearly, and correctly, saw the principal thrust of the resolution as its recommendation for a Jewish state, since Jews were a minority in Palestine. One reason Norway gave for voting to recommend Jewish statehood was "the international undertakings with regard to the Jewish National Home."[4] That was a reference to the Palestine mandate document and to Norway's supposition that the League of Nations had committed the international community to Jewish statehood. There was no push-back to Norway's statement, even though Norway sorely mischaracterized what had been done by the League.

Arab delegates at the United Nations challenged the Palestine mandate as an infringement on Arab self-determination, but they did not explain that Jewish rights never received international endorsement.[5] The Palestine mandate was treated at the United Nations as a document attributing territorial entitlement to the Jewish people.

The Arab delegates did, to be sure, object to relying on what was done in the 1920s as a reason for recommending Jewish statehood. In that vein, they were joined only by India, which at the time was having its own issues with Britain. India objected to the reliance by other member states on the predominant Narrative about the 1920s. "The interpretation of such matters as the Balfour Declaration and the promise of a Jewish National Home," said India's delegate in dismissing the historical argument with a bit of irony, "were of profound interest to the historian and the constitutional lawyer."[6]

When Britain did withdraw from Palestine in 1948 and a Jewish state was declared, Syria asked the Security Council to ask the International Court of Justice for an advisory opinion on the legal status of Palestine. The Security Council declined, though only by the narrowest of margins.[7] Syria then asked the General Assembly to ask for such an opinion and again nearly succeeded. In the General Assembly, the vote on the proposal to ask for an advisory opinion was evenly split, but that meant no majority.[8] No legal opinion was sought that might have found that what was done in the 1920s did not support Jewish entitlement. The legality of Britain's control of Palestine and of the Balfour Declaration was never subjected to a formal legal assessment. The Palestine situation was resolved on the ground by force of arms in 1948, yielding a situation that would fester through periodic wars.

In recent decades, the question has been raised whether Britain should apologize and try to make amends over what it did to Palestine. Other governments have publicly expressed regret over past policies that violated the rights of subordinated populations. The attitude of the British Government towards its role in the 1920s has been a topic of public discussion. A non-governmental group symbolically based in Edinburgh because of A. J. Balfour's Scottish heritage takes as its mission to "acknowledge Britain's historic and continuing responsibilities to uphold equal rights for the Israeli and Palestinian peoples."[9] Far from expressing contrition, the British Government has, as we saw in Chapter 4, doubled down on the correctness of its policy. In 2017, at the centenary of the Balfour Declaration, the Government announced in the House of Lords that it would "mark the centenary of Balfour with pride." The announcement prompted one member to suggest that the centenary would better be marked "with a gracious apology from the British Government and Parliament." "The Balfour Declaration," came the Government reply, "was an historic statement and one for which the United Kingdom has no intention to apologise."[10]

A Government whose actions have resulted in so much harm might be expected to assume a measure of responsibility. Even if the Government deems the promotion of Zionism and the resultant formation of Israel as a positive development, the concomitant deprivation of a people of its country is a consequence that might be expected to give it pause. In the final months of its governance in Palestine, Foreign Secretary Ernest Bevin did try to find a way to remedy the situation Britain had created. By then, however, Britain had allowed the Jewish Agency such a strong factual and diplomatic posture that the Jewish Agency did not need to compromise.

Short of a formal apology or acceptance of an obligation to make amends, there are measures the British Government could take. The Government could acknowledge that its tenure in Palestine lacked a legal foundation. In particular, it could retract the statement it made to the United Nations in 1947 to rationalize its tenure, given the obvious falsehood in that statement. Acceptance of the statehood of Palestine, as flowing directly from the Treaty of Lausanne, would also seem an easy and obvious step for the British Government. That was a treaty that Britain used, albeit wrongly, to base its presence in Palestine. The Government cannot logically accept the Treaty of Lausanne as having given it status in Palestine but then disclaim the Treaty's attribution of statehood to Palestine. Several other states that are parties to the Lausanne treaty presently recognize Palestine as a state.

Another modest step for Britain would be to support prosecution in the International Criminal Court of acts victimizing the Palestinian people. The British Government, however, has objected to the Court assuming jurisdiction for a variety of alleged depredations, on the rationale that Palestine is not a state.[11] The Court itself says that it has such jurisdiction.[12] As a party to the Rome Statute of the International Criminal Court, Britain could ask the Prosecutor to investigate Israeli officials who prevent the repatriation of Arab families forced out of the country in 1948, given that major violations of human rights qualify as crimes against humanity under the Rome Statute.[13] Denying a population access to its own country is such a violation.[14]

An accurate portrayal of the diplomacy of the 1920s has significant ramifications for Israel. Its statehood, to be sure, has been accepted.[15] But Israel has also been at pains to portray that statehood as legitimate. An Israeli law defining Israel's self-conception recites, "The State of Israel is the nation state of the Jewish People, in which it realizes its natural, cultural, religious and historical right to self-determination. The exercise of the right to national self-determination is unique to the Jewish People." That statement posits not only Jewish rights, but the absence of any concomitant rights on the part of the Arabs. An accurate reading of what was done in the 1920s shows that no self-determination right was recognized for the Jewish people and that a self-determination right for the entire population (predominantly Arab) was assumed. Article 22 of the League Covenant, as we saw, regarded Palestine as "provisionally independent."

Jews were, of course, part of the population of Palestine, so they shared the rights to which the population was entitled when Britain took the country. Self-determination applied to the entirety of that population, including any who would later be displaced, in particular the Arabs displaced in 1948. Having found shelter beyond the areas under Israel's control, they and their progeny remain part of the population enjoying a right to self-determination.

The Zionist Organization's assertion of a Jewish territorial entitlement based on Hebrew occupation in ancient times found little resonance on the world stage in the 1920s. Beginning with its draft mandate document of 1919, the Zionist Organization tried to gain the support of governments for the proposition that world Jewry had a legal claim to Palestine based on ancient occupation. The British Government resisted the claim, meeting it halfway in the preamble to the mandate document with the formulation "historical connection" as a basis for "reconstituting their national home," but without wording about a legal claim.

Britain's lack of legitimate legislative authority during its tenure in Palestine undermines reliance by Israel on legislative or regulatory acts adopted by Britain. The Knesset has purported to find in British enactments a legal base for emergency regulations to suppress opposition. Britain had adopted a comprehensive set of emergency laws, promulgated in their last version in 1945.[16] Israel purported to carry them forward.[17] As a matter of Israeli law, they remain in force today. Those enactments were based on legislative authority Britain claimed on the bases we saw in the 1923 Order in Council. A Palestine (Defence) Order in Council of 1937 was the underlying enactment for the 1938 and 1945 emergency regulations. The Order cited the Foreign Jurisdiction Act of 1890 and recited that "by Treaty, grant, usage, sufferance, and other lawful means His Majesty has power and jurisdiction in Palestine."[18] Even by 1937, Britain had none of the potential legal bases listed in the Foreign Jurisdiction Act.

Prior to terminating its mandate in 1948, Britain repealed these emergency regulations, hence for that reason alone they were not open to be applied by Israel.[19] That issue aside, however, Britain had no basis for them, so Israel was attempting to continue in force a set of regulations that were invalidly adopted.

For the United Nations, the lesson from the 1920s is that it has been operating on a false premise since 1947. As much as Britain, it must make amends for misreading what was done in the 1920s, and for accepting the Narrative generated by Britain and the Zionist Organization. For what was done at the United Nations, a particular onus falls on the two major powers of the UN's early period. The Soviet Union had opposed Zionism all through Britain's tenure in Palestine but supported it in 1947 out of considerations of strategic advantage for itself.[20] The United States, which, as we saw, had kept itself apart from the issue of Zionism, decided to support it in 1947 out of considerations of its own domestic politics.[21] Largely as a result of the fact that the two superpowers opposed independence for a single Palestine, the United Nations remained on the sidelines as Zionist militias cleared Palestine of most of its Arab population.[22] The United Nations has the potential of reassuming the central role it played in 1947, now hopefully on the basis of an accurate understanding of the false premises that underlay its earlier approach.

The accepted starting point in diplomatic discussions of recent decades is that each side has territorial rights and that those conflicting rights must be accommodated. The calculus would be quite different if world leaders understood that no concept of a Jewish territorial entitlement was accepted during the mandate era. No particular resolution of the territorial conflict would emerge, but the PLO aspiration for control of only the Gaza Strip and West Bank would be seen as a compromise position that was espoused only after the world community failed to secure self-determination for the entirety of Palestine's population. A repatriation offer to the Arab families forced out of the country in 1948 would be seen as a necessary component in the effectuation of self-determination.

Beginning in 1947, the international community has addressed the conflict over Palestine without comprehending how and why it originated. Jewish territorial entitlement was not accepted during the time of British control. Britain espoused Zionist aspirations in Palestine, seeking advantage for itself from a collaboration that might make Palestine easier to govern. It tried to convince other states to accept the Zionist aspirations. It did not succeed in that project. The other major powers tolerated what Britain was doing, largely because they had their own interests to protect and because they lacked the capacity, once Britain was in control in Palestine, to influence its practices.

Britain has a potential role at present. It is no longer the world power it was in the 1920s, but it occupies a unique position in regard to efforts by the international community to bring an end to the Arab-Israeli conflict. To this day, it allows the Narrative to be accepted by the international community, even though it, better than anyone else, knows it to be false. In the name of achieving peaceful accommodation, Britain should muster the political will to acknowledge that there was no basis for its governance of Palestine. The approach of the international community to the Arab-Israeli conflict would begin from far different premises if world leaders came to understand that Britain ruled Palestine without a legal basis and that the League of Nations never endorsed Jewish territorial rights. Britain's effort to clothe itself in the robes of legality amounted to nothing more than legal chicanery on a world stage.

DOCUMENTS ANNEX

Document 1

League of Nations Covenant, Article 22

To those colonies and territories which as a consequence of the late war have ceased to be under the sovereignty of the States which formerly governed them and which are inhabited by peoples not yet able to stand by themselves under the strenuous conditions of the modern world, there should be applied the principle that the well-being and development of such peoples form a sacred trust of civilisation and that securities for the performance of this trust should be embodied in this Covenant.

The best method of giving practical effect to this principle is that the tutelage of such peoples should be entrusted to advanced nations who by reason of their resources, their experience or their geographical position can best undertake this responsibility, and who are willing to accept it, and that this tutelage should be exercised by them as Mandatories on behalf of the League.

The character of the mandate must differ according to the stage of the development of the people, the geographical situation of the territory, its economic conditions and other similar circumstances.

Certain communities formerly belonging to the Turkish Empire have reached a stage of development where their existence as independent nations can be provisionally recognized subject to the rendering of administrative advice and assistance by a Mandatory until such time as they are able to stand alone. The wishes of these communities must be a principal consideration in the selection of the Mandatory.

Other peoples, especially those of Central Africa, are at such a stage that the Mandatory must be responsible for the administration of the territory under conditions which will guarantee freedom of conscience and religion, subject only to the maintenance of public order and morals, the prohibition of abuses such as the slave trade, the arms traffic and the liquor traffic, and the prevention of the establishment of fortifications or military and naval bases and of military training of the natives for other than police purposes and the defence of territory, and will also secure equal opportunities for the trade and commerce of other Members of the League.

There are territories, such as South-West Africa and certain of the South Pacific Islands, which, owing to the sparseness of their population, or their small size, or their remoteness from the centres of civilisation, or their geographical contiguity to the territory of the Mandatory, and other circumstances, can be best administered under the laws of the Mandatory as integral portions of its territory, subject to the safeguards above mentioned in the interests of the indigenous population.

In every case of mandate, the Mandatory shall render to the Council an annual report in reference to the territory committed to its charge.

The degree of authority, control, or administration to be exercised by the Mandatory shall, if not previously agreed upon by the Members of the League, be explicitly defined in each case by the Council.

A permanent Commission shall be constituted to receive and examine the annual reports of the Mandatories and to advise the Council on all matters relating to the observance of the mandates.

Document 2

Draft Palestine Mandate

supplied to David Hunter Miller by Zionist Organization, Paris, 28 March 1919
as reproduced in
David Hunter Miller, *My Diary at the Conference of Paris with Documents*
(Document 665), vol. 7, at 372 (1924), New York: Appeal Printing Co.
(See Chapter 15 for context)

WHEREAS by a convention between His Majesty the Emperor of the Ottomans on the one hand and ... (hereinafter referred to as the Signatory Powers), on the other hand, signed by their respective plenipotentiaries on ... the territory of Palestine included within the boundaries described in the annexed schedule, (which is hereinafter referred to as Palestine) and all dominions and sovereignty therein possessed, asserted or claimed by the Emperor of the Ottomans was ceded to the Signatory Powers, and

WHEREAS the Signatory Powers have subscribed to the Covenant of the League of Nations, and have agreed that the Government and administration of Palestine, and all rights and powers appropriate to such administration shall be entrusted to a Mandatary selected in accordance with the principles proclaimed in that Covenant, to be exercised by that Mandatary in the manner and subject to the conditions therein described, and

WHEREAS the inhabitants of Palestine are unable at the present time effectively to constitute and to maintain an autonomous commonwealth, and

WHEREAS the League of Nations and the Signatory Powers recognize the historic title of the Jewish People to Palestine and the right of the Jews to reconstitute Palestine as their national Home: and there to establish the foundations of a Jewish Commonwealth; and

WHEREAS it is the wish of the inhabitants of Palestine and of the Jews that governmental and administrative powers to be exercised over the territory and its inhabitants should be confined to Great Britain as the Mandatary of the League of Nations and as trustee of the Signatory Powers.

NOW THEREFORE THE Signatory Powers hereby constitute Great Britain the Mandatary of the League of Nations for the Government and Administration of Palestine, subject to the following limitations and obligations:

I.

All powers hereby conferred shall be exercised subject to the control which now is or hereafter may be vested in the League of Nations.

II.

The establishment of Palestine as the Jewish National Home and its development into an autonomous commonwealth dedicated to the advance of Social Justice shall be the guiding purpose in the execution of the mandate. The Mandatary shall adopt measures appropriate for the creation of such political, administrative and economic conditions as will tend to the realization of these aims, in so far as such measures may be adopted without prejudicing the civil or religious rights and political status enjoyed by the Jews in other countries;

In furtherance of these ends the Mandatary *inter alia:*

(a) shall adopt appropriate measures (not inconsistent with the established rights of existing non-Jewish Communities) to promote the immigration of Jews and their close settlement upon the land;
(b) shall establish the Hebrew tongue as one of the official languages of the land to be employed in all official documents and procedure, and upon the money and coinage of the land; recognize the Jewish Sabbath and holidays as legal holidays for persons of the Jewish faith and permit to them the pursuit of their ordinary vocations on all other days;
(c) shall entrust the organization and administration of a system of education for the Jewish inhabitants to appropriate Jewish agencies;
(d) shall promote the largest measure of local and municipal self-government that conditions may progressively render practicable;
(e) shall make provision for governmental or other public ownership, and development of the natural resources of the Country and for such ownership and operation of the public works and utilities established and to be established therein; and shall adopt effective measures to prevent the exploitation for private profit of any such resources, public works and utilities;
(f) shall adopt effective measures to ensure that all lands shall be owned or controlled for the benefit of the people of Palestine as a whole, and that the rights granted thereinto individuals shall be such only as will stimulate the productive use thereof, and ensure, by proper measures of taxation or otherwise, that every increase in the value of land over that of August 1, 1914, whether now accrued or hereafter accruing, excepting such as is due to improvements made thereon by individuals, shall be appropriated for the benefit of the State and of the People of Palestine as a whole;
(g) shall adopt effective measures to foster the organization of all agricultural, industrial, commercial and financial undertakings upon a cooperative basis;
(h) shall so define the qualifications for citizenship in Palestine as not to exclude any person on the ground of race, religion or sex, nor any person

who shall have been a resident of Palestine within five years prior to the date of this Mandate on any grounds other than those of moral, mental or physical disqualification.

(i) In effectuating these purposes it shall work progressively in cooperation with appropriate Jewish agencies.

III.

No law shall be made respecting the establishment of religion or prohibiting the free exercise thereof, and the free exercise and enjoyment of religious profession and worship without discrimination or preference shall forever be allowed. No political or religious test other than that of Citizenship and an oath of affirmation to support the laws of the land and the Covenants and judgments of the League of Nations shall be required as a qualification to any office or public trust under the Government of Palestine or as a qualification for the exercise of any civil or political rights therein.

IV.

It shall adopt and enforce such measures as shall be adequate to protect both against physical impairment and against profanation the places within the land which are revered as holy by the adherents of the Jewish, Mohammedan and Christian faiths, and to permit access thereto to the adherents of the faith or faiths by which they are held in reverence, and shall from time to time amend such measures to conform to such requirements, not inconsistent with the exercise of the general administrative and governmental functions hereinbefore conferred, as the League of Nations may impose.

V.

All members of the League of Nations and the people thereof shall be assured the same opportunities for trade and commerce therein and with the inhabitants thereof as are assured to the Mandatary and its people.

VI.

Whenever in the opinion of the Mandatary or the League of Nations the inhabitants of Palestine shall be fit to create and maintain an autonomous, representative and responsible government, the Mandatary shall take such steps as will permit them through the exercise of a democratic franchise, without regard to race, sex, or faith, to establish a representative and responsible Government in such form as the people of Palestine may devise.

Document 3

British Mandate for Palestine

(terms as approved provisionally by Council of League of Nations 24 July 1922)
League of Nations, *Official Journal*, vol. 3 (no. 8), at 1007 (1922), Annex 391

The Council of the League of Nations

WHEREAS the Principal Allied Powers have agreed, for the purpose of giving effect to the provisions of Article 22 of the Covenant of the League of Nations, to entrust to a Mandatory selected by the said Powers the administration of the territory of Palestine, which formerly belonged to the Turkish Empire, within such boundaries as may be fixed by them; and

WHEREAS the Principal Allied Powers have also agreed that the Mandatory should be responsible for putting into effect the declaration originally made on November 2nd, 1917, by the Government of His Britannic Majesty, and adopted by the said Powers, in favour of the establishment in Palestine of a national home for the Jewish people, it being clearly understood that nothing should be done which might prejudice the civil and religious rights of existing non-Jewish communities in Palestine, or the rights and political status enjoyed by Jews in any other country; and

WHEREAS recognition has thereby been given to the historical connection of the Jewish people with Palestine and to the grounds for reconstituting their national home in that country; and

WHEREAS the Principal Allied Powers have selected His Britannic Majesty as the Mandatory for Palestine; and

WHEREAS the mandate in respect of Palestine has been formulated in the following terms and submitted to the Council of the League for approval; and

WHEREAS His Britannic Majesty has accepted the mandate in respect of Palestine and undertaken to exercise it on behalf of the League of Nations in conformity with the following provisions; and

WHEREAS by the afore-mentioned Article 22 (paragraph 8), it is provided that the degree of authority, control or administration to be exercised by the Mandatory, not having been previously agreed upon by the Members of the League, shall be explicitly defined by the Council of the League of Nations;

Confirming the said mandate, defines its terms as follows:

Article 1. The Mandatory shall have full powers of legislation and of administration, save as they may be limited by the terms of this mandate.

Article 2. The Mandatory shall be responsible for placing the country under such political, administrative and economic conditions as will secure the establishment of the Jewish national home, as laid down in the preamble, and the development of self-governing institutions, and also for safeguarding the civil and religious rights of all the inhabitants of Palestine, irrespective of race and religion.

Article 3. The Mandatory shall, so far as circumstances permit, encourage local autonomy.

Article 4. An appropriate Jewish agency shall be recognised as a public body for the purpose of advising and co-operating with the Administration of Palestine in such economic, social and other matters as may affect the establishment of the Jewish national home and the interests of the Jewish population in Palestine, and, subject always to the control of the Administration, to assist and take part in the development of the country.

The Zionist organization, so long as its organisation and constitution are in the opinion of the Mandatory appropriate, shall be recognised as such agency. It shall take steps in consultation with His Britannic Majesty's Government to secure the co-operation of all Jews who are willing to assist in the establishment of the Jewish national home.

Article 5. The Mandatory shall be responsible for seeing that no Palestine territory shall be ceded or leased to, or in any way placed under the control of, the Government of any foreign Power.

Article 6. The Administration of Palestine, while ensuring that the rights and position of other sections of the population are not prejudiced, shall facilitate Jewish immigration under suitable conditions and shall encourage, in co-operation with the Jewish agency referred to in Article 4, close settlement by Jews on the land, including State lands and waste lands not required for public purposes.

Article 7. The Administration of Palestine shall be responsible for enacting a nationality law. There shall be included in this law provisions framed so as to facilitate the acquisition of Palestinian citizenship by Jews who take up their permanent residence in Palestine.

Article 8. The privileges and immunities of foreigners, including the benefits of consular jurisdiction and protection as formerly enjoyed by Capitulation or usage in the Ottoman Empire, shall not be applicable in Palestine.

Unless the Powers whose nationals enjoyed the afore-mentioned privileges and immunities on August 1st, 1914, shall have previously renounced the right to their re-establishment, or shall have agreed to their non-application for a specified period, these privileges and immunities shall, at the expiration of the mandate, be immediately re-established in their entirety or with such modifications as may have been agreed upon between the Powers concerned.

Article 9. The Mandatory shall be responsible for seeing that the judicial system established in Palestine shall assure to foreigners, as well as to natives, a complete guarantee of their rights.

Respect for the personal status of the various peoples and communities and for their religious interests shall be fully guaranteed. In particular, the control and administration of Wakfs shall be exercised in accordance with religious law and the dispositions of the founders.

Article 10. Pending the making of special extradition agreements relating to Palestine, the extradition treaties in force between the Mandatory and other foreign Powers shall apply to Palestine.

Article 11. The Administration of Palestine shall take all necessary measures to safeguard the interests of the community in connection with the development of the country, and, subject to any international obligations accepted by the Mandatory, shall have full power to provide for public ownership or control of any of the natural resources of the country or of the public works, services and utilities established or to be established therein. It shall introduce a land system appropriate to the needs of the country, having regard, among other things, to the desirability of promoting the close settlement and intensive cultivation of the land.

The Administration may arrange with the Jewish agency mentioned in Article 4 to construct or operate, upon fair and equitable terms, any public works, services and utilities, and to develop any of the natural resources of the country, in so far as these matters are not directly undertaken by the Administration. Any such arrangements shall provide that no profits distributed by such agency, directly or indirectly, shall exceed a reasonable rate of interest on the capital, and any further profits shall be utilised by it for the benefit of the country in a manner approved by the Administration.

Article 12. The Mandatory shall be entrusted with the control of the foreign relations of Palestine and the right to issue exequaturs to consuls appointed by foreign Powers. He shall also be entitled to afford diplomatic and consular protection to citizens of Palestine when outside its territorial limits.

Article 13. All responsibility in connection with the Holy Places and religious buildings or sites in Palestine, including that of preserving existing rights and of securing free access to the Holy Places, religious buildings and sites and the free exercise of worship, while ensuring the requirements of public order and decorum, is assumed by the Mandatory, who shall be responsible solely to the League of Nations in all matters connected herewith, provided that nothing in this article shall prevent the Mandatory from entering into such arrangements as he may deem reasonable with the Administration for the purpose of carrying the provisions of this article into effect; and provided also that nothing in this mandate shall be construed as conferring upon the Mandatory authority to interfere with the fabric or the management of purely Moslem sacred shrines, the immunities of which are guaranteed.

Article 14. A special Commission shall be appointed by the Mandatory to study, define and determine the rights and claims in connection with the Holy Places and the rights and claims relating to the different religious communities in Palestine. The method of nomination, the composition and the functions of this Commission shall be submitted to the Council of the League for its approval, and the Commission shall not be appointed or enter upon its functions without the approval of the Council.

Article 15. The Mandatory shall see that complete freedom of conscience and the free exercise of all forms of worship, subject only to the maintenance of public order and morals, are ensured to all. No discrimination of any kind shall be made between the inhabitants of Palestine on the ground of race, religion or language. No person shall be excluded from Palestine on the sole ground of his religious belief.

The right of each community to maintain its own schools for the education of its own members in its own language, while conforming to such educational requirements of a general nature as the Administration may impose, shall not be denied or impaired.

Article 16. The Mandatory shall be responsible for exercising such supervision over religious or eleemosynary bodies of all faiths in Palestine as may be required for the maintenance of public order and good government. Subject to such supervision, no measures shall be taken in Palestine to obstruct or interfere with the enterprise of such bodies or to discriminate against any representative or member of them on the ground of his religion or nationality.

Article 17. The Administration of Palestine may organise on a voluntary basis the forces necessary for the preservation of peace and order, and also for the defence of the country, subject, however, to the supervision of the Mandatory, but shall not use them for purposes other than those above specified save with the consent of the Mandatory. Except for such purposes, no military, naval or air forces shall be raised or maintained by the Administration of Palestine.

Nothing in this article shall preclude the Administration of Palestine from contributing to the cost of the maintenance of the forces of the Mandatory in Palestine.

The Mandatory shall be entitled at all times to use the roads, railways and ports of Palestine for the movement of armed forces and the carriage of fuel and supplies.

Article 18. The Mandatory shall see that there is no discrimination in Palestine against the nationals of any State Member of the League of Nations (including companies incorporated under its laws) as compared with those of the Mandatory or of any foreign State in matters concerning taxation, commerce or navigation, the exercise of industries or professions, or in the treatment of merchant vessels or civil aircraft. Similarly, there shall be no discrimination in Palestine against goods originating in or destined for any of the said States, and there shall be freedom of transit under equitable conditions across the mandated area.

Subject as aforesaid and to the other provisions of this mandate, the Administration of Palestine may, on the advice of the Mandatory, impose such taxes and customs duties as it may consider necessary, and take such steps as it may think best to promote the development of the natural resources of the country and to safeguard the interests of the population. It may also, on the advice of the Mandatory, conclude a special customs agreement with any State the territory of which in 1914 was wholly included in Asiatic Turkey or Arabia.

Article 19. The Mandatory shall adhere on behalf of the Administration of Palestine to any general international conventions already existing, or which may be concluded hereafter with the approval of the League of Nations, respecting the slave traffic, the traffic in arms and ammunition, or the traffic in drugs, or relating to commercial equality, freedom of transit and navigation, aerial navigation and postal, telegraphic and wireless communication or literary, artistic or industrial property.

Article 20. The Mandatory shall co-operate on behalf of the Administration of Palestine, so far as religious, social and other conditions may permit, in the execution of any common policy adopted by the League of Nations for preventing and combating disease, including diseases of plants and animals.

Article 21. The Mandatory shall secure the enactment within twelve months from this date, and shall ensure the execution of a Law of Antiquities based on the following rules. This law shall ensure equality of treatment in the matter of excavations and archaeological research to the nationals of all States Members of the League of Nations.

1. "Antiquity" means any construction or any product of human activity earlier than the year 1700 A. D.
2. The law for the protection of antiquities shall proceed by encouragement rather than by threat.

   Any person who, having discovered an antiquity without being furnished with the authorization referred to in paragraph 5, reports the same to an official of the competent Department, shall be rewarded according to the value of the discovery.
3. No antiquity may be disposed of except to the competent Department, unless this Department renounces the acquisition of any such antiquity.

   No antiquity may leave the country without an export licence from the said Department.
4. Any person who maliciously or negligently destroys or damages an antiquity shall be liable to a penalty to be fixed.
5. No clearing of ground or digging with the object of finding antiquities shall be permitted, under penalty of fine, except to persons authorised by the competent Department.
6. Equitable terms shall be fixed for expropriation, temporary or permanent, of lands which might be of historical or archaeological interest.
7. Authorisation to excavate shall only be granted to persons who show sufficient guarantees of archaeological experience. The Administration of Palestine shall not, in granting these authorisations, act in such a way as to exclude scholars of any nation without good grounds.
8. The proceeds of excavations may be divided between the excavator and the competent Department in a proportion fixed by that Department. If division seems impossible for scientific reasons, the excavator shall receive a fair indemnity in lieu of a part of the find.

Article 22. English, Arabic and Hebrew shall be the official languages of Palestine. Any statement or inscription in Arabic on stamps or money in Palestine shall be repeated in Hebrew and any statement or inscription in Hebrew shall be repeated in Arabic.

Article 23. The Administration of Palestine shall recognise the holy days of the respective communities in Palestine as legal days of rest for the members of such communities.

Article 24. The Mandatory shall make to the Council of the League of Nations an annual report to the satisfaction of the Council as to the measures taken during the year to carry out the provisions of the mandate. Copies of all laws and regulations promulgated or issued during the year shall be communicated with the report.

Article 25. In the territories lying between the Jordan and the eastern boundary of Palestine as ultimately determined, the Mandatory shall be entitled, with the consent of the Council of the League of Nations, to postpone or withhold application of such provisions of this mandate as he may consider inapplicable to the existing local conditions, and to make such provision for the administration of the territories as he may consider suitable to those conditions, provided that no action shall be taken which is inconsistent with the provisions of Articles 15, 16 and 18.

Article 26. The Mandatory agrees that, if any dispute whatever should arise between the Mandatory and another member of the League of Nations relating to the interpretation or the application of the provisions of the mandate, such dispute, if it cannot be settled by negotiation, shall be submitted to the Permanent Court of International Justice provided for by Article 14 of the Covenant of the League of Nations.

Article 27. The consent of the Council of the League of Nations is required for any modification of the terms of this mandate.

Article 28. In the event of the termination of the mandate hereby conferred upon the Mandatory, the Council of the League of Nations shall make such arrangements as may be deemed necessary for safeguarding in perpetuity, under guarantee of the League, the rights secured by Articles 13 and 14, and shall use its influence for securing, under the guarantee of the League, that the Government of Palestine will fully honour the financial obligations legitimately incurred by the Administration of Palestine during the period of the mandate, including the rights of public servants to pensions or gratuities.

The present instrument shall be deposited in original in the archives of the League of Nations and certified copies shall be forwarded by the Secretary-General of the League of Nations to all members of the League.

Done at London the twenty-fourth day of July, one thousand nine hundred and twenty-two.

NOTES

Setting the Stage: Was Britain's Rule in Palestine Legal?

1 Jonathan Schneer, *The Balfour Declaration: The Origins of the Arab-Israeli Conflict* (London: Bloomsbury, 2010), at 48.
2 *Sir Edward Grey to M. Cambon*, 16 May 1916 (Correspondence embodying the Sykes-Picot Agreement), *Documents on British Foreign Policy 1919–1939*, 1st series, vol. 4, at 245.
3 Schneer, *The Balfour Declaration*, at 54.
4 Palestine for the Jews: Official sympathy, *The Times*, 9 November 1917, at 7.
5 *President Wilson's State Papers and Addresses* (New York: Review of Reviews Co., 1918), at 468–70.
6 Surrender of Turkey: The terms of armistice, *The Times*, 1 November 1918, at 6. Terms to Turkey: Text of armistice, *The Times*, 2 November 1918, at 7.
7 Covenant of the League of Nations, art. 22, Part I of Treaty of Peace between the Allied and Associated Powers and Germany, Versailles, 28 June 1919, League of Nations, *Official Journal*, vol. 1 (no. 1), at 3 (1920).
8 Paul Pic, *Syrie et Palestine: mandats français et anglais dans le Proche-Orient* (Paris: Librairie ancienne Édouard Champion, 1924), at 4–5.
9 Paul Pic, Le régime du mandat d'après le traité de Versailles; son application dans le Proche Orient; mandats français en Syrie, Anglais en Palestine et Mésopotamie, *Revue de droit international public*, vol. 30 (2nd series, vol. 5), 321, at 324 (1923).
10 Henri Rolin (1874–1946), Le système des mandats coloniaux, *Revue de droit international et de législation comparée*, 3rd series, vol. 1, at 329 (1920) (translation from French by author).
11 Gregory S. Mahler, *The Arab-Israeli Conflict: An Introduction and Documentary Reader* (New York: Routledge, 2019), at 70.
12 Theodor Herzl, *Der Judenstaat: Versuch einer modernen Lösung der Judenfrage* (Leipzig: M. Breitenstein's Verlags-Buchhandlung, 1896).
13 Raphael Patai (ed.), *The Complete Diaries of Theodor Herzl* (New York: Herzl Press, 1960), vol. 2, at 720.
14 Ibid., vol. 3, at 1114.
15 D. Edward Knox, *The Making of a New Eastern Question: British Palestine Policy and the Origins of Israel, 1917–1925* (Washington, DC: Catholic University of America Press, 1981), at 18.
16 Bernard Wasserstein, *The British in Palestine: The Mandatory Government and the Arab-Jewish Conflict 1917–1929* (London: Royal Historical Society, 1978), at 15.

1 The Balfour Declaration Is the Focal Point for the Legal Situation of Palestine

1 Declaration of the Establishment of the State of Israel, *Laws of the State of Israel*, vol. 1, at 3 (from *Official Gazette*, no. 1, 14 May 1948).
2 Yoram Dinstein, The International Legal Dimensions of the Arab-Israeli Conflict, in Alfred Kellerman, Kurt Siehr, and Talia Einhorn (eds.), *Israel among the Nations: International and Comparative Law Perspectives on Israel's 50th Anniversary* (The Hague: Kluwer, 1998), 137, at 138.
3 Palestine for the Jews: Official sympathy, *The Times*, 9 November 1917, at 7.
4 League of Nations, *Official Journal*, vol. 1 (Special Supplement No. 3), 3, at 6 (October 1920), Report of the Committee of Jurists Entrusted by the Council of the League of Nations with the Task of Giving an Advisory Opinion upon the Legal Aspects of the Aaland Islands Question.

2 The Balfour Declaration Was a Binding Commitment to the Jewish People

1 Yoram Dinstein, The International Legal Dimensions of the Arab-Israeli Conflict, in Alfred Kellerman, Kurt Siehr, and Talia Einhorn (eds.), *Israel among the Nations: International and Comparative Law Perspectives on Israel's 50th Anniversary* (The Hague: Kluwer, 1998), 137, at 139.
2 Permanent Court of International Justice, *Legal Status of Eastern Greenland*, Judgment of April 5th, 1933, series A/B, no. 53.
3 *Legal Status of Eastern Greenland*, Judgment, at 71.
4 Report on Middle East Conference Held in Cairo and Jerusalem, 12 to 30 March 1921, Appendix 23: Deputation of Executive Committee of the Haifa Congress received by the Secretary of State for the Colonies at Government House, Monday, 28 March 1921, 142, at 144, United Kingdom, National Archives No. CAB 24/126, at 189.
5 Ibid., at 145.
6 Jean Allain, *International Law in the Middle East: Closer to Power than Justice* (Aldershot: Ashgate, 2004), at 79.
7 Boris Johnson, *The Churchill Factor: How One Man Made History* (New York: Riverhead Books, 2014), at 304–05.
8 War Cabinet 298, Minutes of a Meeting of the War Cabinet held at 10, Downing Street, S.W., on Friday, 14 December 1917, at 11 a.m., at 2, Secret, United Kingdom, National Archives No. CAB 23/4.
9 Palestine for the Jews: Official sympathy, *The Times*, 9 November 1917, at 7.
10 J. M. N. Jeffries, *The Palestine Deception: 'Daily Mail' Inquiry on the Spot* (London: Daily Mail, 1923), at 26.
11 International Law Commission, Guiding Principles applicable to unilateral declarations of States capable of creating legal obligations, with commentaries thereto 2006, para. 1, *Yearbook of the International Law Commission*, 2006, vol. II, Part Two, at 161.
12 International Court of Justice, *Nuclear Tests* (Australia v. France), Reports (1974), 253, at 268–69.

3 The Jewish National Home Meant a Jewish State

1 War Cabinet 261, Minutes of a Meeting of the War Cabinet held at 10, Downing Street, S.W., on Wednesday, 31 October 1917, at noon, at 6, Secret, United Kingdom, National Archives No. CAB 23/4.

2 J. M. N. Jeffries, *Palestine: The Reality: The Inside Story of the Balfour Declaration 1917–1938* (Northampton, MA: Olive Branch Press, 2017) (originally London: Longmans, Green & Co., 1939), at 170–71. Jonathan Schneer, *The Balfour Declaration: The Origins of the Arab-Israeli Conflict* (London: Bloomsbury, 2010), at 335.

3 Jay Pilzer, *The League of Nations and the Jewish Question*, Thesis (Ph.D.), Duke University, Microfiche. Ann Arbor, MI, University Microfilms (1976), at 90.

4 Minorities Treaty between the Principal Allied and Associated Powers (The British Empire, France, Italy, Japan and the United States) and Poland, Versailles, 28 June 1919, art. 9. *British and Foreign State Papers 1919*, vol. 112, at 232.

5 Report of a Committee set up to consider certain correspondence between Sir Henry McMahon [His Majesty's High Commissioner in Egypt] and the Sharif of Mecca in 1915 and 1916, 16 March 1939, presented by the Secretary of State for the Colonies to Parliament by Command of His Majesty March 1939, London, Annex F: The Hogarth Message of January, 1918, United Kingdom, Command Paper 5974.

6 D. Edward Knox, *The Making of a New Eastern Question: British Palestine Policy and the Origins of Israel, 1917–1925* (Washington, DC: Catholic University of America Press, 1981), at 41.

7 Report of a Committee set up to consider certain correspondence between Sir Henry McMahon [His Majesty's High Commissioner in Egypt] and the Sharif of Mecca in 1915 and 1916, 16 March 1939, presented by the Secretary of State for the Colonies to Parliament by Command of His Majesty March 1939, London, Annex B: The McMahon-Husain Correspondence. Victor Kattan, *From Coexistence to Conquest: International Law and the Origins of the Arab-Israeli Conflict, 1891–1949* (New York: Pluto Press, 2009), at 98–116.

8 British Empire Report No. 4, at 3, 12 November 1919, Secret, United Kingdom, National Archives No. CAB 24/156.

9 No. 5: The Colonial Office to the Zionist Organisation, 3 June 1922, Correspondence with the Palestine Arab Delegation and the Zionist Organisation, Enclosure in No. 5: British Policy in Palestine, United Kingdom, Command Paper 1700 [italics in original].

10 Palestine: Statement of Policy Presented by the Secretary of State for the Colonies to Parliament by Command of His Majesty, May 1939, ¶4, United Kingdom, Command Paper 6019.

11 Constitution of the Permanent Mandates Commission, 29 November 1920, League of Nations, *Official Journal*, vol. 1 (no. 8), at 87 (1920).

12 League of Nations, Permanent Mandates Commission, Minutes of the Thirty-Sixth Session Held at Geneva from 8 to 29 June 1939 (12th meeting, 15 June 1939), at 98, League of Nations Doc. C.170.M.100.1939.VI.

13 United Nations, General Assembly, Res. 106 (S-1), 15 May 1947.

14 United Nations, General Assembly, 2nd session, Special Committee on Palestine, Report to the General Assembly, 3 September 1947, vol. 1, at 20–21, United Nations Doc. A/364. quoting Palestine Royal Commission, Report, July 1937, United Kingdom, Command Paper 5479 (London: His Majesty's Stationery Office, 1937), at 33.

15 United Nations, General Assembly, 2nd session, Special Committee on Palestine, Report to the General Assembly, 3 September 1947, vol. 1, at 47, United Nations Doc. A/364.
16 United Nations, General Assembly, Future Government of Palestine, Res. 181, 29 November 1947.
17 United Nations, General Assembly, 2nd session, Special Committee on Palestine, Report to the General Assembly, 3 September 1947, vol. 1, at 20–21, United Nations Doc. A/364.
18 Ibid., at 24.
19 Abba Eban, *Abba Eban: An Autobiography* (New York: Random House, 1977), at 78.
20 Robert St. John, *Eban* (Garden City, NY: Doubleday, 1972), at 167.
21 Brian Urquhart, *Ralph Bunche: An American Life* (New York: W.W. Norton, 1993), at 144–45.
22 Yoram Dinstein, The International Legal Dimensions of the Arab-Israeli Conflict, in Alfred Kellerman, Kurt Siehr, and Talia Einhorn (eds.), *Israel among the Nations: International and Comparative Law Perspectives on Israel's 50th Anniversary* (The Hague: Kluwer, 1998), 137, at 138–39.

4 The Balfour Declaration Was Issued to Affirm Jewish Rights in Palestine

1 Full text of May's speech at Balfour Declaration centenary dinner, *Times of Israel*, 3 November 2017.
2 Declaration of the Establishment of the State of Israel, *Laws of the State of Israel*, vol. 1, at 3 (from *Official Gazette*, no. 1, 14 May 1948).
3 J. M. N. Jeffries, *Palestine: The Reality: The Inside Story of the Balfour Declaration 1917–1938* (Northampton, MA: Olive Branch Press, 2017) (originally London: Longmans, Green & Co., 1939), at 171.
4 Leonard Stein, *The Balfour Declaration* (New York: Simon & Schuster, 1961), at 428.
5 Palestine and the Balfour Declaration: History of the Negotiations leading up to the Balfour Declaration of 2 November 1917, at 2, Cabinet Paper 60 (23), 23 January 1923, Secret, United Kingdom, National Archives No. CAB 24/158, at 465.
6 War Cabinet 227, Minutes of a Meeting of the War Cabinet held at 10, Downing Street, S.W., on Monday, 3 September 1917, at 11:30 a.m., at 2–3, Secret, United Kingdom, National Archives No. CAB 23/4.
7 Ibid., at 3.
8 Stein, *The Balfour Declaration*, at 516–17, 533–34.
9 Richard Ned Lebow, Woodrow Wilson and the Balfour Declaration, *Journal of Modern History*, vol. 40, 501, at 511–12 (1968).
10 Palestine and the Balfour Declaration: History of the Negotiations leading up to the Balfour Declaration of 2 November 1917, at 2, Cabinet Paper 60 (23), 23 January 1923, Secret, United Kingdom, National Archives No. CAB 24/158, at 465.
11 Ibid., at 2.
12 James Renton, *The Zionist Masquerade: The Birth of the Anglo-Zionist Alliance 1914–1918* (New York: Palgrave Macmillan, 2007), at 65.
13 Palestine and the Balfour Declaration: History of the Negotiations leading up to the Balfour Declaration of 2 November 1917, at 3, Cabinet Paper 60 (23), 23 January 1923, Secret, United Kingdom, National Archives No. CAB 24/158, at 465.

14 Jonathan Schneer, *The Balfour Declaration: The Origins of the Arab-Israeli Conflict* (London: Bloomsbury, 2010), at 339.
15 War Cabinet 245, Minutes of a Meeting of the War Cabinet held at 10, Downing Street, S.W. on Thursday, 4 October 1917, at 5, Secret, United Kingdom, National Archives No. CAB 23/4.
16 Palestine and the Balfour Declaration: History of the Negotiations leading up to the Balfour Declaration of 2 November 1917, at 2, Cabinet Paper 60 (23), 23 January 1923, Secret, United Kingdom, National Archives No. CAB 24/158, at 465. Esco Foundation for Palestine, *Palestine: A Study of Jewish, Arab, and British Policies* (New Haven: Yale University Press, 1947), vol. 1, at 83–84. Doreen Ingrams, *Palestine Papers 1917–1922: Seeds of Conflict* (London: John Murray, 1970), at 7.
17 War Cabinet 245, Minutes of a Meeting of the War Cabinet held at 10, Downing Street, S.W. on Thursday, 4 October 1917, at 5, Secret, United Kingdom, National Archives No. CAB 23/4.
18 Ibid., at 3.
19 Ibid., at 6.
20 Curzon, The Future of Palestine, at 1, GT 2406, 26 October 1917, Secret, United Kingdom, National Archives No. CAB 24/30.
21 Ibid., at 1–3.
22 Ibid., at 2–3.
23 David Gilmour, The Unregarded Prophet: Lord Curzon and the Palestine Question, *Journal of Palestine Studies*, vol. 25 (no. 3), at 60 (1996).
24 Stein, *The Balfour Declaration*, at 546.
25 Ibid., at 546.
26 War Cabinet 261, Minutes of a Meeting of the War Cabinet held at 10, Downing Street, S.W., on Wednesday, 31 October 1917, at noon, at 5, Secret, United Kingdom, National Archives No. CAB 23/4.
27 Ibid., at 6.
28 Ibid.
29 Ibid.
30 Palestine: Memorandum by the Secretary of State for the Colonies (Devonshire), at 3, Cabinet Paper 106 (23), 17 February 1923, Secret, United Kingdom, National Archives No. CAB 24/159.
31 Ibid., at 3.
32 Palestine: Memorandum by Middle East Department, Colonial Office, ¶3, Cabinet Paper 21 (24), 12 February 1924, Secret, United Kingdom, National Archives No. CAB 24/165.
33 Stein, *The Balfour Declaration*, at 568.
34 Ibid., at 579–80.
35 Ibid., at 568.
36 Aharon Cohen, *Israel and the Arab World* (New York: Funk and Wagnalls, 1970), at 124.
37 Stein, *The Balfour Declaration*, at 587–601. Palestine, Cabinet Paper 149 (23), 13 March 1923, Secret, United Kingdom, National Archives No. CAB 24/159.
38 David Rechter, *The Jews of Vienna and the First World War* (Oxford: Littman Library of Jewish Civilization, 2008), at 55.

5 The Paris Peace Conference Raised Jewish Statehood to the International Level

1 Tom Segev, *One Palestine Complete: Jews and Arabs Under the British Mandate* (New York: Henry Holt, 1999), at 116.
2 Chaim Weizmann, *Trial and Error: The Autobiography of Chaim Weizmann* (New York: Harper & Brothers, 1949), at 245.
3 Statement of the Zionist Organization regarding Palestine, 3 February 1919, Paris Peace Conf. Doc. 180.03101/48, in Secretary's Notes of a Conversation Held in M. Pichon's Room at the Quai d'Orsay, Paris, on Thursday, 27 February 1919, at 3 p.m., *Foreign Relations of the United States: Paris Peace Conference 1919*, vol. 4, 159, at 161–62.
4 Ibid., at 161–62.
5 Secretary's Notes of a Conversation Held in M. Pichon's Room at the Quai d'Orsay, Paris, on Thursday, 27 February 1919, at 3 p.m., *Foreign Relations of the United States: Paris Peace Conference 1919*, vol. 4, 159, at 161–62.
6 Herbert Adams Gibbons, Zionism and the World Peace, *The Century*, vol. 97, 368, at 374 (January 1919).
7 Segev, *One Palestine, Complete*, at 16.
8 Ibid., at 69.
9 Chaim Weizmann, *Trial and Error: The Autobiography of Chaim Weizmann* (New York: Harper & Brothers, 1949), at 125.
10 Secretary's Notes of a Conversation Held in M. Pichon's Room at the Quai d'Orsay, Paris, on Thursday, 27 February 1919, at 3 p.m., *Foreign Relations of the United States: Paris Peace Conference 1919*, vol. 4, 159, at 162.
11 Ibid., at 163.
12 Ibid.
13 Ibid.
14 Simcha Kling, *The Mighty Warrior: The Life Story of Menahem Ussishkin* (New York: Jonathan David, 1965), at 1–3.
15 Secretary's Notes of a Conversation Held in M. Pichon's Room at the Quai d'Orsay, Paris, on Thursday, 27 February 1919, at 3 p.m., *Foreign Relations of the United States: Paris Peace Conference 1919*, vol. 4, at 165.
16 Joseph Klausner, *Menahem Ussishkin: His Life and Work* (New York: Scopus, 1942), at 108.
17 Nahum Sokolow, *History of Zionism 1600–1918* (New York: Ktav Publishing House, 1969), vol. 2, at 38–39.
18 Leon Shapiro, Outline of the History of Russian and Soviet Jewry 1912–1974, in Simon M. Dubnow, *History of the Jews in Russia and Poland from the Earliest Times until the Present Day* (New York: Ktav Publishing House, 1975), vol. 3, 413, at 419.
19 Salo Baron, *The Russian Jew under Tsars and Soviets* (New York: Macmillan, 1976), at 182.
20 Joseph Schechtman, *Zionism and Zionists in Soviet Russia: Greatness and Drama* (New York: Zionist Organization of America, 1966), at 18.
21 Secretary's Notes of a Conversation Held in M. Pichon's Room at the Quai d'Orsay, Paris, on Thursday, 27 February 1919, at 3 p.m., *Foreign Relations of the United States: Paris Peace Conference 1919*, vol. 4, 159, at 170.
22 Shlomo Sand, *The Invention of the Jewish People* (London: Verso, 2009), at 251–52.
23 Secretary's Notes of a Conversation Held in M. Pichon's Room at the Quai d'Orsay, Paris, on Thursday, 27 February 1919, at 3 p.m., *Foreign Relations of the United States: Paris Peace Conference 1919*, vol. 4, 159, at 164.

24 Ibid., at 165.
25 Ibid.
26 Ibid., at 169.
27 J. M. N. Jeffries, *Palestine: The Reality: The Inside Story of the Balfour Declaration 1917–1938* (Northampton, MA: Olive Branch Press, 2017) (originally London: Longmans, Green & Co., 1939), at 279.
28 D. Edward Knox, *The Making of a New Eastern Question: British Palestine Policy and the Origins of Israel, 1917–1925* (Washington, DC: Catholic University of America Press, 1981), at 111–12.
29 Yehoshua Porath, *The Emergence of the Palestinian-Arab National Movement 1918–1929* (London: Frank Cass, 1974), at 82.
30 Ibid., at 85.
31 Secretary's Notes of a Conversation Held at Mr. Pichon's Room at the Quai d'Orsay, Paris, on Thursday, 30 January 1919, at 11 a.m., *Foreign Relations of the United States: Paris Peace Conference 1919*, vol. 3, 785, at 795.
32 Ibid., at 785.
33 Secretary''s Notes of a Meeting of the Supreme Council of the Allied and Associated Powers Held in the Salle de l'Horloge, Quai d'Orsay, on Tuesday, 17 June 1919, at 11 a.m., *Foreign Relations of the United States: Paris Peace Conference 1919*, vol. 4, 508, at 511.
34 Memorandum Submitted to the Council by Mr. Lloyd George, Scheme for settlement in the Turkish Empire, 21 May 1919, *Foreign Relations of the United States: Paris Peace Conference 1919*, vol. 5, at 770.
35 Notes of a Meeting Held in President Wilson's House, Place des Etats-Unis, Paris, on Wednesday, 21 May 1919, at 11 a.m., *Foreign Relations of the United States: Paris Peace Conference 1919*, vol. 5, 754, at 762.
36 Bernard Wasserstein, *The British in Palestine: The Mandatory Government and the Arab-Jewish Conflict 1917–1929* (London: Royal Historical Society, 1978), at 36.
37 For full text of Article 22, see Documents Annex.

6 Britain's Allies Made the Balfour Declaration an International Commitment

1 Jerusalem Center for Public Affairs, 100 years since the San Remo conference (video), 6 May 2020.
2 Dore Gold, 100 years since the San Remo conference which shaped Middle East, *Jerusalem Post*, 26 April 2020.
3 French Note and Memoranda by the British Peace Delegation regarding Turkish Settlement. December 1919. Note communicated by M. Berthelot to Lord Curzon of Kedleston. London, 12 December 1919, at 13, Cabinet Paper 391, United Kingdom, National Archives No. CAB 24/95/94.
4 Will invite America on Turkish question: Allies meet in London soon to settle Turks' fate, *Boston Daily Globe*, 22 January 1920, at 6.
5 Peace discussions shift across Channel to London, *Washington Post*, 13 February 1920, at 6. British Secretary's Notes of an Allied Conference, held at 10, Downing Street, London, S.W. 1, on Tuesday, 17 February 1920, at 3.30 p.m., Great Britain, Foreign Office, *Documents on British Foreign Policy 1919–1939*, 1st series, vol. 7, at 99.

6 Jackson Fleming, Why the Allies do not want us in the Near East: One observer who is convinced that France and England had just as soon play poker for the pieces of the Ottoman Empire without our sitting in the game, *The New York Times*, 25 January 1920, at 43.
7 British Secretary's Notes of an Allied Conference, held at 10, Downing Street, London, S.W. 1, on Tuesday, 17 February 1920, at 3.30 p.m., Great Britain, Foreign Office, *Documents on British Foreign Policy 1919–1939*, 1st series, vol. 7, 99, at 102.
8 Ibid., at 103.
9 Ibid.
10 Ibid., at 104.
11 Ibid.
12 Ibid., at 108.
13 Ibid., at 111.
14 Ibid., at 103.
15 Peace with Turkey: Points of Settlement: Future of Palestine: A Jewish National Home?, *Times of India*, 17 February 1920, at 9.
16 Treaty of Peace between the Allied and Associated Powers and Germany, Versailles, 28 June 1919, preamble, *Foreign Relations of the United States: Paris Peace Conference 1919*, vol. 13, at 57.
17 British Secretary's Notes of a Meeting of the Supreme Council, held at the Villa Devachan, San Remo, on Saturday, 24 April 1920, at 4 p.m., Great Britain, Foreign Office, *Documents on British Foreign Policy 1919–1939*, 1st series, vol. 8, 156, at 165.
18 Thomas W. Burkman, *Japan and the League of Nations: Empire and World Order, 1914–1938* (Honolulu: University of Hawaii Press, 2008), at 62.
19 Notes of a Meeting of the Heads of the British, French and Italian Delegations, held at the Villa Devachan, San Remo, on Sunday, 18 April 1920, at 11 a.m., *Documents on British Foreign Policy 1919–1939*, 1st series, vol. 8, at 1.
20 Jun Morikawa, *Japan and Africa: Big Business and Diplomacy* (Trenton, NJ: Africa World Press, 1997), at 47.
21 *Report on the Work of the Department of Propaganda in Enemy Countries* (private and confidential) (London: His Majesty's Stationery Office, no date: 1919?), at 22.
22 Minutes of a meeting held at 23 Rue Nitot at 3 p.m. on Monday 19 May 1919, at 4, Secret, United Kingdom, National Archives No. CAB 23/44B/9.
23 Philip Marshall Brown, The Mandate over Armenia, *American Journal of International Law*, vol. 14, 396, at 398 (1920).
24 Allies offer the core: They do not want Armenia because it is an unprofitable morsel, *San Francisco Chronicle*, 27 April 1920, at 24.
25 Mandate over Armenia (message from President), *Congressional Record*, vol. 59, Part 7, at 7533, 24 May 1920.
26 Senate rejects mandate, 52 to 23, *The New York Times*, 2 June 1920.
27 British Secretary's Notes of a Meeting of the Supreme Council, held at the Villa Devachan, San Remo, on Sunday, 25 April 1920, at 11 a.m., *Documents on British Foreign Policy 1919–1939*, 1st series, vol. 8, 172, at 177.
28 Id. at 177. Notes du secrétaire prises au cours de la reunion tenue le 25 avril à 11 heures à la Villa Devachan, Doc. 19, Ministère des Affaires Étrangères, *Documents diplomatiques français 1921* (annexes 10 janvier 1920–31 décembre 1921), at 176.
29 British Secretary's Notes of a Meeting of the Supreme Council, held at the Villa Devachan, San Remo, on Sunday, 25 April 1920, at 11 a.m., Great Britain, Foreign Office, *Documents on British Foreign Policy 1919–1939*, 1st series, vol. 8, 172 at 177.

30 Covenant of the League of Nations, art. 18, Part I of Treaty of Peace between the Allied and Associated Powers and Germany, Versailles, 28 June 1919, League of Nations, *Official Journal*, vol. 1 (no. 1), at 3 (1920).
31 Memorandum of agreement between M. Philippe Berthelot, Directeur des affaires politiques et commerciales au Ministère des Affaires Étrangères, and Professor Sir John Cadman, K.C.M.G., Director in Charge of His Majesty's Petroleum Department, San Remo, 24 April 1920, *League of Nations Treaty Series*, vol. 1, at 282.
32 Eugene Kontorovich, San Remo's Promise Fulfilled, 25 April 2020, www.youtube.com.
33 M. Millerand, Ministre des Affaires étrangères, à M. Paléologue, Secrétaire general du Ministère des Affaires étrangères, San Remo, 27 April 1920, Doc. 404, Ministère des Affaires Étrangères, *Documents diplomatiques français 1920*, vol. 1 (10 janvier–18 mai), at 564 (translation from French by author).
34 Hersch Lauterpacht (ed.), *Lassa Oppenheim, International Law: A Treatise* (London: Longmans, Green & Co., 1948), vol. 1, at 197.
35 United Nations, General Assembly, 2nd session, Special Committee on Palestine, Report to the General Assembly, 3 September 1947, vol. 1, at 18, United Nations Doc. A/364.
36 British Secretary's Notes of a Meeting of the Supreme Council, held at the Villa Devachan, San Remo, on Sunday, 25 April 1920, at 11 a.m., Great Britain, Foreign Office, *Documents on British Foreign Policy 1919–1939*, 1st series, vol. 8, 172 at 177 (as recorded in French by the British Secretary; translation from French by author).
37 Earl Curzon to Mr. Vansittart (Paris), 30 September 1920, No. 157 [E 11698/4164/44], Great Britain, Foreign Office, *Documents on British Foreign Policy 1919–1939*, 1st series, vol. 13, at 349.
38 L. Oppenheim, *International Law: A Treatise* (London: Longmans, Green & Co., 1920), vol. 1, at 363. Charles Rousseau, Les frontières de la France, *Revue générale de droit international public*, vol. 58 (1954), at 23–52 and 345–74.
39 Convention on Certain Points connected with the mandates for Syria and the Lebanon, Palestine and Mesopotamia (France-United Kingdom), Paris, 23 December 1920, art. 1, *League of Nations Treaty Series*, vol. 22, at 355.

7 Britain's Allies Endorsed Jewish Rights

1 Dore Gold, 100 years since the San Remo conference which shaped Middle East, *Jerusalem Post*, 26 April 2020.
2 British Secretary's Notes of a Meeting of the Supreme Council, held at the Villa Devachan, San Remo, on Saturday, 24 April 1920, at 4 p.m., Great Britain, Foreign Office, *Documents on British Foreign Policy 1919–1939*, 1st series, vol. 8, 156, at 159.
3 Ibid., at 159.
4 Nahum Sokolow, *History of Zionism 1600–1918* (New York: Ktav Publishing House, 1969), vol. 2, at 127.
5 Ibid., at 129. See also Leonard Stein, *The Balfour Declaration* (New York: Simon & Schuster, 1961), at 592–93.
6 Sokolow, *History of Zionism 1600–1918*, vol. 2, at 128 (translation from French by author). See also Edy Kaufman, The French Pro-Zionist Declarations of 1917–1918, *Middle Eastern Studies*, vol. 15 (no. 3), 374, at 391 (1979).
7 Sokolow, *History of Zionism 1600–1918*, vol. 2, at 127.
8 Stein, *The Balfour Declaration*, at 660–61.

9 British Secretary's Notes of a Meeting of the Supreme Council, held at the Villa Devachan, San Remo, on Saturday, 24 April 1920, at 4 p.m., Great Britain, Foreign Office, *Documents on British Foreign Policy 1919–1939*, 1st series, vol. 8, 156, at 160.

10 Ibid., at 163.

11 Ibid., at 167. Jehuda Reinharz, The Balfour Declaration and Its Maker: A reassessment, *Journal of Modern History*, vol. 64, 455, at 498 (1992) (citing a note solicited by Weizmann: Chinda to Weizmann, 6 January 1919, CZA ZR/2039).

12 As explained in a notation in *Documents diplomatiques français* titled Procès-verbaux de la Conférence de San Remo, 18–26 avril 1920, *Documents diplomatiques français 1921* (annexes 10 janvier 1920–31 décembre 1921), at 58.

13 British Secretary's Notes of a Meeting of the Supreme Council, held at the Villa Devachan, San Remo, on Saturday, 24 April 1920, at 4 p.m., Great Britain, Foreign Office, *Documents on British Foreign Policy 1919–1939*, 1st series, vol. 8, 156, at 163.

14 Notes du secrétaire prises au cours de la réunion tenue le 24 avril à 16 heures à la Villa Devachan, Doc. 18, Ministère des Affaires Étrangères, *Documents diplomatiques français 1921* (annexes 10 janvier 1920–31 décembre 1921), 24 April 1920, at 167–68.

15 Notes du secrétaire prises au cours de la réunion tenue le 24 avril à 16 heures à la Villa Devachan, Doc. 18, Ministère des Affaires Étrangères, *Documents diplomatiques français 1921* (annexes 10 janvier 1920–31 décembre 1921), 24 April 1920, at 164. And Berthelot to the same effect in British Secretary's Notes of a Meeting of the Supreme Council, held at the Villa Devachan, San Remo, on Saturday, 24 April 1920, at 4 p.m., Great Britain, Foreign Office, *Documents on British Foreign Policy 1919–1939*, 1st series, vol. 8, 156, at 168.

16 Notes du secrétaire prises au cours de la réunion tenue le 24 avril à 16 heures à la Villa Devachan, Doc. 18, Ministère des Affaires Étrangères, *Documents diplomatiques français 1921* (annexes 10 janvier 1920–31 décembre 1921), 24 April 1920, at 166.

17 Ibid., at 173 (translation from French by author).

18 British Secretary's Notes of a Meeting of the Supreme Council, held at the Villa Devachan, San Remo, on Saturday, 24 April 1920, at 4 p.m., Great Britain, Foreign Office, *Documents on British Foreign Policy 1919–1939*, 1st series, vol. 8, 156, at 169.

19 Notes du secrétaire prises au cours de la réunion tenue le 24 avril à 16 heures à la Villa Devachan, Ministère des Affaires Étrangères, *Documents diplomatiques français 1921* (annexes 10 janvier 1920–31 décembre 1921), 24 April 1920, Doc. 18, at 174 (translation from French by author).

20 British Secretary's Notes of a Meeting of the Supreme Council, held at the Villa Devachan, San Remo, on Saturday, 24 April 1920, at 4 p.m., Great Britain, Foreign Office, *Documents on British Foreign Policy 1919–1939*, 1st series, vol. 8, 156, at 169.

21 Notes du secrétaire prises au cours de la réunion tenue le 24 avril à 16 heures à la Villa Devachan, Ministère des Affaires Étrangères, *Documents diplomatiques français 1921* (annexes 10 janvier 1920–31 décembre 1921), 24 April 1920, Doc. 18, at 174 (translation from French by author).

22 Agreement between France, Russia, Great Britain and Italy, London, 26 April 1915, art. 9, United Kingdom, Command Paper 671.

23 Accord sur les pétroles signé par MM. Millerand et Lloyd George, 18 April 1920, Doc. 400, Ministère des Affaires Étrangères, *Documents diplomatiques français 1920*, vol. 1 (10 janvier – 18 mai), at 557.

24 Note from the Italian Ambassador to Earl Curzon, 23 October 1920, No. 2202 [E 13385/20/44], Great Britain, Foreign Office, Great Britain, Foreign Office, *Documents on British Foreign Policy 1919–1939*, 1st series, vol. 13, 363, at 364.

25 British Secretary's Notes of a Meeting of the Supreme Council, held at the Villa Devachan, San Remo, on Friday, 23 April 1920, at 4 p.m., Great Britain, Foreign Office, *Documents on British Foreign Policy 1919–1939*, 1st series, vol. 8, at 141.
26 British Secretary's Notes of a Meeting of the Supreme Council, held at the Villa Devachan, San Remo, on Saturday, 24 April 1920, at 4 p.m., Great Britain, Foreign Office, *Documents on British Foreign Policy 1919–1939*, 1st series, vol. 8, 156, at 162.
27 David Lloyd George, *The Truth About the Peace Treaties* (London: V. Gollancz, 1938), vol. 2, at 1173–74.
28 Treaty of Peace between the Allied and Associated Powers and Germany, Versailles, 28 June 1919, art. 119, *Foreign Relations of the United States: Paris Peace Conference 1919*, vol. 13, at 57.
29 Sumitra Rattan, The Yap Controversy and Its Significance, *Journal of Pacific History*, vol. 7, at 124 (1972). Thomas W. Burkman, *Japan and the League of Nations: Empire and World Order, 1914–1938* (Honolulu: University of Hawaii Press, 2008), at 69–70.
30 Timothy P. Maga, Prelude to War? The United States, Japan, and the Yap Crisis, 1918–1922, *Diplomatic History*, vol. 9 (no. 3), 215, at 223 (1985).
31 Treaty between the United States of America and Japan concerning the Yap Island and the other islands under mandate situated in the Pacific north of the Equator, Washington, 11 February 1922, art. 4, *League of Nations Treaty Series*, vol. 12, at 212.
32 Preliminary Peace Conference, Protocol No. 5, 28 April 1919, Plenary Session of 28 April 1919, *Foreign Relations of the United States: Paris Peace Conference 1919*, vol. 3, 285, at 291.
33 Conferences of Ministers on Miscellaneous Matters, S.Series, vol. 2, Subject Index, secret (Japanese note dated 2 August 1920), United Kingdom, National Archives No. CAB 23/36, at 299–300.
34 Paul Pic, *Syrie et Palestine: mandats français et anglais dans le Proche-Orient* (Paris: Librairie ancienne Édouard Champion, 1924), at 88–92.
35 British Secretary's Notes of a Meeting of the Supreme Council, held at the Villa Devachan, San Remo, on Saturday, 24 April 1920, at 4 p.m., Great Britain, Foreign Office, *Documents on British Foreign Policy 1919–1939*, 1st series, vol. 8, 156, at 163.
36 Ibid., at 159.
37 Ibid., at 167.
38 British Secretary's Notes of a Meeting of the Supreme Council, held at the Villa Devachan, San Remo, on Sunday, 25 April 1920, at 11 a.m., *Documents on British Foreign Policy 1919–1939*, 1st series, vol. 8, 172, at 176.
39 Lloyd George, *The Truth About the Peace Treaties*, vol. 2, at 1175.
40 Edwin L. James, Palestine under Britain, *The New York Times*, 26 April 1920, at 1.
41 Denies San Remo rumors: Curzon protests against press reports of serious disagreements, *The New York Times*, 27 April 1920, at 1.
42 M. Millerand, Ministre des Affaires étrangères, au Général Gouraud, Haut-commissaire français à Beyrouth. T. n. 445–46, Paris, 7 May 1920, Doc. 450, Ministère des Affaires Étrangères, *Documents diplomatiques français 1920*, vol. 1 (10 janvier – 18 mai), at 617 (translation from French by author).
43 Ibid., at 617.

8 Britain Took on Palestine Because of the League's Mandate System

1 Yoram Dinstein, The International Legal Dimensions of the Arab-Israeli Conflict, in Alfred Kellerman, Kurt Siehr, and Talia Einhorn (eds.), *Israel among the Nations: International and Comparative Law Perspectives on Israel's 50th Anniversary* (The Hague: Kluwer, 1998), 137, at 139.

2 The Earl of Derby (Paris) to Earl Curzon (Received May 12, 10.20 a.m.), No. 568 Telegraphic [E 4614/56/44], 11 May 1920, Great Britain, Foreign Office, *Documents on British Foreign Policy 1919–1939*, 1st series, vol. 13, at 70.

3 Bernard Wasserstein, *The British in Palestine: The Mandatory Government and the Arab-Jewish Conflict 1917–1929* (London: Royal Historical Society, 1978), at 24. Tom Segev, *One Palestine Complete: Jews and Arabs under the British Mandate* (New York: Henry Holt, 1999), at 64.

4 Wasserstein, *The British in Palestine*, at 24–25 (quoting Foreign Office to Sir Reginald Wingate, 13 February 1918, United Kingdom Foreign Office 371/3392/419).

5 Henry Cattan, *The Question of Jerusalem* (London: Third World Centre for Research and Publishing, 1980), at 26.

6 Great Britain, Foreign Office. Administration of occupied enemy territory in Palestine (O.E.T.A. South): report by Col. C.N. French, August 1919, No. T 1/12367/35457. John J. McTague, The British Military Administration in Palestine 1917–1920, *Journal of Palestine Studies*, vol. 7 (no. 3), 55, at 57 (1978).

7 Convention (IV) respecting the Laws and Customs of War on Land: Annex: Regulations concerning the Laws and Customs of War on Land, The Hague, 18 October 1907, art. 43, US Congress, Statutes at Large, vol. 36, at 2277.

8 United Kingdom, *Manual of Military Law* (1914), Chapter XIV, art. 354.

9 Norman Bentwich, The Legal Administration of Palestine under the British Military Occupation, *British Year Book of International Law*, vol. 1, at 139 (1920–1921).

10 D. Edward Knox, *The Making of a New Eastern Question: British Palestine Policy and the Origins of Israel, 1917–1925* (Washington, DC: Catholic University of America Press, 1981), at 75.

11 Note by Dr. Weizmann, dated 6 September 1919, Martin Bunton (ed.), *Land Legislation in Mandate Palestine* (Cambridge: Cambridge University Press, 2009), vol. 5, at 17.

12 An ordinance to provide for the licensing of veterinary surgeons, 2 March 1919, *Legislation of Palestine 1918–1925: Including the Orders-in-Council, Ordinances, Public Notices, Proclamations, Regulations, etc.* (Alexandria: Printed for the Government of Palestine by Whitehead Morris, 1926), vol. 1, at 52.

13 An ordinance to provide for the registration of partnerships, 29 May 1919, *Legislation of Palestine 1918–1925: Including the Orders-in-Council, Ordinances, Public Notices, Proclamations, Regulations, etc.* (Alexandria: Printed for the Government of Palestine by Whitehead Morris, 1926), vol. 1, at 53.

14 An ordinance to provide for the registration of marriage and divorce, 23 September 1919, *Legislation of Palestine 1918–1925: Including the Orders-in-Council, Ordinances, Public Notices, Proclamations, Regulations, etc.* (Alexandria: Printed for the Government of Palestine by Whitehead Morris, 1926), vol. 1, at 57.

15 Bentwich, The Legal Administration of Palestine under the British Military Occupation, at 139.

16 Ibid., at 145.

17 Ibid., at 146.
18 Ibid., at 148.
19 Norman and Helen Bentwich, *Mandate Memories 1918–1948* (London: Hogarth Press, 1965), at 46.
20 Occupied Enemy Territory Administration (South), Report of the Court of Enquiry convened by order of H.E. the High Commissioner and Commander-in-Chief, dated the 12th day of April, 1920 (secret) (Palin Report), at 29, 1 July 1920, United Kingdom Foreign Office 371/5121.
21 Norman and Helen Bentwich, *Mandate Memories 1918–1948* (London: Hogarth Press, 1965), at 36, 52.
22 Telegram to Lord Allenby Cairo, 29 April 1920, United Kingdom, National Archives No. CAB 800/156/49 (CAB 800/156, at 149).
23 Ibid., at 149. Copy of a letter from Mr. Herbert Samuel, 31, Porchester Terrace, Hyde Park, W.2, to Lord Curzon, 14 May 1920, United Kingdom, National Archives No. CAB 800/156/49 (CAB 800/156, at 151). Howard M. Sachar, *The Emergence of the Middle East: 1914–1924* (New York: Alfred A. Knopf, 1969), at 394.
24 United Kingdom, Parliamentary Debates, House of Lords, 29 June 1920, 5th series, vol. 40, column 1015.
25 The new era in Palestine: King's message, *The Times*, 12 July 1920, at 13.
26 Ibid.
27 Zionists' celebration, *The Times*, 7 July 1920, at 11.
28 *The Political History of Palestine under British Administration: Memorandum by His Britannic Majesty's Government Presented in 1947 to the United Nations Special Committee on Palestine Published at Jerusalem, 1947* (reprinted New York: British Information Services, 1947), at 1.
29 United Kingdom, Parliamentary Debates, House of Lords, 23 December 1920, 5th series, vol. 39, column 950.
30 Speech of the King on the closing of the British Parliament, 28 December 1920, *British and Foreign State Papers 1920*, vol. 113, at 251.
31 A Survey of Palestine Prepared in December 1945 and January 1946 for the information of the Anglo-American Committee of Inquiry (Washington, DC: Institute for Palestine Studies, 1991) [reprinted from London: Her Majesty's Stationery Office], vol. 1, at 3.
32 Palestine Muslims and Sir H. Samuel, *The Times*, 7 July 1920, at 13.
33 An ordinance to regulate the transfer of land, September 1920, *Legislation of Palestine 1918–1925: Including the Orders-in-Council, Ordinances, Public Notices, Proclamations, Regulations, etc.* (Alexandria: Printed for the Government of Palestine by Whitehead Morris, 1926), vol. 1, at 62. Bernard Wasserstein, *The British in Palestine: The Mandatory Government and the Arab-Jewish Conflict 1917–1929* (London: Royal Historical Society, 1978), at 91. Bernard Regan, *The Balfour Declaration: Empire, the Mandate and Resistance in Palestine* (London: Verso, 2017), at 87.
34 Immigration Ordinance, 26 August 1920, *Legislation of Palestine 1918–1925: Including the Orders-in-Council, Ordinances, Public Notices, Proclamations, Regulations, etc.* (Alexandria: Printed for the Government of Palestine by Whitehead Morris, 1926), vol. 1, at 637. Bernard Wasserstein, *The British in Palestine: The Mandatory Government and the Arab-Jewish Conflict 1917–1929* (London: Royal Historical Society, 1978), at 91.
35 John J. McTague, Zionist-British Negotiations over the Draft Mandate for Palestine, 1920, *Jewish Social Studies*, vol. 42 (no. 3/4), 281, at 290 (Summer-Autumn 1980).

36 Alfred Hyamson, *Palestine under the Mandate 1920–1948*, (London: Methuen & Co., 1950), at 33.
37 Ibid., at 35.
38 United Kingdom, *Manual of Military Law* (1914), Chapter XIV, art. 361.
39 John J. McTague, *British Policy in Palestine, 1917–1922* (Lanham, MD: University Press of America, 1983), at 137–38.
40 Palestine Arab Congress, Haifa. Kazem al-Husseini, President, to Mandates Section, Secretariat, League of Nations, 12 February 1921, League of Nations Doc. 11228.
41 Ibid.
42 League of Nations, Draft Mandate for Palestine, Letters dated 2 and 10 September 1921 from the Palestine Arab Delegation, 27 September 1921, League of Nations Doc. C-372-M.-260.1921.VI.
43 Report on Middle East Conference Held in Cairo and Jerusalem, 12 to 30 March 1921, Appendix 23: Deputation of Executive Committee of the Haifa Congress received by the Secretary of State for the Colonies at Government House, Monday, 28 March 1921, 142, at 150, United Kingdom, National Archives No. CAB 24/126, at 192.
44 Howard M. Sachar, *The Emergence of the Middle East: 1914–1924* (New York: Alfred A. Knopf, 1969), at 392.
45 Occupied Enemy Territory Administration (South), Report of the Court of Enquiry convened by order of H.E. the High Commissioner and Commander-in-Chief, dated the 12th day of April, 1920 (secret) (Palin Report), at 38, 1 July 1920, United Kingdom Foreign Office 371/5121.
46 Ibid., at 4–5.
47 Ibid., at 12.
48 Ibid., at 79.

9 The League of Nations Protected Palestine's Arab Population

1 The new era in Palestine: King's message, *The Times*, 12 July 1920, at 13.
2 United Kingdom, Parliamentary Debates, House of Commons, 24 November 1920, 5th series, vol. 135, column 432.
3 Norman Bentwich, Mandated Territories: Palestine and Mesopotamia (Iraq), *British Year Book of International Law*, vol. 2, at 48 (1921–1922).
4 Margaret E. Burton, *The Assembly of the League of Nations* (Chicago: University of Chicago Press, 1941), at 79–81.
5 Susan Pedersen, *The Guardians: The League of Nations and the Crisis of Empire* (Oxford: Oxford University Press, 2015), at 51.
6 Constitution of the Permanent Mandates Commission, approved by the Council on 29 November 1920, League of Nations, *Official Journal*, vol. 1 (no. 8), at 87 (1920).
7 Obligations falling upon the League of Nations under the terms of Article 22 of the Covenant (mandates): Report presented by the Belgian Representative, M. Hymans, and adopted by the Council of the League of Nations, League of Nations, *Official Journal*, vol. 1 (no. 6), 334, at 339–40 (1920), Council, 8th session, 5 August 1920.
8 Permanent Court of International Justice, Statute, art. 65.

9 United Kingdom, Parliamentary Debates, House of Lords, 21 June 1922, 5th series, vol. 50, column 1011.
10 Pedersen, *The Guardians*, at 102.
11 Observations by the Permanent Mandates Commission on the Petition Discussed at Its Fifth Session, Annex 711, League of Nations, *Official Journal*, vol. 6 (no. 2), at 219 (1925).
12 League of Nations, *Official Journal*, vol. 6 (no. 2), at 133 (1925), Council, 32nd session, 6th meeting, 10 December 1924.
13 League of Nations, *Official Journal*, vol. 5 (no. 2), at 335 (1924), Council, 27th session, 4th meeting, 12 December 1923.
14 Giulio Diena, Les mandats internationaux, Hague Academy of International Law, *Recueil des cours*, vol. 5 (1924-IV), 211, at 235.
15 Covenant of the League of Nations, art. 5, Part I of Treaty of Peace between the Allied and Associated Powers and Germany, Versailles, 28 June 1919, League of Nations, *Official Journal*, vol. 1 (no. 1), at 3 (1920).
16 Barriedale Keith, Mandates, *Journal of Comparative Legislation and International Law*, 3rd series, vol. 4, part I, 71, at 80 (1922).
17 International Court of Justice, *South West Africa Cases* (Liberia v. South Africa, Ethiopia v. South Africa), Second Phase, Reports (1966), 6, at 46.
18 Bentwich, Mandated Territories, at 56.
19 Keith, Mandates, at 81. Permanent Court of International Justice, *Mavrommatis Palestine Concessions*, Judgment of 30 August 1924, series A, no. 2, at 11–12.
20 Alberto Vallani, *I mandati internazionali della Società delle nazioni* (Milano: Editore - Libraio della Real casa, 1923), at 23.
21 Henri Rolin (1874–1946), Le système des mandats coloniaux, *Revue de droit international et de législation comparée*, 3rd series, vol. 1, 329, at 333 (1920) (translation from French by author).
22 Quincy Wright, *Mandates under the League of Nations* (Chicago: University of Chicago Press, 1930), at 3.
23 Procès-verbal d'une conversation entre M. Millerand et M. Lloyd George, San Remo, 18 April 1920, Doc. 382, Ministère des Affaires Étrangères, *Documents diplomatiques français 1920*, vol. 1 (10 janvier–18 mai), 534, at 539 (translation from French by author).
24 Giulio Diena, Les mandats internationaux, Hague Academy of International Law, *Recueil des cours*, vol. 5 (1924-IV), 211, at 236.
25 France, Code civil (1804), §1984: "*un acte par lequel une personne donne à une autre le pouvoir de faire quelque chose pour le mandant et en son nom. Le contrat ne se forme que par l'acceptation du mandataire.*"
26 Henri Rolin (1874–1946), Le système des mandats coloniaux, *Revue de droit international et de législation comparée*, 3rd series, vol. 1, 329, at 334 (1920).
27 Henri A. Rolin (1891–1973), La pratique des mandats internationaux, Hague Academy of International Law, *Recueil des cours*, vol. 19 (1927-IV), 497, at 506 (translation from French by author).
28 Ibid., at 507.
29 Mr. Vansittart (Paris) to Earl Curzon (Received August 5), No. 71 A [E 9427/4164/44], Great Britain, Foreign Office, *Documents on British Foreign Policy 1919–1939*, 1st series, vol. 13, 326, at 327–28.

30 Draft Mandates for Mesopotamia and Palestine as Submitted for the approval of the League of Nations (London: His Majesty's Stationery Office, 1921), Foreign Office Misc. no. 3, United Kingdom, Command Paper 1176.

31 M. Cambon, Ambassadeur de France à Londres, à M. Millerand, Ministre des Affaires étrangères, London, 11 May 1920, Doc. 463, Ministère des Affaires Étrangères, *Documents diplomatiques français 1920*, vol. 1 (10 janvier–18 mai), at 630.

32 Treaty of Peace between the Allied and Associated Powers and Turkey, Sèvres, 10 August 1920, arts. 94, 95, 96, 132, Treaty Series (United Kingdom), no. 11 (1920), United Kingdom, Command Paper 964.

33 Ibid., art. 433.

34 Jacob Stoyanovsky, *The Mandate for Palestine* (London: Longmans, 1928), at 19.

35 Draft Mandates for Mesopotamia and Palestine as Submitted for the approval of the League of Nations (London: His Majesty's Stationery Office, 1921), Foreign Office Misc. no. 3, United Kingdom, Command Paper 1176. For full text of the Zionist Organization draft, see Documents Annex.

36 Norman Bentwich, Mandated Territories: Palestine and Mesopotamia (Iraq), *British Year Book of International Law*, vol. 2, 48, at 50 (1921–1922).

37 United Kingdom, Parliamentary Debates, House of Commons, 8 November 1920, 5th series, vol. 134, column 826.

38 Ibid., column 826.

10 Britain Was Given Palestine by the League of Nations

1 League of Nations, *Official Journal*, vol. 3 (no. 8), at 825 (1922), Council, 19th session, 13th meeting, 24 July 1922.

2 Abraham Bell and Eugene Kontorovich, Palestine, *Uti Possidetis Juris*, and the Borders of Israel, *Arizona Law Review*, vol. 58, 633, at 667–668 (2016). Compare W. F. Boustany, *The Palestine Mandate: Invalid and Impracticable* (Beirut: American Press, 1936), at 114, noting "that it was the Mandatory himself who sought such obligations to be imposed upon him."

3 Elihu Lauterpacht, *Jerusalem and the Holy Places* (London: Anglo-Israel Association, 1968), at 13.

4 Rashid Khalidi, The Iron Cage: *The Story of the Palestinian Struggle for Statehood* (Boston: Beacon Press, 2006), at 31.

5 Giulio Diena, Les mandats internationaux, Hague Academy of International Law, *Recueil des cours*, vol. 5 (1924-IV), 211, at 233.

6 Henri Rolin (1874–1946), Le système des mandats coloniaux, *Revue de droit international et de législation comparée*, 3rd series, vol. 1, 329, at 335 (1920).

7 League of Nations, *Official Journal*, vol. 3 (no. 8), at 825 (1922), Council, 19th session, 13th meeting, 24 July 1922.

8 Ibid., at 825.

9 United Kingdom, Parliamentary Debates, House of Lords, 25 June 1920, 5th series, vol. 40, column 877.

10 A Survey of Palestine Prepared in December 1945 and January 1946 for the information of the Anglo-American Committee of Inquiry (Washington, DC: Institute for Palestine Studies, 1991) [reprinted from London: Her Majesty's Stationery Office], vol. 1, at 4.

11 For full text of the Palestine mandate document, see Documents Annex.

12 Treaty of Peace between the Allied and Associated Powers and Germany, Versailles, 28 June 1919, art. 119, *Foreign Relations of the United States: Paris Peace Conference 1919*, vol. 13, at 57.
13 Treaty of Peace between the Allied and Associated Powers and Turkey, Sèvres, 10 August 1920, Treaty Series (United Kingdom), no. 11 (1920), United Kingdom, Command Paper 964.
14 To Robert G. Vansittart, London, 1 March 1920, in Jehuda Reinharz (ed.), *The Letters and Papers of Chaim Weizmann*, vol. 9, Series A (October 1918–July 1920), at 320.
15 Ibid., at 321.
16 Ibid., at 321. Weizmann's reference to the Peace Conference reflected the fact that the discussions of early 1920 among the Principal Allied Powers were regarded as a continuation from Paris.
17 Ibid., at 321.
18 Obligations falling upon the League of Nations under the terms of Article 22 of the Covenant (mandates): Report presented by the Belgian Representative, M. Hymans, and adopted by the Council of the League of Nations, League of Nations, *Official Journal*, vol. 1 (no. 6), 334, at 336 (1920), Council, 8th session, 5 August 1920.
19 United Kingdom, Parliamentary Debates, House of Lords, 21 June 1922, 5th series, vol. 50, column 1011.
20 Note from Earl Curzon to the Italian Ambassador, No. E 15728/4164/44, 28 December 1920, Great Britain, Foreign Office, *Documents on British Foreign Policy 1919–1939*, 1st series, vol. 13, 426, at 427.
21 League of Nations, *Records of the Second Assembly*: Plenary Meetings (Meetings held from the 5th of September to the 5th of October 1921), at 343.
22 Ibid., at 357.
23 The British Foreign Office (Crowe) to the American Ambassador (Harvey), No. E 14259/37/88, 29 December 1921, reprinted in U.S. Department of State, *The Palestine Mandate* (Salisbury, NC: Documentary Publications, 1977) (originally published as *Mandate for Palestine* (Washington, DC: United States Government Printing Office, 1927), at 54–55.
24 Lancelot Oliphant (in the absence of the Secretary of State), The British Secretary of State for Foreign Affairs to the American Ambassador (Harvey), 29 April 1922, ibid. at 65–66.
25 Ibid., at 66.
26 Status of Palestine: Mandate and treaty, *The Times*, 12 May 1922, at 9.
27 League of Nations, *Official Journal*, vol. 3 (no. 6, Part II), at 518 (1922), Council, 18th session, 1st meeting, 11 May 1922.
28 Ibid., at 518.
29 Ibid.
30 League of Nations, *Official Journal*, vol. 3 (no. 6, Part II), at 546 (1922), Council, 18th session, 11th meeting, 17 May 1922.
31 Ibid., at 547.
32 Ibid.
33 Obligations falling upon the League of Nations under the terms of Article 22 of the Covenant (mandates): Report presented by the Belgian Representative, M. Hymans, and adopted by the Council of the League of Nations, League of Nations, *Official Journal*, vol. 1 (no. 6), 334, at 338 (1920), Council, 8th session, 5 August 1920.

34 Treaty of Alliance (Britain-Iraq), Baghdad, 10 October 1922, art. 1, with Protocol, signed respectively, at Baghdad, 10 October 1922, and 30 April 1923, *League of Nations Treaty Series*, vol. 35, at 14.
35 British Mandate for Iraq. Consideration of the draft. Instrument submitted by the British Government, League of Nations, *Official Journal*, vol. 5 (no. 10), at 1314 (1924), Council, 13th session, 7th meeting, 19 September 1924.
36 British Mandate for Iraq. Adoption of the Draft Instrument submitted by the British Government, League of Nations, *Official Journal*, vol. 5 (no. 10), at 1346–1347 (1924), Council, 13th session, 14th meeting, 27 September 1924. Quincy Wright, *Mandates under the League of Nations* (Chicago: University of Chicago Press, 1930), at 60.
37 Henri Rolin (1874–1946), Le système des mandats coloniaux, *Revue de droit international et de législation comparée*, 3rd series, vol. 1, 329, at 338 (1920) (translation from French by author).
38 Henri A. Rolin (1891–1973), La pratique des mandats internationaux, Hague Academy of International Law, *Recueil des cours*, vol. 19 (1927-IV), 497, at 508.
39 Obligations falling upon the League of Nations under the terms of Article 22 of the Covenant (mandates): Report presented by the Belgian Representative, M. Hymans, and adopted by the Council of the League of Nations, League of Nations, *Official Journal*, vol. 1 (no. 6), 334, at 337 (1920), Council, 8th session, 5 August 1920.
40 Ibid., at 335.
41 Ibid., at 340–41.
42 Le Règlement de la paix, *Le Temps*, 16 December 1920, at 1.
43 Wm. Rogers Louis, The United Kingdom and the Beginning of the Mandates System, 1919–1922, *International Organization*, vol. 23 (no. 1), 73, at 76 (1969).
44 League of Nations, *Official Journal*, vol. 3 (no. 8), at 1007 (1922), Annex 391: British Mandate for Palestine, art. 1.
45 Earl Curzon to Lord Hardinge (Paris), No. 1319 Telegraphic [E 16035/4164/44], 26 December 1920, Great Britain, Foreign Office, *Documents on British Foreign Policy 1919–1939*, 1st series, vol. 13, at 425.
46 Note of a conversation held at 10, Downing Street, London, S.W. 1, on Monday, 3 July 1922, at 12 Noon, Secret S.49, Appendix: Memorandum by Signor Schanzer, Annex No. 1, United Kingdom, National Archives No. CAB 23/36/10, at 102–03.
47 Ibid., at 104, 106–07.
48 The British Foreign Office (Oliphant) to Mr. LeClercq, No. E 7948/78/65, Confidential, 11 August 1922, reprinted in U.S. Department of State, *The Palestine Mandate* (Salisbury, NC: Documentary Publications, 1977) (originally published as *Mandate for Palestine* (Washington, DC: United States Government Printing Office, 1927), at 79. (F. D. K. LeClercq was at the US Department of State.)
49 Note of a conversation held at 10, Downing Street, London, S.W. 1, on Monday, 3 July 1922, at 12 Noon, Secret S.49, United Kingdom, National Archives No. CAB 23/36/10, at 95.
50 Colonial Office, 18 July 1922, United Kingdom, National Archives No. CAB 800/156/49 (CAB 800/156, at 176).
51 League of Nations, *Official Journal*, vol. 3 (no. 8), 798, at 799 (1922), Council, 19th session, 5th meeting (private), 19 July 1922.
52 Ibid., at 798.
53 Ibid., at 799.
54 League of Nations, *Official Journal*, vol. 3 (no. 8), at 818 (1922), Council, 19th session, 11th meeting, 22 July 1922. Wright, *Mandates under the League of Nations*, at 59.

55 M. Poincaré, Ministre des Affaires étrangères à M. de Saint-Aulaire, Ambassadeur de France à Londres, 19 July 1922 Doc. 45, *Documents diplomatiques français 1922*, vol. 2 (1 juillet–31 décembre), at 63.
56 League of Nations, *Official Journal*, vol. 3 (no. 8), at 824 (1922), Council, 19th session, 13th meeting, 24 July 1922. Wm. Roger Louis, The United Kingdom and the Beginning of the Mandates System, 1919–1922, *International Organization*, vol. 23 (no. 1), 73, at 90 (1969).
57 M. Poincaré, Ministre des Affaires étrangères à M. de Saint-Aulaire, Ambassadeur de France à Londres, 20 July 1922 Doc. 49, *Documents diplomatiques français 1922*, vol. 2 (1 juillet–31 décembre), at 68.
58 League of Nations, *Official Journal*, vol. 3 (no. 8), at 825 (1922), Council, 19th session, 13th meeting, 24 July 1922.
59 The British Secretary of State for Foreign Affairs (Curzon) to the American Ambassador (Harvey), 2 October 1922, reprinted in U.S. Department of State, *The Palestine Mandate* (Salisbury, NC: Documentary Publications, 1977) (originally published as *Mandate for Palestine* (Washington, DC: United States Government Printing Office, 1927), at 80 (¶10).

11 The League of Nations Put the Palestine Mandate into Legal Force

1 *The Political History of Palestine under British Administration Memorandum by His Britannic Majesty''s Government presented in 1947 to the United Nations Special Committee on Palestine Published at Jerusalem, 1947* (reprinted New York: British Information Services, 1947), at 1.
2 Shabtai Rosenne, Revisiting Some Legal Aspects of the Transition from Mandate to Independence: December 1947–15 May 1948, in Alfred Kellerman, Kurt Siehr, and Talia Einhorn (eds.), *Israel among the Nations: International and Comparative Law Perspectives on Israel's 50th Anniversary* (The Hague: Kluwer, 1998), 311, at 313.
3 A Survey of Palestine Prepared in December 1945 and January 1946 for the information of the Anglo-American Committee of Inquiry (Washington, DC: Institute for Palestine Studies, 1991) [reprinted from London: Her Majesty's Stationery Office], vol. 1, at 4.
4 The Secretary of State to the Ambassador in France (Herrick), 30 October 1922, *Foreign Relations of the United States 1923*, vol. 2, at 884.
5 U.S. refuses to join Lausanne peace parley, *Atlanta Constitution*, 29 October 1922, at A1.
6 Turkish National Pact, 28 January 1920, in Arnold J. Toynbee (ed.), *The Western Question in Greece and Turkey: A Study in the Contact of Civilisations* (London: Constable & Co., 1923), at 209.
7 Ernest Hemingway, They All Made Peace – What Is Peace?, *Little Review: Quarterly Journal of Art and Letters*, vol. 9 (no. 3), at 20 (1923).
8 William L. Cleveland, *A History of the Modern Middle East* (Boulder: Westview, 2004), at 178.
9 No. 37. The Marquess Curzon of Kedleston to Sir Eyre Crowe, Lausanne, 5 January 1923, Further Correspondence respecting Turkey, Part III, January to March 1923, Foreign Office 424/256, at 84.

10 Paul Pic, *Syrie et Palestine: mandats français et anglais dans le Proche-Orient* (Paris: Librairie ancienne Édouard Champion, 1924), at 30.
11 Draft Treaty of Peace, art. 16, Further Correspondence respecting Turkey, Part III, January to March 1923, Foreign Office 424/256, at 282.
12 Treaty of Peace, Lausanne, 24 July 1923, art. 16, *League of Nations Treaty Series*, vol. 28, at 12.
13 Ibid., art. 143.
14 Under Secretary of State for Foreign Affairs to Secretary-General, 16 August 1923, League of Nations Doc. C.536.1923.VI.
15 Ibid.
16 Ibid.
17 Note pour le représentant de la France à la 26e session du Conseil de la SDN, 29 August 1923, Doc. 19, Ministère des Affaires Étrangères, *Documents diplomatiques français 1923*, vol. 2 (annexes 1 janvier –31 décembre), at 198.
18 League of Nations, *Official Journal*, vol. 4 (no. 11), at 1355 (1923), Council, 26th session, 23rd meeting, 29 September 1923, Agenda Item 1092: British Mandate for Palestine.
19 Obligations falling upon the League of Nations under the terms of Article 22 of the Covenant (mandates): Report presented by the Belgian Representative, M. Hymans, and adopted by the Council of the League of Nations, League of Nations, *Official Journal*, vol. 1 (no. 6), 334, at 336 (1920), Council, 8th session, 5 August 1920.
20 Société des nations, *Journal officiel*, vol. 4 (no. 11), at 1355 (1923), Council, 26th session, 23rd meeting, 29 September 1923, Agenda Item 1092: Mandat britannique pour la Palestine.
21 Treaty of Peace, Lausanne, 24 July 1923, *League of Nations Treaty Series*, vol. 28, at 13, note 1 (showing ratification by Turkey, 31 March 1924, and by Britain, Japan, and Italy 6 August 1924; see art. 143 for stipulation on date of entry into force).
22 Permanent Court of International Justice, *Mavrommatis Palestine Concessions*, series C, Annex 3: Speech by Sir Cecil Hurst (Great Britain) at the public sitting on 15 July 1924, 20, at 22.
23 *The Political History of Palestine under British Administration Memorandum by His Britannic Majesty's Government presented in 1947 to the United Nations Special Committee on Palestine Published at Jerusalem, 1947* (reprinted New York: British Information Services, 1947), at 1.
24 The Imperial Conference. Colonial Policy. Duke of Devonshire's Speech, *The Times*, 4 October 1923, at 7.
25 Imperial and Foreign News Items, *The Times*, 10 October 1923, at 9.
26 Palestine: Report on Palestine Administration, 1923 (London: His Majesty's Stationery Office, 1924), at 3, reprinted in *Palestine and Transjordan Administration Reports 1918–1948* (London: Archive Editions, 1995), vol. 1 (1918–1924), at 393.
27 Palestine Arabs: Government offer rejected, *The Times*, 13 October 1923, at 12. Amin Said, *The Great Arab Revolt: A Detailed and Comprehensive History of the Arab Cause in a Quarter Century* (Cairo: Madbouly Bookshop, 1934), vol. 3, at 86 (in Arabic).
28 League of Nations, Permanent Mandates Commission, Minutes of the Fifth Session (Extraordinary) held at Geneva from 23 October to 6 November 1924, League of Nations Document C.617.M.216 (1924) VI, 20 November 1924, at 54: Examination of the Annual Report of the British Government for 1923 on the Administration of the Mandated Territory of Palestine, 28 October 1924.
29 Henry Cattan, *Palestine and International Law: The Legal Aspects of the Arab-Israeli Conflict* (London: Longman, 1976), at 65–68.

30 Report by His Britannic Majesty's Government on the Administration under Mandate of Palestine and Transjordan for the year 1924, Section I, Report by His Britannic Majesty's Government on the Administration under Mandate of Palestine, 8 July 1925, League of Nations Document C. 452 (i). M, 166 (i), 1925. VI.

31 *The Political History of Palestine under British Administration: Memorandum by His Britannic Majesty's Government presented in 1947 to the United Nations Special Committee on Palestine Published at Jerusalem, 1947* (reprinted New York: British Information Services, 1947), at 1.

32 Henri Rolin (1874–1946), Le système des mandats coloniaux, *Revue de droit international et de législation comparée*, 3rd series, vol. 1, 329, at 339 (1920).

33 Ibid., at 346.

34 United Nations, General Assembly, 2nd session, Special Committee on Palestine, Report to the General Assembly, 3 September 1947, vol. 1, at 18, United Nations Doc. A/364.

35 A Survey of Palestine Prepared in December 1945 and January 1946 for the information of the Anglo-American Committee of Inquiry (Washington: Institute for Palestine Studies, 1991) [reprinted from London: Her Majesty's Stationery Office], vol. 1, at 3.

12 The Peace Treaty with Turkey Legalized Britain's Status in Palestine

1 Treaty of Peace, Lausanne, 24 July 1923, art. 16, *League of Nations Treaty Series*, vol. 28, at 12.

2 *League of Nations Treaty Series*, vol. 28, at 12–13.

3 Jean Baleyte et al., *Dictionnaire économique et juridique* (Paris: LGDJ, 1992) (a vested interest in an enterprise). Interesse | Definition of Interesse by Merriam-Webster (a legal interest in property).

4 Elihu Lauterpacht, *Jerusalem and the Holy Places* (London: Anglo-Israel Association, 1968), at 13.

5 James Crawford, *The Creation of States in International Law* (Oxford: Clarendon Press, 2006), at 549.

6 Robbie Sabel, The Right to Self-determination and the 1922 League of Nations Mandate for Palestine, *Israel Law Review*, vol. 49, at 420 (2016). The quotation is from a reporter's rendition of an oral statement, hence may not represent Sabel's exact words.

7 Robbie Sabel, *International Law and the Arab-Israeli Conflict* (Cambridge: Cambridge University Press, 2022), at 61, 65.

8 Albert Millot, *Les Mandats Internationaux: étude sur l'application de l'Article 22 du Pacte de la Société des Nations* (Paris: Larose 1924), at 92. Jacob Stoyanovsky, *The Mandate for Palestine* (London: Longmans, 1928), at 233.

9 Treaty of Peace, Lausanne, art. 46.

10 Treaty of Peace between the Allied and Associated Powers and Turkey, Sèvres, 10 August 1920, art. 241, Treaty Series (United Kingdom), no. 11 (1920), United Kingdom, Command Paper 964.

11 Ottoman Public Debt Case (1925), United Nations, *Reports of International Arbitral Awards*, vol. 1, 529, esp. at 609–10.

12 Treaty of Peace, Lausanne, Protocol XII, art. 9.

13 Permanent Court of International Justice, *Mavrommatis Palestine Concessions*, Judgment of 30 August 1924, series A, no. 2.

14 Permanent Court of International Justice, *Mavrommatis Jerusalem Concessions*, Judgment of 26 March 1925, series A, no. 5, at 32.
15 Treaty of Peace, Lausanne, art. 30.
16 Treaty of Peace between the Allied and Associated Powers and Turkey, Sèvres, art. 123.
17 Jacob Stoyanovsky, *The Mandate for Palestine: A Contribution to the Theory and Practice of International Mandates* (London: Longmans, Green and Co., 1928), at 264.
18 United Kingdom, Court of Criminal Appeal, *King v. Ketter* [1940] 1 Kings Bench 787, at 789–90.
19 Georg Schwarzenberg, British and Palestinian Nationalities (Notes of Cases), *Modern Law Review*, vol. 3, at 164 (1939).
20 Permanent Court of International Justice, *Mavrommatis Palestine Concessions*, series C, Annex 3: Speech by Sir Cecil Hurst (Great Britain) at the public sitting on 15 July 1924, 20, at 24–25.
21 Ibid., at 25.
22 Ibid.
23 Ibid.
24 C. J. B. Hurst, *International Law: The Collected Papers of Sir Cecil Hurst* (London: Stevens & Son, 1950).
25 Secretary's Notes of a Conversation Held at Mr. Pichon's Room at the Quai d'Orsay, Paris, on Thursday, 30 January 1919, at 11 a.m., *Foreign Relations of the United States: Paris Peace Conference 1919*, vol. 3, at 785.
26 Mr. Vansittart (Paris) to Earl Curzon (Received 5 August 1920), No. 71 A [E 9427/4164/44], Great Britain, Foreign Office, *Documents on British Foreign Policy 1919–1939*, 1st series, vol. 13, at 326 (note 1).
27 Permanent Court of International Justice, *Mavrommatis Jerusalem Concessions*, Judgment of 26 March 1925, series A, no. 5, at 32.
28 United Kingdom, Palestine Order in Council, 1922 (August 10), Statutory Rules & Orders No. 1282, at 362.
29 United Nations, General Assembly, 2nd session, Special Committee on Palestine, Report to the General Assembly, 3 September 1947, vol. 1, at 19, United Nations Doc. A/364.
30 An Act to consolidate the Foreign Jurisdiction Acts, 4 August 1890, 53 &54 Victoria, chap. 37.
31 United Kingdom, Parliamentary Debates, House of Commons, 20 March 1923, 5th series, vol. 161, column 2388W.
32 Privy Council, Jerusalem-Jaffa District Governor v. Suleiman Murra, 1926 Law Reports 321, at 324.
33 Boustany, W. F. *The Palestine Mandate: Invalid and Impracticable* (Beirut: American Press, 1936), at 131–138.
34 Arab Higher Committee, *The Palestine Arab Case: A Statement by the Arab Higher Committee (The body representing the Palestine Arabs)* (Cairo: Arab Higher Committee, 1947), at 22–23.

13 The Palestine Mandate Document Was a Treaty between Britain and the League

1 United Nations, General Assembly, 2nd session, *Ad Hoc* Committee on the Palestinian Question, 17th meeting, 17 October 1947, at 110, United Nations Doc. A/AC.14/SR.17.

2 Yoram Dinstein, The International Legal Dimensions of the Arab-Israeli Conflict, in Alfred Kellerman, Kurt Siehr, and Talia Einhorn (eds.), *Israel among the Nations: International and Comparative Law Perspectives on Israel's 50th Anniversary* (The Hague: Kluwer, 1998), 137, at 139.
3 Vienna Convention on the Law of Treaties, Vienna, 23 May 1969, art. 2(a), *United Nations Treaty Series*, vol. 1155, at 331.
4 Research in International Law: Draft Convention on the Law of Treaties, art. 5, *American Journal of International Law*, vol. 29 Supplement, 657 at 732 (1935).
5 Ibid., art. 6.
6 Covenant of the League of Nations, art. 18, Part I of Treaty of Peace between the Allied and Associated Powers and Germany, Versailles, 28 June 1919, League of Nations, *Official Journal*, vol. 1 (no. 1), at 3 (1920).
7 Francesco Capotorti, L'extinction et la suspension des traités, Hague Academy of International Law, *Recueil des cours*, vol. 134 (1971-III), 417, at 533. Research in International Law, Draft Convention on the Law of Treaties, art. 33(b), *American Journal of International Law*, vol. 29 Supplement, 657, at 739 (1935).
8 Giulio Diena, Les mandats internationaux, Hague Academy of International Law, *Recueil des cours*, vol. 5 (1924-IV), 211, at 236.
9 Palestine Act: Act of Parliament to make provision with respect to the termination of His Majesty's jurisdiction in Palestine and for purposes connected therewith – 11 & 12 Geo. 6, c. 27, 29 April 1948, *The Statutes Third Revised Edition*, vol. 31, at 239, also in *British and Foreign State Papers 1948*, Part I, vol. 150, at 278.
10 United Kingdom, Parliamentary Debates, House of Commons, 10 March 1948, 5th series, vol. 448, columns 1319–20.
11 Giulio Diena, Les mandats internationaux, Hague Academy of International Law, *Recueil des cours*, vol. 5 (1924-IV), 211, at 232.
12 Henri Rolin (1874–1946), Le système des mandats coloniaux, *Revue de droit international et de législation comparée*, 3rd series, vol. 1, 329, at 334 (1920).
13 Communications from the Swiss Federal Council concerning the diplomatic immunities to be accorded to the staff of the League of Nations and of the International Labour Office, League of Nations Doc. C 555.X926.V, League of Nations, *Official Journal*, vol. 7 (no. 10) at 1422 (1926).
14 Agreement concerning the execution of the transfer to the United Nations of certain assets of the League of Nations, Geneva, 19 July 1946, *United Nations Treaty Series*, vol. 1, at 109.
15 League of Nations, *Official Journal*, vol. 3 (no. 8), at 1007 (1922), Annex 391: British Mandate for Palestine, art. 26.
16 Ibid., art. 18.
17 Permanent Court of International Justice, Statute, art. 36.
18 Permanent Court of International Justice, *Mavrommatis Palestine Concessions*, Judgment of 30 August 1924, series A, no. 2, at 11.
19 Dinstein, The International Legal Dimensions of the Arab-Israeli Conflict, at 139.
20 International Court of Justice, *South West Africa Cases* (Ethiopia v. South Africa, Liberia v. South Africa), Preliminary Objections, Reports (1962), at 319.
21 International Court of Justice, Statute, art. 37.
22 International Court of Justice, *South West Africa Cases* (Ethiopia v. South Africa, Liberia v. South Africa), Preliminary Objections, Reports (1962), 319, at 330.
23 Ibid., at 462.

24 Ibid., at 492.
25 Ibid., at 490.
26 Ibid.
27 Ibid., at 332.
28 International Court of Justice, *Legal Consequences for States of the Continued Presence of South Africa in Namibia (South West Africa) notwithstanding Security Council Resolution 276 (1970)*, Advisory Opinion, Reports (1971), 16, at 46–47.
29 *The Political History of Palestine under British Administration Memorandum by His Britannic Majesty's Government presented in 1947 to the United Nations Special Committee on Palestine Published at Jerusalem, 1947* (reprinted New York: British Information Services, 1947), at 1–2.
30 League of Nations, *Official Journal*, vol. 3 (no. 6, Part II), at 547 (1922), Council, 18th session, 11th meeting, 17 May 1922. The mention of the term "instrument" and the phrase "It is not they who invented the system of the Mandates" do not appear in the recorder's edited version of Balfour's remarks in the *Official Journal.* They appear in what was apparently a verbatim account of Balfour's remarks that was obtained by the *Daily Mail.* J. M. N. Jeffries, *Palestine: The Reality: The Inside Story of the Balfour Declaration 1917–1938* (Northampton, MA: Olive Branch Press, 2017) (originally London: Longmans, Green & Co., 1939), at 574.

14 The League of Nations Required Britain to Implement the Balfour Declaration

1 Felix Frankfurter, The Palestine Situation Restated, *Foreign Affairs*, vol. 9 (no. 3), 409, at 414 (April 1931).
2 Jean Allain, *International Law in the Middle East: Closer to Power than Justice* (Aldershot: Ashgate, 2004), at 79.
3 United Nations, General Assembly, 2nd session, Special Committee on Palestine, Report to the General Assembly, 3 September 1947, vol. 1, at 18, United Nations Doc. A/364.
4 Introduction, *Israel Law Review*, vol. 49, at 285 (2016).
5 Yuval Shany, Legal Entitlements, Changing Circumstances and Intertemporality: A Comment on the Creation of Israel and the Status of Palestine, *Israel Law Review*, vol. 49, 391, at 394 (2016).
6 Ibid., at 395.
7 League of Nations, *Official Journal*, vol. 3 (no. 8), at 825 (1922), Council, 19th session, 13th meeting, 24 July 1922.
8 James Crawford, *The Creation of States in International Law* (Oxford: Clarendon Press, 2006), at 423 (note 177).
9 League of Nations, *Official Journal*, vol. 3 (no. 8), at 818–20 (1922), Council, 19th session, 11th meeting, 22 July 1922.
10 Yuval Shany, Legal Entitlements, Changing Circumstances and Intertemporality: A Comment on the Creation of Israel and the Status of Palestine, *Israel Law Review*, vol. 49, 391, at 395 (2016).
11 Ibid., at 401–02.
12 Chaim Weizmann, Arabs and Zionists: The Pact of 1919, *The Times*, 10 June 1936, at 15, column 1.

13 Secretary's Notes of a Conversation Held in M. Pichon's Room at the Quai d'Orsay, Paris, on Thursday, 6 February 1919, at 3 p.m., *Foreign Relations of the United States: Paris Peace Conference 1919*, vol. 3, at 889–94.

14 Ibid., at 891.

15 Memorandum by the Emir Feisal, 1 January 1919, in David Hunter Miller, *My Diary of the Conference of Paris, with Documents* (New York: Appeal Printing Co., 1924), vol. 4, at 298–99 (Document 250). The Memorandum is referenced in Secretary's Notes of a Conversation Held in M. Pichon's Room at the Quai d'Orsay, Paris, on Thursday, 6 February 1919, at 3 p.m., *Foreign Relations of the United States: Paris Peace Conference 1919*, vol. 3, at 889.

16 Chaim Weizmann, Arabs and Zionists: The Pact of 1919, *The Times*, 10 June 1936, at 15, column 1.

17 League of Nations, *Official Journal*, vol. 3 (no. 6, Part II), at 547 (1922), Council, 18th session, 11th meeting, 17 May 1922.

18 Yaël Ronen, The Legal Relevance of the Mandate for Palestine to the Israeli-Palestinian Conflict: Mapping the Debate, *Israel Law Review*, vol. 49, 417, at 418 (2016).

15 The Palestine Mandate Document Implemented the League Covenant

1 Hersch Lauterpacht (ed.), *Lassa Oppenheim, International Law: A Treatise* (London: Longmans, Green & Co., 1948), vol. 1, at 197.

2 J. M. N. Jeffries, *Palestine: The Reality: The Inside Story of the Balfour Declaration 1917–1938* (Northampton MA: Olive Branch Press, 2017) (originally London: Longmans, Green & Co., 1939), at 551.

3 Palestine Royal Commission (Peel Commission), Report, July 1937, United Kingdom, Command Paper 5479 (London: His Majesty's Stationery Office, 1937), at 28.

4 Melvin I. Urofsky, *Felix Frankfurter: Judicial Restraint and Individual Liberties* (Boston: G.K. Hall, 1991), at 17.

5 *Felix Frankfurter Reminisces: Recorded in Talks with Dr. Harlan B. Phillips* (New York: Reynal, 1960), at 155.

6 David Hunter Miller, *My Diary at the Conference of Paris with Documents* (New York: Appeal Printing Co., 1924), vol. 7, at 369.

7 Ibid., at 372–74. Esco Foundation for Palestine, *Palestine: A Study of Jewish, Arab, and British Policies* (New Haven: Yale University Press, 1947), vol. 1, at 167.

8 Miller, *My Diary at the Conference of Paris*, vol. 7, at 372–73.

9 The Political Report: Palestine Mandate, *The New Palestine* (Zionist Organization of America), vol. 1, no. 35, at 13 (9 September 1921). See also Esco Foundation for Palestine, *Palestine: A Study of Jewish, Arab, and British Policies* (New Haven: Yale University Press, 1947), vol. 1, at 164 (listing some of the same names).

10 John J. McTague, Zionist-British Negotiations over the Draft Mandate for Palestine, 1920, *Jewish Social Studies*, vol. 42 (no.3/4) 281, at 283–84 (Summer-Autumn 1980).

11 Chaim Weizmann, *Trial and Error: The Autobiography of Chaim Weizmann* (New York: Harper & Brothers, 1949), at 290.

12 Esco Foundation for Palestine, *Palestine: A Study of Jewish, Arab, and British Policies* (New Haven: Yale University Press, 1947), vol. 1, at 172.

13 The Political Report: Palestine Mandate, *The New Palestine* (Zionist Organization of America), vol. 1, no. 35, at 13 (9 September 1921).
14 Weizmann, *Trial and Error*, at 290–91.
15 Mandates A. Memorandum by the Secretary of State for Foreign Affairs. Printed for the Cabinet. November 1920, at 1, Cabinet Paper 2197, Secret, United Kingdom, National Archives No. CAB 24/115. The letter "A" refers to the fact that the mandates for Turkey's Arab territories were called "Class A" mandates.
16 Ibid., at 1.
17 Ibid., at 2.
18 Ibid., at 2.
19 Mr. Vansittart (Paris) to Earl Curzon (Received August 5), No. 71 A [E 9427/4164/44], Great Britain, Foreign Office, *Documents on British Foreign Policy 1919–1939*, 1st series, vol. 13, 326, at 328 (note 4).
20 Letter from Dr. Weizmann to Earl Curzon, 30 October 1920 [E 13514/464/44], Great Britain, Foreign Office, *Documents on British Foreign Policy 1919–1939*, 1st series, vol. 13, 373, at 376 (note 4, quoting unprinted letter of Curzon to Lloyd George of 29 October 1920).
21 Felix Frankfurter, The Palestine Situation Restated, *Foreign Affairs*, vol. 9 (no. 3), 409, at 411 (April 1931).
22 International Court of Justice, *Minquiers and Ecrehos* (France/United Kingdom), Reports (1953), 47, at 56–57.
23 Weizmann, *Trial and Error*, at 280.
24 Mandates A. Memorandum by the Secretary of State for Foreign Affairs. Printed for the Cabinet. November 1920, at 2, Cabinet Paper 2197, Secret, United Kingdom, National Archives No. CAB 24/115.
25 Draft Mandates for Mesopotamia and Palestine as Submitted for the approval of the League of Nations (London: His Majesty's Stationery Office, 1921), United Kingdom, Command Paper 1176.
26 Weizmann, *Trial and Error*, at 280.
27 Secretary's Notes of a Conversation Held in M. Pichon's Room at the Quai d'Orsay, Paris, on Thursday, 27 February 1919, at 3 p.m., *Foreign Relations of the United States: Paris Peace Conference 1919*, vol. 4, at 162.
28 League of Nations, *Official Journal*, vol. 3 (no. 8), at 1007 (1922), Annex 391: British Mandate for Palestine, art. 4.
29 Statement of the Zionist Organization regarding Palestine, 3 February 1919, Paris Peace Conf. Doc. 180.03101/48, reprinted in Secretary's Notes of a Conversation Held in M. Pichon's Room at the Quai d'Orsay, Paris, on Thursday, 27 February 1919, at 3 p.m., *Foreign Relations of the United States: Paris Peace Conference 1919*, vol. 4, at 162.
30 Akram Zua'iter, *The Palestine Question* (Damascus: Palestine Arab Refugees Institution, 1958), at 51.
31 League of Nations, *Official Journal*, vol. 3 (no. 8), at 1007 (1922), Annex 391: British Mandate for Palestine, art. 1.
32 Gérard D. Khoury, *Une tutelle coloniale: Le mandat français en Syrie et au Liban, Écrits politiques de Robert de Caix* (Paris: Éditions Belin, 2006), at 247.
33 David Hunter Miller, *My Diary at the Conference of Paris with Documents* (New York: Appeal Printing Co., 1924), vol. 7, at 370.

34 A Survey of Palestine Prepared in December 1945 and January 1946 for the information of the Anglo-American Committee of Inquiry (Washington: Institute for Palestine Studies, 1991) [reprinted from London: Her Majesty's Stationery Office], vol. 1, at 3.
35 Report of the American Section of the International Commission on Mandates in Turkey (King-Crane Commission), *Foreign Relations of the United States: Paris Peace Conference 1919*, vol. 12, 751, at 772. Victor Kattan, *From Coexistence to Conquest: International Law and the Origins of the Arab-Israeli Conflict, 1891–1949* (New York: Pluto Press, 2009), at 122-124.
36 Memorandum by Mr. Balfour (Paris) respecting Syria, Palestine, and Mesopotamia, 11 August 1919 [132187/2117/44[A], United Kingdom Foreign Office 371/4183, *Documents on British Foreign Policy 1919–1939*, 1st series, vol. 4, 340, at 345.
37 Eastern Report No. CXX, 15 May 1919, Printed for the War Cabinet, at 5, Secret, United Kingdom, National Archives No. CAB 24/145.
38 Quincy Wright, *Mandates under the League of Nations* (Chicago: University of Chicago Press, 1930), at 62.
39 Jean Allain, *International Law in the Middle East: Closer to Power than Justice* (Aldershot: Ashgate, 2004), at 84–85. And see W. F. Boustany, *The Palestine Mandate: Invalid and Impracticable* (Beirut: American Press, 1936), at 33, criticizing the Council for approving a mandate document at odds with the Covenant.
40 League of Nations, *Official Journal*, vol. 3 (no. 6, Part II), at 547 (1922), Council, 18th session, 11th meeting, 17 May 1922.
41 United Nations, General Assembly, 2nd session, Special Committee on Palestine, Report to the General Assembly, 3 September 1947, vol. 1, at 35, United Nations Doc. A/364.
42 Ibid., at 35.
43 Program, General Syrian Congress, Damascus, 2 July 1919, in Report of the American Section of the International Commission on Mandates in Turkey (King-Crane Commission), *Foreign Relations of the United States: Paris Peace Conference 1919*, vol. 12, 751, at 780.
44 United Nations, General Assembly, 2nd session, Special Committee on Palestine, Report to the General Assembly, 3 September 1947, vol. 1, at 35, United Nations Doc. A/364.
45 Program, General Syrian Congress, Damascus, 2 July 1919, in Report of the American Section of the International Commission on Mandates in Turkey (King-Crane Commission), *Foreign Relations of the United States: Paris Peace Conference 1919*, vol. 12, 751, at 780.
46 Declaration of the Establishment of the State of Israel, *Laws of the State of Israel*, vol. 1, at 3 (from *Official Gazette*, no. 1, 14 May 1948).

16 The Palestine Mandate Document Recognized Jews as a National Group

1 Joel Kovel, *Overcoming Zionism: Creating a Single Democratic State in Israel/Palestine* (London: Pluto Press, 2007), at 34.
2 Jacob Stoyanovsky, *The Mandate for Palestine: A Contribution to the Theory and Practice of International Mandates* (London: Longmans, Green & Co., 1928), at 42.
3 Ruth Gavison, The National Rights of Jews, in Alan Baker (ed.), *Israel's Rights as a Nation-State in International Diplomacy* (Jerusalem: Jerusalem Center for Public Affairs, 2011), 9, at 12.

4 Minorities Treaty between the Principal Allied and Associated Powers (The British Empire, France, Italy, Japan and the United States) and Poland, Versailles, 28 June 1919, *British and Foreign State Papers 1919*, vol. 112, at 232.
5 United Nations Charter, arts. 1, 55.
6 International Covenant on Civil and Political Rights, art. 1, *United Nations Treaty Series*, vol. 999, at 171.
7 Gavison, The National Rights of Jews, at 12.
8 Israel, Law of Return, 5 July 1950.
9 Israel, Law of Return (Amendment No. 2), 10 March 1970, art. 4B.
10 Israel, Supreme Court, Rufeisen v. Minister of the Interior, 7 December 1962. HCJ 72/62, 16 PD 2428 [1962], translated in *Selected Judgments of the Supreme Court of Israel*, special vol. 1, at 34 (1971).

17 The Palestine Mandate Document Bound Britain to the Balfour Declaration

1 United Nations, General Assembly, 2nd session, *Ad Hoc* Committee on the Palestinian Question, 17th meeting, 17 October 1947, at 110, United Nations Doc. A/AC.14/SR.17.
2 Yoram Dinstein, The International Legal Dimensions of the Arab-Israeli Conflict, in Alfred Kellerman, Kurt Siehr, and Talia Einhorn (eds.), *Israel among the Nations: International and Comparative Law Perspectives on Israel's 50th Anniversary* (The Hague: Kluwer, 1998), 137, at 139.
3 Palestine Arab Congress, Haifa. Kazem al-Husseini, President, to Mandates Section, Secretariat, League of Nations, 12 February 1921, League of Nations Doc. 11228.
4 Palestine. Disturbances in May 1921, Reports of the Commission of Enquiry (Haycraft Commission), October 1921, United Kingdom, Command Paper 1540.
5 Conclusions of a Meeting of the Cabinet held at 10, Downing Street, S.W., on Thursday, 18 August 1921, at 11.30 a.m., at 8, Cabinet Paper 70 (21), 18 August 1921, Secret, United Kingdom, National Archives No. CAB 23/26.
6 Ibid., at 8.
7 Ibid., at 8–9.
8 United Kingdom, Report on Palestine Administration 1922, 31 December 1922, at 2, accessible at https://unispal.un.org/UNISPAL.NSF/0/A682CABF739FEBAA052565E8006D907C
9 Palestine: Memorandum by the Secretary of State for the Colonies (Devonshire), at 11, Cabinet Paper 106 (23), 17 February 1923, Secret, United Kingdom, National Archives No. CAB 24/159.
10 Ibid., at 11.
11 Ibid., at 13.
12 Ibid., at 13–14.
13 Ibid., at 12.
14 Palestine Committee, Cabinet Paper 293 (23), 27 June 1923, Secret, United Kingdom, National Archives No. CAB 24/160.
15 Bernard Wasserstein, *The British in Palestine: The Mandatory Government and the Arab-Jewish Conflict 1917–1929* (London: Royal Historical Society, 1978), at 126.
16 Committee on Palestine, The Future of Palestine, at 5, Cabinet Paper 351 (23), 27 July 1923, Secret, United Kingdom, National Archives No. CAB 24/161. See also Wasserstein, *The British in Palestine*, at 126–127.

17 Committee on Palestine, The Future of Palestine, at 3, Cabinet Paper 351 (23), 27 July 1923, Secret, United Kingdom, National Archives No. CAB 24/161.
18 Ibid., at 3.
19 Wasserstein, *The British in Palestine*, at 127.
20 Committee on Palestine, The Future of Palestine, at 4, Cabinet Paper 351 (23), 27 July 1923, Secret, United Kingdom, National Archives No. CAB 24/161.
21 Conclusions of a Meeting of the Cabinet held at the House of Commons, S.W. 1 on Tuesday, 31 July 1923, at 5.30 p.m., Cabinet Paper 43 (23), 31 July 1923, Secret, United Kingdom, National Archives No. CAB 23/46.

18 The International Community Committed Itself to the Balfour Declaration

1 Felix Frankfurter, The Palestine Situation Restated, *Foreign Affairs*, vol. 9 (no. 3), 409, at 414 (April 1931).
2 Yoram Dinstein, The International Legal Dimensions of the Arab-Israeli Conflict, in Alfred Kellerman, Kurt Siehr, and Talia Einhorn (eds.), *Israel among the Nations: International and Comparative Law Perspectives on Israel's 50th Anniversary* (The Hague: Kluwer, 1998), 137, at 140.
3 Ibid., at 140.
4 Maurice Hirsch, Palestinians sue Britain – as thanks for over half a billion dollars in aid, 6 December 2020, Palestinian Media Watch.
5 Covenant of the League of Nations, art. 15, Part I of Treaty of Peace between the Allied and Associated Powers and Germany, Versailles, 28 June 1919, League of Nations, *Official Journal*, vol. 1 (no. 1), at 3 (1920).
6 Dinstein, The International Legal Dimensions of the Arab-Israeli Conflict, at 140.
7 Convention between the United States and Great Britain with respect to rights in Palestine, London, 3 December 1924, US Congress, Statutes at Large, vol. 44, at 2184. (Ratifications were required. They followed in 1925.)
8 League of Nations, *Official Journal*, vol. 3 (no. 8), at 1007 (1922), Annex 391: British Mandate for Palestine, art. 18.
9 Convention between the United States and Great Britain with respect to rights in Palestine, London, 3 December 1924, art. 1, US Congress, Statutes at Large, vol. 44, at 2184.
10 Convention between the United States and France respecting rights in Syria and the Lebanon, Paris, 4 April 1924, US Treaty Series, no. 695, US Statutes at Large, vol. 43, at 1821.
11 Frank E. Manuel, *The Realities of American-Palestine Relations* (Washington, DC: Public Affairs Press, 1949), at 273.
12 Ibid., at 285.
13 The British Secretary of State for Foreign Affairs (Curzon) to the American Ambassador (Harvey), No. E 9865/78/65, 2 October 1922, reprinted in U.S. Department of State, *The Palestine Mandate* (Salisbury, NC: Documentary Publications, 1977) (originally published as *Mandate for Palestine* (Washington, DC: United States Government Printing Office, 1927), at 80 (¶2).
14 The British Secretary of State for Foreign Affairs (Curzon) to the American Chargé (Wheeler), No. E 11386/1899/65, 29 November 1923, *Foreign Relations of the United States 1923*, vol. 2, at 228, reprinted in US Department of State, *The Palestine Mandate*

(Salisbury, NC: Documentary Publications, 1977) (originally published as *Mandate for Palestine* (Washington, DC: United States Government Printing Office, 1927), at 85.

15 Manuel, *The Realities of American-Palestine Relations*, at 273, 284.

16 Carl J. Friedrich, *American Policy toward Palestine* (Washington, DC: Public Affairs Press, 1944), at 23.

17 Manuel, *The Realities of American-Palestine Relations*, at 273.

18 Ibid., at 273, 296.

19 The American Ambassador (Kellogg) to the British Secretary of State for Foreign Affairs (MacDonald), No. 187, 30 April 1924, reprinted in U.S. Department of State, *The Palestine Mandate* (Salisbury, NC: Documentary Publications, 1977) (originally published as *Mandate for Palestine* (Washington, DC: United States Government Printing Office, 1927), at 86–87.

20 Manuel, *The Realities of American-Palestine Relations*, at 286.

21 Friedrich, *American Policy toward Palestine*, at 20. Esco Foundation for Palestine, *Palestine: A Study of Jewish, Arab, and British Policies* (New Haven: Yale University Press, 1947), vol. 1, at 177 and 252.

22 State Department Statement [Treaty With Great Britain Respecting Palestine], 3 December 1924, *Supplement to the Messages and Papers of the Presidents Covering the Term of Warren G. Harding, March 4, 1921 to August 2, 1923 and the First Term of Calvin Coolidge, August 3, 1923 to March 4, 1925* (New York: Bureau of National Literature, 1925), at 9469–70.

23 The Anglo-American Treaty: Palestine as Jewish national home ignored, *American Israelite*, 11 December 1924, at 4.

19 Britain Held Legal Status in Palestine

1 United Kingdom, Import Duties Act, 1932, §1, 22 Geo. 5, c. 8. David L. Glickman, The British Imperial Preference System, *Quarterly Journal of Economics*, vol. 61 (no. 3), 439, at 442 (1947).

2 United Kingdom, Import Duties Act, 1932 §5.

3 United Kingdom, Import Duties (Mandated Territories) Preference Order, 1932, No. 133, 17 March 1932, in *Statutory Rules and Orders and Statutory Instruments Revised to December 31, 1948* (London: His Majesty's Stationery Office 1950), vol. 5, at 490.

4 John Rogers Herod, *Favored Nation Treatment, An Analysis of the Most Favored Nation Clause* (New York: Banks Law Publishing, 1901), at 3–4.

5 Meeting of the Cabinet to be held at No. 10, Downing Street, at 2, C.P. 25 (32), 27 April 1932, Secret, United Kingdom, National Archives No. CAB 23/71.

6 Ibid., at 3.

7 Ibid.

8 Ibid., at 2.

9 Ibid.

10 United Kingdom, Parliamentary Debates, House of Commons, 14 March 1932, 5th series, vol. 263, column13.

11 League of Nations, Permanent Mandates Commission, Minutes of the 22d session, held at Geneva, 11th meeting, 10 November 1932. League of Nations, Permanent Mandates Commission, Minutes of the 23d session, Geneva, 13th meeting, 27 June 1933.

12 A Convention To regulate the Commerce between the Territories of the United States and of his Britannick Majesty, 3 July 1815, art. 2, US Congress, Statutes at Large, vol. 8, at. 228.

13 The British Ambassador (Lindsay) to the Secretary of State, Washington, 15 July 1932, Doc. 641.67n3/2, in *Foreign Relations of the United States 1932*, vol. 2, at 29.
14 The Secretary of State to the British Chargé (Osborne), Washington, 27 August 1932, Doc. 641.67n3/11, id. at 32. Also in Imperial Preference for Palestine: Memorandum by the Secretary of State for the Colonies, C.P. 333 (32), 7 October 1932, Secret, United Kingdom, National Archives No. CAB 24/233. Referenced in Green Hackworth, *Digest of International Law* (Washington, DC: US Government Printing Office 1940), vol. 1, at 115.
15 Treaty of Commerce and Navigation, Madrid, 31 October 1922, art. 1, *League of Nations Treaty Series*, vol. 28, at 340.
16 Memorandum by the Secretary of State for the Colonies, Imperial Preference for Palestine, Annexure V, C.P. 333 (32), 7 October 1932, Secret, United Kingdom, National Archives No. CAB 24/33.
17 The Ambassador in Spain (Laughlin) to the Secretary of State, Madrid, 28 October 1932, Doc. 641.67n3/18, *Foreign Relations of the United States 1932*, vol. 2, at 36–37 (reporting on Spain's reply to the United Kingdom).
18 Memorandum by the Secretary of State for the Colonies, Imperial Preference for Palestine, Annexure IV, C.P. 333 (32), 7 October 1932, Secret, United Kingdom, National Archives No. CAB 24/33. See also The Chargé in Great Britain (Atherton) to the Secretary of State, Doc. 641.67n3/9, *Foreign Relations of the United States 1932*, vol. 2, at 33, and The Chargé in Italy (Kirk) to the Secretary of State, Rome, 22 October 1932, Doc. 641.67n3/17, *Foreign Relations of the United States 1932*, vol. 2, at 35–36 (both reporting on Italy's reply to the United Kingdom).
19 Memorandum by the Secretary of State for the Colonies, Imperial Preference for Palestine, Annexure VI, C.P. 333 (32), 7 October 1932, Secret, United Kingdom, National Archives No. CAB 24/33.
20 David L. Glickman, The British Imperial Preference System, *Quarterly Journal of Economics*, vol. 61 (no. 3), 439, at 455–56.
21 Memorandum by the Secretary of State for the Colonies, Imperial Preference for Palestine, Annexure VII, C.P. 333 (32), 7 October 1932, Secret, United Kingdom, National Archives No. CAB 24/33.
22 Ibid., Annexure I.
23 Ibid., at 1.
24 Foreign Office, Suggested Extension of Imperial Preference to Palestine, at 1, No. E 5478/606/31, C.P. 363 (32), 20 October 1932, Secret, CAB 24/234.
25 Ibid., at 2.
26 Ibid., at 1.
27 Foreign Office, Suggested Extension of Imperial Preference to Palestine, at 1, No. E 5478/606/31, C.P. 363 (32), 20 October 1932, Secret, CAB 24/234. Roza I. M. El-Eini, Trade Agreements and the Continuation of Tariff Protection Policy in Mandate Palestine in the 1930s, *Middle Eastern Studies*, vol. 34 (no. 1), 164, at 183.
28 Committee on Imperial Preference for Palestine, Report, C.P. 367 (32), 28 October 1932, Secret, United Kingdom, National Archives No. CAB 24/234.
29 Note: Chargé in Britain, Dispatch No. 433, 15 January 1934, Doc. 641.67n3/20, *Foreign Relations of the United States 1932*, vol. 2, at 37.
30 Paul Pic, Le régime du mandat d'après le traité de Versailles; son application dans le Proche Orient; mandats français en Syrie, Anglais en Palestine et Mésopotamie, *Revue de droit international public*, vol. 30 (2nd series, vol. 5), 321, at 331 (1923).

31 Traité pour l'organisation du protectorat français dans l'Empire chérifien, Fez, 30 March 1912, *British and Foreign State Papers 1913*, vol. 106, at 1023. *Consolidated Treaty Series*, vol. 216, at 20.

20 The United Nations Charter Carried Forward a Jewish Entitlement to Statehood

1 Francesco Capotorti, L'extinction et la suspension des traités, Hague Academy of International Law, *Recueil des cours*, vol. 134 (1971-III), 417, at 533. Research in International Law, Draft Convention on the Law of Treaties, art. 33(b), *American Journal of International Law*, vol. 29 Supplement at 657 (1935).

2 League of Nations, *Official Journal*, Special Supplement No. 194, Records of the Twentieth (Conclusion) and Twenty-First Ordinary Sessions of the Assembly, 18 April 1946, Annex 27: Resolutions adopted by the Assembly at Its Twenty-first Ordinary Session: Mandates, at 278.

3 League of Nations, *Official Journal*, Special Supplement No. 194, Records of the Twentieth (Conclusion) and Twenty-First Ordinary Sessions of the Assembly, 7th meeting, 18 April 1946, at 59.

4 League of Nations, *Official Journal*, Special Supplement No. 194, Records of the Twentieth (Conclusion) and Twenty-First Ordinary Sessions of the Assembly, 18 April 1946, Annex 27: Resolutions adopted by the Assembly at Its Twenty-first Ordinary Session: Mandates, at 278–79.

5 Paul S. Riebenfeld, The Legitimacy of Jewish Settlement in Judea, Samaria and Gaza, in Edward M. Siegel (ed.), *Israel's Legitimacy in Law and History: Proceedings of the Conference on International Law and the Arab-Israeli Conflict Sponsored by the Louis D. Brandeis Society of Zionist Lawyers, October 21, 1990, New York* (New York: Center for Near East Policy Research, 1993), 39, at 41.

6 Hersch Lauterpacht, Article 18 of the Mandate for Palestine and the Dissolution of the League of Nations [a paper written in November 1946], in Elihu Lauterpacht (ed.), *International Law Being the Collected Papers of Hersch Lauterpacht*, vol. 3, 101, at 105 (1977).

7 Patrick C.R. Terry, Britain in Palestine (1917–1948)—Occupation, the Palestine Mandate, and International Law, *University of Bologna Law Review*, vol. 2 (no. 2), at 243 (2017).

8 Ruth B. Russell, *A History of the United Nations Charter: The Role of the United States 1940–1945* (Washington, DC: Brookings Institution, 1958), at 494–95.

9 Leland M. Goodrich, Edvard Hambro, and Anne Patricia Simons, *Charter of the United Nations: Commentary and Documents* (New York: Columbia University Press, 1969), at 494.

10 Ibid.

Postscript: Why History Matters

1 League of Nations, *Official Journal*, Special Supplement No. 194, Records of the Twentieth (Conclusion) and Twenty-First Ordinary Sessions of the Assembly, 7th meeting, 18 April 1946, at 58–59.

2 United Nations, General Assembly, 1st special session, General Committee, 29th meeting, 29 April 1947, at 13, United Nations Doc. A/BUR/SR.29.
3 Kenneth Stein, Introduction of the Mandatory System (2009), Center for Israel Education, accessible at https://israeled.org/resources/documents/mandate-palestine/
4 United Nations, General Assembly, 2nd session, *Ad Hoc* Committee on the Palestinian Question, 16th meeting, 16 October 1947, at 108, United Nations Doc. A/AC.14/SR.16.
5 *The Palestine Arab Case: A Statement by the Arab Higher Committee (The body representing the Palestine Arabs)* (Cairo: Arab Higher Committee, 1947), at 22–23. Issa Nakhleh, *Encyclopedia of the Palestine Problem* (New York: Intercontinental Books, 1991).
6 United Nations, General Assembly, 2nd session, *Ad Hoc* Committee on the Palestinian Question, 11th meeting, 11 October 1947, at 61, United Nations Doc. A/AC.14/SR.11.
7 United Nations, Security Council, 340th meeting, 27 July 1948, at 34.
8 United Nations, General Assembly, 3rd session, 1st Committee, 228th meeting, 4 December 1948, at 932–33, United Nations Doc. A/C.1/SR.228.
9 https://balfourproject.org/
10 United Kingdom, Parliamentary Debates, House of Lords, 3 April 2017, vol. 782 https://hansard.parliament.uk › *html › Lords › 2017-04-03*
11 Boris Johnson, Letter to MP Stephen Crabb et al., 9 April 2021.
12 International Criminal Court, Pre-Trial Chamber I, Decision on the 'Prosecution request pursuant to article 19(3) for a ruling on the Court's territorial jurisdiction in Palestine,' ICC-01/18-143, 5 February 2021.
13 Rome Statute of the International Criminal Court, arts. 7, 14, *United Nations Treaty Series*, vol. 2187, at 3.
14 Universal Declaration of Human Rights, art. 13(2), United Nations, General Assembly Res. 217A, 10 December 1948. International Covenant on Civil and Political Rights, art. 12(4), *United Nations Treaty Series*, vol. 999, at 171.
15 United Nations, General Assembly, Admission of Israel to membership in the United Nations, Res. 273, 11 May 1949.
16 Defense (Emergency) Regulations, Official Gazette of the Government of Palestine, No. 1442, Supplement No. 2, 27 September 1945, at 1083–85.
17 Law and Administration Ordinance, art. 11, *Laws of the State of Israel*, vol. 1, at 7 (1948).
18 Palestine (Defence) Order in Council, 18 March 1937, Supplement No. 2 to the Palestine Gazette Extraordinary No. 675 of 24 March 1937.
19 Palestine (Revocations) Order in Council, § 2, ¶2, Statutory Instrument No. 1004 (1948).
20 Arnold Krammer, *The Forgotten Friendship: Israel and the Soviet Bloc, 1947–1953* (Urbana IL: University of Illinois Press, 1974), at 51–52. Galia Golan, *Soviet Policies in the Middle East from World War Two to Gorbachev* (Cambridge: Cambridge University Press, 1990), at 35. Pavel Sudoplatov and Anatoli Sudoplatov, *Special Tasks: The Memoirs of an Unwanted Witness – A Soviet Spymaster* (Boston: Little, Brown, 1994) at 292–93.
21 John Snetsinger, *Truman, the Jewish Vote, and the Creation of Israel* (Stanford: Hoover Institution Press, 1974), at 103, citing Clifford to Truman, Memorandum: The Politics of 1948, 19 November 1947, Clark M. Clifford Papers, Harry S. Truman Library, Independence, Missouri. Michael J. Cohen, *Truman and Israel* (Berkeley: University of California Press, 1990), at 60.

22 Israel Defense Force, Intelligence Service (Arab section), Migration of Eretz Yisrael Arabs between 1 December 1947 and 1 June 1948 (30 June 1948), English translation, Akevot Institute for Israeli-Palestinian Conflict Research, from Hashomer Hatzair (Yad Yaari) Archive, file 95–35.27(3), reproduced in Seth Anziska, Special Document File, *Journal of Palestine Studies*, vol. 49 (no.1), at 64 (2019). Benny Morris, The Causes and Character of the Arab Exodus from Palestine: the Israel Defence Forces Intelligence Analysis of June 1948, *Middle Eastern Studies*, vol. 22, 5, at 10 (1986). Erskine Childers, The Wordless Wish: From Citizens to Refugees, in Ibrahim Abu-Lughod, *The Transformation of Palestine: Essays on the Origin and Development of the Arab-Israeli Conflict* (Evanston: Northwestern University Press, 1971), at 165. Ari Shavit, *My Promised Land: The Triumph and Tragedy of Israel* (New York: Spiegel and Grau, 2013), at 108. Shay Hazkani, *Dear Palestine: A Social History of the 1948 War* (Stanford: Stanford University Press, 2021), at 163–64. Adam Raz, Classified Docs Reveal Massacres of Palestinians in '48 – and What Israeli Leaders Knew, *Ha'aretz*, 9 December 2021. Gideon Levy, The ghosts of Tantura, *Ha'aretz*, 23 January 2022.

BIBLIOGRAPHY

Allain, Jean. *International Law in the Middle East: Closer to Power than Justice* (Aldershot: Ashgate, 2004).

Baron, Salo. *The Russian Jew under Tsars and Soviets* (New York: Macmillan, 1976).

Bell, Abraham and Eugene Kontorovich. Palestine, *Uti Possidetis Juris*, and the Borders of Israel, *Arizona Law Review*, vol. 58 (2016).

Bentwich, Norman. The Legal Administration of Palestine under the British Military Occupation, *British Year Book of International Law*, vol. 1 (1920–1921).

Bentwich, Norman. Mandated Territories: Palestine and Mesopotamia (Iraq), *British Year Book of International Law*, vol. 2 (1921–1922).

Bentwich, Norman, and Helen Bentwich. *Mandate Memories 1918–1948* (London: Hogarth Press, 1965).

Boustany, W. F. *The Palestine Mandate: Invalid and Impracticable* (Beirut: American Press, 1936).

Brown, Philip Marshall. The Mandate over Armenia, *American Journal of International Law*, vol. 14 (1920).

Burkman, Thomas W. *Japan and the League of Nations: Empire and World Order, 1914–1938* (Honolulu: University of Hawaii Press, 2008).

Burton, Margaret E. *The Assembly of the League of Nations* (Chicago: University of Chicago Press, 1941).

Cattan, Henry. *Palestine and International Law: The Legal Aspects of the Arab-Israeli Conflict* (London: Longman, 1976).

Cohen, Aharon. *Israel and the Arab World* (New York: Funk and Wagnalls, 1970).

Crawford, James. *The Creation of States in International Law* (Oxford: Clarendon Press, 2006).

Diena, Giulio. Les mandats internationaux, Hague Academy of International Law, *Recueil des cours*, vol. 5 (1924-IV).

Dinstein, Yoram. The International Legal Dimensions of the Arab-Israeli Conflict, in Alfred Kellerman, Kurt Siehr, and Talia Einhorn (eds.), *Israel among the Nations: International and Comparative Law Perspectives on Israel's 50th Anniversary* (The Hague: Kluwer, 1998).

Eban, Abba. *Abba Eban: An Autobiography* (New York: Random House, 1977).

Esco Foundation for Palestine. *Palestine: A Study of Jewish, Arab, and British Policies* (New Haven: Yale University Press, 1947).

Felix Frankfurter Reminisces: Recorded in Talks with Dr. Harlan B. Phillips (New York: Reynal, 1960).

Gavison, Ruth. The National Rights of Jews, 9–22, in Alan Baker (ed.), *Israel's Rights as a Nation-State in International Diplomacy* (Jerusalem: Jerusalem Center for Public Affairs, 2011).

Gibbons, Herbert Adams. Zionism and the World Peace, *The Century*, vol. 97 (1919).

Gilmour, David. The Unregarded Prophet: Lord Curzon and the Palestine Question, *Journal of Palestine Studies*, vol. 25 (no. 3) (1996).

Gold, Dore. 100 years since the San Remo conference which shaped Middle East, *Jerusalem Post*, 26 April 2020.

Goodrich, Leland M., Edvard Hambro, and Anne Patricia Simons. *Charter of the United Nations: Commentary and Documents* (New York: Columbia University Press, 1969).

Hyamson, Alfred. *Palestine under the Mandate 1920–1948* (London: Methuen & Co., 1950).

Ingrams, Doreen. *Palestine Papers 1917–1922: Seeds of Conflict* (London: John Murray, 1970).

Jeffries, J. M. N. *Palestine: The Reality: The Inside Story of the Balfour Declaration 1917–1938* (Northampton, MA: Olive Branch Press, 2017) (originally London: Longmans, Green & Co., 1939).

Jeffries, J. M. N. *The Palestine Deception: "Daily Mail" Inquiry on the Spot* (London: Daily Mail, 1923).

Kattan, Victor. *From Coexistence to Conquest: International Law and the Origins of the Arab-Israeli Conflict, 1891–1949* (New York: Pluto Press, 2009).

Kaufman, Edy. The French Pro-Zionist Declarations of 1917–1918, *Middle Eastern Studies*, vol. 15 (no. 3) (1979).

Keith, Barriedale. Mandates, *Journal of Comparative Legislation and International Law*, 3rd series, vol. 4, part I (1922).

Khalidi, Rashid. *The Iron Cage: The Story of the Palestinian Struggle for Statehood* (Boston: Beacon Press, 2006).

Khoury, Gérard D. *Une tutelle coloniale: Le mandat français en Syrie et au Liban, Écrits politiques de Robert de Caix* (Paris: Éditions Belin, 2006).

Klausner, Joseph. *Menahem Ussishkin: His Life and Work* (New York: Scopus, 1942).

Kling, Simcha. *The Mighty Warrior: The Life Story of Menahem Ussishkin* (New York: Jonathan David, 1965).

Knox, D. Edward. *The Making of a New Eastern Question: British Palestine Policy and the Origins of Israel, 1917–1925* (Washington, DC: Catholic University of America Press, 1981).

Kovel, Joel. *Overcoming Zionism: Creating a Single Democratic State in Israel/Palestine* (London: Pluto Press, 2007).

Lauterpacht, Elihu. *Jerusalem and the Holy Places* (London: Anglo-Israel Association, 1968).

Lauterpacht, Hersch. Article 18 of the Mandate for Palestine and the Dissolution of the League of Nations [a paper written in November 1946], 101–105, in Elihu Lauterpacht (ed.), *International Law Being the Collected Papers of Hersch Lauterpacht* (Cambridge: Cambridge University Press, 1977), vol. 3.

Lauterpacht, Hersch (ed.). *Lassa Oppenheim, International Law: A Treatise* (London: Longmans, Green & Co., 1948).

Lebow, Richard Ned. Woodrow Wilson and the Balfour Declaration, *Journal of Modern History*, vol. 40 (1968).

Lloyd George, David. *The Truth about the Peace Treaties* (London: V. Gollancz, 1938).

Maga, Timothy P. Prelude to War? The United States, Japan, and the Yap Crisis, 1918–22, *Diplomatic History*, vol. 9 (no. 3) (1985).

Manuel, Frank E. *The Realities of American-Palestine Relations* (Washington, DC: Public Affairs Press, 1949).

McTague, John J. *British Policy in Palestine, 1917–1922* (Lanham, MD: University Press of America, 1983).

McTague, John J. The British Military Administration in Palestine 1917–1920, *Journal of Palestine Studies*, vol. 7 (no. 3) (1978).

McTague, John J. Zionist-British Negotiations over the Draft Mandate for Palestine, 1920, *Jewish Social Studies*, vol. 42 (no. 3/4) (1980).
Miller, David Hunter. *My Diary at the Conference of Paris with Documents* (New York: Appeal Printing Co., 1924), vol. 7.
Millot, Albert. *Les Mandats Internationaux: étude sur l'application de l'Article 22 du Pacte de la Société des Nations* (Paris: Larose, 1924).
Morikawa, Jun. *Japan and Africa: Big Business and Diplomacy* (Trenton, NJ: Africa World Press, 1997).
Nakhleh, Issa. *Encyclopedia of the Palestine Problem* (New York: Intercontinental Books, 1991).
Pedersen, Susan. *The Guardians: The League of Nations and the Crisis of Empire* (Oxford: Oxford University Press, 2015).
Pic, Paul. Le régime du mandat d'après le traité de Versailles; son application dans le Proche Orient; mandats français en Syrie, anglais en Palestine et Mésopotamie, *Revue de droit international public*, vol. 30 (2nd series, vol. 5, 1923).
Pic, Paul. *Syrie et Palestine: mandats français et anglais dans le Proche-Orient* (Paris: Librairie ancienne Édouard Champion, 1924).
Pilzer, Jay. *The League of Nations and the Jewish Question*, Thesis (Ph.D.), Duke University, Microfiche. Ann Arbor, MI, University Microfilms (1976).
Porath, Yehoshua. *The Emergence of the Palestinian-Arab National Movement 1918–1929* (London: Frank Cass, 1974).
Rattan, Sumitra. The Yap Controversy and Its Significance, *Journal of Pacific History*, vol. 7 (1972).
Rechter, David. *The Jews of Vienna and the First World War* (Oxford: Littman Library of Jewish Civilization, 2008).
Regan, Bernard. *The Balfour Declaration: Empire, the Mandate and Resistance in Palestine* (London: Verso, 2017).
Reinharz, Jehuda (ed.). *The Letters and Papers of Chaim Weizmann*, vol. 9, Series A (October 1918–July 1920).
Renton, James. *The Zionist Masquerade: The Birth of the Anglo-Zionist Alliance 1914–1918* (New York: Palgrave Macmillan, 2007).
Riebenfeld, Paul S. The Legitimacy of Jewish Settlement in Judea, Samaria and Gaza, 39–41, in Edward M. Siegel (ed.), *Israel's Legitimacy in Law and History: Proceedings of the Conference on International Law and the Arab-Israeli Conflict Sponsored by the Louis D. Brandeis Society of Zionist Lawyers, October 21, 1990, New York* (New York: Center for Near East Policy Research, 1993).
Rolin, Henri (1874–1946). Le système des mandats coloniaux, *Revue de droit international et de législation comparée*, 3rd series, vol. 1 (1920).
Rolin, Henri A. (1891–1973). La pratique des mandats internationaux, Hague Academy of International Law, *Recueil des cours*, vol. 19 (1927-IV).
Ronen, Yaël. The Legal Relevance of the Mandate for Palestine to the Israeli-Palestinian Conflict: Mapping the Debate, *Israel Law Review*, vol. 49 (2016).
Rosenne, Shabtai. Revisiting Some Legal Aspects of the Transition from Mandate to Independence: December 1947–15 May 1948, in Alfred Kellerman, Kurt Siehr, and Talia Einhorn (eds.), *Israel among the Nations: International and Comparative Law Perspectives on Israel's 50th Anniversary* (The Hague: Kluwer, 1998).
Russell, Ruth B. *A History of the United Nations Charter: The Role of the United States 1940–1945* (Washington, DC: Brookings Institution, 1958).

Sabel, Robbie. The Right to Self-determination and the 1922 League of Nations Mandate for Palestine, *Israel Law Review*, vol. 49 (2016).
Sabel, Robbie. *International Law and the Arab-Israeli Conflict* (Cambridge: Cambridge University Press, 2022).
Sachar, Howard M. *The Emergence of the Middle East: 1914–1924* (New York: Alfred A. Knopf, 1969).
Sand, Shlomo. *The Invention of the Jewish People* (London: Verso, 2009).
Schechtman, Joseph. *Zionism and Zionists in Soviet Russia: Greatness and Drama* (New York: Zionist Organization of America, 1966).
Schneer, Jonathan. *The Balfour Declaration: The Origins of the Arab-Israeli Conflict* (London: Bloomsbury, 2010).
Schwarzenberg, Georg. British and Palestinian Nationalities (Notes of Cases), *Modern Law Review*, vol. 3 (1939).
Segev, Tom. *One Palestine Complete: Jews and Arabs under the British Mandate* (New York: Henry Holt, 1999).
Shany, Yuval. Legal Entitlements, Changing Circumstances and Intertemporality: A Comment on the Creation of Israel and the Status of Palestine, *Israel Law Review*, vol. 49 (2016).
Shapiro, Leon. Outline of the History of Russian and Soviet Jewry 1912–1974, in Simon M. Dubnow, *History of the Jews in Russia and Poland from the Earliest Times until the Present Day* (New York: Ktav Publishing House, 1975).
Sokolow, Nahum. *History of Zionism 1600–1918* (New York: Ktav Publishing House, 1969), vol. 2.
Stein, Leonard. *The Balfour Declaration* (New York: Simon & Schuster, 1961).
Stoyanovsky, Jacob. *The Mandate for Palestine* (London: Longmans, Green & Co., 1928).
Strawson, John. *Partitioning Palestine: Legal fundamentalism in the Palestinian-Israeli conflict* (London: Pluto, 2010).
Terry, Patrick C. R. Britain in Palestine (1917–1948)—Occupation, the Palestine Mandate, and International Law, *University of Bologna Law Review*, vol. 2 (no. 2) (2017).
Urofsky, Melvin I. *Felix Frankfurter: Judicial Restraint and Individual Liberties* (Boston: G.K. Hall, 1991).
Urquhart, Brian. *Ralph Bunche: An American Life* (New York: W.W. Norton, 1993).
Vallani, Alberto. *I mandati internazionali della Società delle nazioni* (Milano: Editore – Libraio della Real Casa, 1923).
Wasserstein, Bernard. *The British in Palestine: The Mandatory Government and the Arab-Jewish Conflict 1917–1929* (London: Royal Historical Society, 1978).
Weizmann, Chaim. *Trial and Error: The Autobiography of Chaim Weizmann* (New York: Harper & Brothers, 1949).
Wright, Quincy. *Mandates under the League of Nations* (Chicago: University of Chicago Press, 1930).

INDEX

www.ingramcontent.com/pod-product-compliance
Ingram Content Group UK Ltd.
Pitfield, Milton Keynes, MK11 3LW, UK
UKHW041831100926
8556IPUK00002B/114

9 781839 984631